Praise for
the
possibility of
everything

"Hope Edelman possesses a voice that embeds itself in your mind."
—*USA Today*

"Edelman writes eloquently about her struggle. . . . With vivid descriptions of Belize and its Mayan history, *The Possibility of Everything* is an intimate account of the struggles of parenting, partnering and faith."
—*People*

"*The Possibility of Everything* is a well-crafted tale of skepticism versus spirituality. . . . Edelman's writing soars highest when depicting her family's eye-opening encounters in the humid tropical jungle with—just possibly—the supernatural."
—*Entertainment Weekly*

"Part mystery, part travelogue, part memoir, the book explores the gaps between science and faith, children and parents, and what we believe and what we wish for."
—*Redbook*

"From its gripping opening to its moving conclusion, *The Possibility of Everything* takes you on a spirited journey that gracefully interweaves details of early motherhood with reflections on faith and transformation, all set against the beauty and wonder of a foreign place. A thoughtful and compelling read by the accomplished Hope Edelman."

—CATHI HANAUER, author of *Sweet Ruin* and editor of *The Bitch in the House*

"To write memoir well, one must surrender fear and reveal all dimensions of the inner truth—from gorgeous to heinous and what lies in between. In search of faith she can wrap her arms around, Edelman set down fear and has revealed all of herself with beauty and candor, innocence and intelligence, wisdom and clarity. In this fascinating and honest account of one woman's quest for wholeness and healing for her daughter, herself, and her family, Edelman gives us hope."

—JENNIFER LAUCK, author of *Still Waters* and *Blackbird: A Childhood Lost and Found*

"Ask any mother: there isn't any role that so consistently demands of us what we know we don't have. Enough patience, enough wisdom, enough energy and grace. The ability to discern between what we can fix and what we can't. Hope Edelman takes her readers on the kind of journey every mother will make—into hope over reason, faith without understanding. *Motherless Daughters* gave us what no other book did—honesty and solace and companionship—from someone who'd been there, too. Readers will say the same of *The Possibility of Everything*."

—KATHRYN HARRISON, author of *The Kiss*

the
possibility of
everything

the possibility *of* everything

a memoir

HOPE EDELMAN

ballantine books trade paperbacks   new york

The Possibility of Everything is a work of nonfiction. Some names and identifying details have been changed.

2010 Ballantine Books Trade Paperback Edition

Copyright © 2009 by Hope Edelman
Reading group guide copyright © 2010 by Random House, Inc.

Published in the United States by Ballantine Books, an imprint of The Random House Publishing Group, a division of Random House, Inc., New York.

BALLANTINE and colophon are registered trademarks of Random House, Inc.

RANDOM HOUSE READER'S CIRCLE and colophon is a registered trademark of Random House, Inc.

Originally published in hardcover in the United States by Ballantine Books, an imprint of The Random House Publishing Group, a division of Random House, Inc., in 2009.

Grateful acknowledgment is made to HarperCollins Publishers for permission to reprint three lines from "Prayer," used as an epigraph, from *Never* by Jorie Graham. Copyright © 2002 by Jorie Graham. Reprinted by permission of HarperCollins Publishers.

LIBRARY OF CONGRESS CATALOGING-IN-PUBLICATION DATA
Edelman, Hope.
The possibility of everything: a memoir/Hope Edelman.
p. c.m.
ISBN 978-0-345-50651-1
eBook ISBN 978-0-345-51701-2
1. Hope. 2. Faith. I. Title.
BD216.E34 2009
972.82'505092—dc22
[B]   2009028303

Printed in the United States of America

www.randomhousereaderscircle.com

2 4 6 8 9 7 5 3 1

Book design by Susan Turner

For Uzi

My husband, my partner,
my prince

. . . this is freedom. This is the force of faith. Nobody gets what they want. Never again are you the same. The longing is to be pure. What you get is to be changed.

—Jorie Graham

You cannot solve problems with the same level of consciousness that created them.

—Albert Einstein

contents

introduction

Cayo District, Belize
December 24, 2000

A ragged dirt road twists through six miles of rain forest in western Belize, linking the villages of Cristo Rey and San Antonio. If you make this drive the day after a heavy December rain, as my husband, Uzi, and I do, the road will still be gluey and ripe. Its surface will be the color and consistency of mango pudding. You might focus intensely on these two elements, *mango* and *pudding*, to divert your attention from how the white van you're riding in keeps sashaying across the slippery road. And you might look down at the three-year-old lying across your lap and think about how she is a child who loves mangoes and loves pudding but that you have never thought to put the two together for her before. You might look at her and think, *Mango pudding! Great idea! Let's find a way to make some tonight!* Or you might think, *If you'll be okay, I'll make you mango pudding every night for the rest of your life.* Or you might look down at her and just think, *Please*, and leave it at that.

Victor, our driver for this ride, maneuvers the eleven-seat passenger van with more skill and less caution than I could safely manage. "Hee-yah!" he calls out as he deftly steers us out of a skid. Every time the van's back end fishtails, I spring for the door handle. I don't know what I'm thinking: grabbing the door handle in an unlocked car is only going to result in an open door on a muddy road, but when you're ricocheting around in the back of a van without seat belts, with a sick child lying across your thighs, the impulse is to lunge for something solid.

I tighten my right arm around my daughter Maya's waist. *Everything's fine*, I tell myself. *She's going to be fine.* I press my left hand against the window and watch the landscape stream by between my fingertips. The jungle grows flush against both sides of the road, tangled and pristine. The bulldozers of American expatriates chewing up the Caribbean coast haven't found their way back here yet. Fat, squat cohune palms burst up from ground level like Las Vegas fountains spraying out of the forest floor. Thick, serpentine vines encircle tree trunks like lush maypole ribbons. The biodiversity here is astounding. I never imagined there could be so many different kinds of leaves in one place, or so many shades of green.

The air outside is like nothing I've encountered before: energetic and molecular and intense. A few hours ago, when we were sitting on the front steps of our cabana at Victor's resort, I took in deep gulps of the jungle's bright, wet promise, the loamy, rich animation of the dirt marrying with chlorophyll to form air so dense it tempts you to take a bite.

At lunch, we ate family style in an open-air dining hall lined with rectangular wooden tables, under the thatched roof Victor and his sons had woven from local palm fronds. While his wife and daughters served heaping plates of rice and beans and bowls of fried plantains, Victor meandered between the tables with a small pad of paper in one hand and a bottle of orange Fanta dangling between the thumb and forefinger of the other. As he approached each table he flipped a chair around and sat on it backward, pulled a pen from behind his ear, and scribbled down each family's travel request for the day. A foursome of fresh-scrubbed Brits—mother, father, daughter, son—wanted to go canoeing on the Macal River. Two bearded men who looked too old to still be backpackers wanted to see the nearby Maya ruins at Xunantunich. A family from Montreal with two college-age daughters opted for a few hours in the neighboring town of San Ignacio, a few miles downriver.

"Sure, sure," Victor said to everyone, tossing back swigs from his bottle. "We take you. No problem." Victor quickly established himself as part hotelier, part chauffeur, and part general contractor, a rainforest Renaissance man in an olive green baseball cap. At our table, he rested a hand on Uzi's shoulder. We'd already put in our afternoon request.

"Two o'clock," Victor told us. "I'll take you, or my son will."

This drive to San Antonio rolls on. Our tires make loud sucking noises as they peel away from the gummy earth. Off to our right, an animal lets loose with what sounds like a familiar, plaintive howl. Maya raises her head in recognition, pivots it around like a slow periscope, then lets it drop back down against my thigh.

"You have coyotes here?" Uzi asks. He's riding up front with Victor, one hand braced against the glove compartment for support.

"What?" Victor maneuvers the van around a wide puddle.

"Coyotes," Uzi says. "You know, like little wolves. We have them at home."

"Oh, yeah," Victor says, swatting the air with his hand. "We got anything you want here."

Anything? Maya coughs her raspy cough against my leg, the sound of gravel rattling between her ribs. I press my palm against her forehead. I'm guessing 101, maybe 101.5, better than yesterday, but not by much. I tuck a sprig of dark curls behind her ear.

Mi vida, I think. My life.

These words that come to me are not the words of my own country, but those of a language I struggled to learn for years, a language that both exhilarates me and breaks my heart. *Mi vida*. At home in Los Angeles, it is the language of the hardworking and the oppressed, of the woman who cleans my house with care once a week, of the man with the white pickup truck who trims the palm trees that line our driveway, of the childless nanny who loves my daughter with a selfless passion while I spend hours in front of a computer screen rearranging words. But here in Belize it is the language of conquerors, the language that overtook the indigenous Maya and then, centuries later, turned around and pushed out the imperial British masters. A language that says, "Here. This. Mine."

Victor sits calmly behind the van's steering wheel. Perhaps he's made this drive for dozens of guests before. I imagine a steady parade of Americans traipsing into the jungle in their Lakers caps and Teva sandals, acting entitled to their cures. Yet surely, we must stand out from the pack. There's Uzi, who's forty, though so boyish no one can believe his age, with an Israeli accent so slight it barely dusts the surface of his speech. He's a quintessentially low-impact kind of guy, soft-spoken, careful to tread lightly on the earth. Not like me, who can't help leaving footprints and food wrappers in my wake everywhere I go. And there's Maya, three feet tall with a mop of dark curls, carrying two rubber baby dolls tucked under her right arm, refusing to eat anything but cucumbers and water for the past three days because everything else hurts going down.

And me? How might I look to someone I've just met? Probably like a medium-aged American woman in striped cotton pants who's equal parts grateful and unsure about being here and who can't stop hovering over her three-year-old—checking, fixing, trying to coax forkfuls of food past the child's tightly shut lips. Or maybe I'm wrong. Maybe I don't make an impression at all. Maybe I'm just another tourist messing up the bedsheets, acting as if I have a right to benefit from knowledge that took Victor's ancestors millennia to learn.

The low, brightly painted buildings of San Antonio Village appear in the distance, like a handful of colorful marbles scattered across the valley's gentle bowl. The Maya Mountains rise blue-gray in the distance. Maya coughs again.

"Ay, *raina*," Victor sighs. He calls her "queen."

Here in the land of the Maya, where body, mind, and spirit are tightly intertwined, physical and spiritual illness are considered one and the same. Physical symptoms, the Maya believe, erupt when the life force that surrounds a person's body, the *ch'ulel*, is damaged by trauma or stress. Those who are sick in body are believed to first be sick in spirit, and so Maya healers always treat both.

Uzi glances at me over his left shoulder, searching my face for a sign. My gentle husband, always gauging my moods, always trying to position himself on the safe side of conflict. *Are you still okay with this?* his expression asks. I crimp the left side of my mouth and shrug my shoulder slightly. I'm deliberately impossible to read.

Even now, eight years later, I cannot tell you if I traveled down that road as a whole person, held intact by my own convictions, or if I went there as a broken woman, mechanically following my husband's lead. I can tell you only what it is like to be riding in that van, on that mango road, rolling past dense fields of brown and green. It is to be a thirty-six-year-old woman, a mother and a wife, who is willing to do anything—*anything*—to help her child.

Mi vida. I will tell you. This is how it feels. As if my life is lying across my lap and I am bringing it into the jungle, to the man who speaks with spirits, so it can be healed.

the
possibility of
everything

chapter one
Topanga Canyon, California
September 2000

The soft clinks of a metal spoon against stainless steel filter upstairs from the kitchen as Carmen prepares Maya's dinner. Tonight it's pasta with red sauce and a side dish of peas. Carmen hums as she cooks, low thrumming vibrations occasionally broken by a string of high-pitched *la-la-la-la*s. I glance at the digital clock at the bottom of my computer screen. Five twenty-six P.M. In four minutes, I'll go down to sit with Maya for dinner, and relieve Carmen for the evening. Then I'll give Maya her bath and read her *The Red Balloon*, for the fourth time this week. I'll put her to sleep, watch some TV, get into bed with a book, and wait for Uzi to come home.

The ceiling fan churns above my head in determined, repetitive circles. I pinch the fabric of my white cotton tank top away from my chest and angle an exhale between my breasts, trying to dry the thin film of sweat that's settled there. It's late September in southern California, our hottest month of the year, and heat rises precipitously in a house with a wall of windows downstairs.

I move my fingers across the keyboard faster, as if the speed of my fingers might stir up a breeze. Today I'm working on a dual review for the *Chicago Tribune*, two Jewish-themed books that have little in common beyond the religious angle. Whoever paired them probably didn't realize that, and it's my job to figure out how to make them work together in the same review. The first book is a history of New York's Lower East Side, packed with detail and research. The second is a memoir by an American psychotherapist, a single mother who moved to Jerusalem with her school-age daughter to jump-start a new phase of her life. I felt predisposed to like this one, as the American wife of an Israeli-born husband, but each time the mother wrote about putting her rapturous love for her adopted country ahead of her daughter's well-being, I had to force myself to keep reading. As a reviewer I'm supposed to be objective and keep my focus on the text, but I've had to work hard at that with this one. As a mother I found too many times in the book when I wanted to grab the author by the shoulders and shout, "Snap out of it! And put your daughter on a plane back to the United States!" I'm trying to figure out if my reaction reveals a weakness in the book or if it's just a reflection of my parenting and the different choices I imagine I'd make. I know how much sweat and lost sleep goes into every book that's written, and I'm loath to review one harshly until I'm certain my criticism is valid.

Downstairs, Carmen sets Maya's sectional plate and sippy cup on the dining table, the sound of plastic kissing wood. Then there's the scuff of a wooden chair being dragged back across the red tile floor.

"La *Ma*-ya!" Carmen sings out. "It is time for dinner now, please!"

I'm still not used to this, having someone else take charge in our kitchen. For the first few weeks after Carmen came to work for us four days a week, we kept circling each other awkwardly at the refrigerator at breakfast, bumping elbows in front of the sink at dinnertime, unsure of who should be doing what and when. Before I moved in with Uzi I'd lived alone for ten years, and I'd developed a highly particular way of getting things done. This is not to say I'm tidy or organized by nature—sadly, I am not—but I've always maintained a semblance of order in the kitchen. It's the singular achievement that gives me a sense of domestic competence, as if being able to find the cutting board in the same place every time I need it offers proof that no matter what kind of sorry state the living room might be in at that moment, I do know how to manage a household, after all. Now, whenever I find the bread knife lying in the silverware drawer instead of poking out of its designated slot in the wooden knife block or see leftovers stored in glass bowls covered with plastic wrap instead of locked into the Tupperware containers I've been using since college, I feel a surge of disoriented panic, as if I've somehow been rendered unnecessary in my own home.

Uzi says I struggle with this because I have trouble relinquishing control. I don't entirely disagree, but I think it's more that I have trouble giving up responsibility. For Maya's first two years, while Uzi was pulling ninety-hour weeks launching a dot-com start-up, I did all the evening shifts at home alone. I was the one who mashed Maya's peas with the blue whale fork, cut her chicken into bite-size cubes, and wiped ketchup smears from her chin with a damp paper towel. Before I went back to teaching and Carmen moved in to help, I was the one who scraped the dinner residue off all the plates, sponged down the table, and refrigerated the leftovers. In the Tupperware I've had since college. Isn't that what mothers are supposed to do?

"La *Ma*-ya!" Carmen sings again, slightly louder this time. "Where is La *Ma*-ya?"

I press the "save" icon on my computer. Where *is* Maya? Probably in her room, getting into costume. Yesterday she was Snow White. The day before, a black-and-gray bat.

"Maya," I call out. "Carmen is looking for you."

God, it's hot in this room. I pluck my tank top away from my chest and let it snap back again a couple of times, just for the tiny rush of air under my chin. I reach down to shut off the computer—and there's a sudden blur of red and purple to my left and a blunt, painful collision of bone against bone on my left thigh.

"Ow!" I cry out, instinctively.

She's gone as quickly as she was upon me. I press the heel of my left hand hard into my leg. The pain echoes harshly, then fades into a dull ache. I can tell I'll have a bruise tomorrow.

"You *hit* me!" I say loud enough for Maya to hear, rising from the desk. "*Maya!*"

"Maya?" Carmen calls from the bottom of the stairs, her voice sounding a lot less certain now.

I find Maya in her bedroom, backed into the corner between her nightstand and the mirrored closet door. She's wearing a red-and-purple gypsy dress with a gold-coin sash, a hand-me-down from my college roommate's daughter. She holds her hands pinned tightly behind her back, an edgy Esmeralda, all pent-up energy and tension and doubt.

She thrusts her chin at me defiantly, as if she's expecting punishment, and that softens me a little. I'm not a mean mother. At least I don't want to be a mean mother. Or the kind of mother prone to frustrated, spontaneous outbursts, which, more and more frequently these past few months, I seem to have become.

Stay calm, I tell myself. *Remember. To breathe.*

I sit on top of the Pooh comforter stretched across Maya's double bed and fold my hands in my lap.

"So," I say. "Do you want to tell Mom what that was about?"

She uncoils in a rush. "It. Wasn't. Me!" she shouts, pounding her clenched little fists against her thighs to emphasize each word. When she does this, I see four fists pumping up and down, her two real ones and the two reflected in the mirror. It's like watching Maya and her angry, identical twin throwing perfectly synchronized tantrums.

"What do you mean, it wasn't you? I was sitting there and you ran in and hit me. I *saw* you."

"Mommy," she wails, and her face crumples into a pinched-up wad. "It wasn't me! It was Dodo!"

"It was *who*?"

She rushes at me, and I rear back a little, anticipating another hit. But this time she hurls her arms around my knees and clings to them.

"I didn't want to," she sobs. "Dodo *made* me."

"Who's Dodo?" The kid has an imagination the size of Guam, but I've never heard mention of a Dodo before.

"He's just . . . *Dodo!*" She smashes her face into my leg. The cries erupt from her in jagged little sobs.

"It's okay," I tell her, rubbing the back of her head. "I'm not hurt. Shh. It's okay." I stare at the image of us in her closet-door mirror, the sobbing child and the mother with her dark eyebrows knit into the cartoon symbol for "confused." Maya can be stubborn and difficult to manage, but she's never been physically aggressive before, especially not toward an adult. She hit me with the intent to hurt: there was no ambiguity there. I'm already thinking about whether to tell Uzi about this later and, if I do, how to avoid putting a worrisome spin on it. The last thing he needs right now is hyperbole or drama from me, and the last thing I need tonight is hearing about how hard it is to live with someone who thrives on hyperbole and drama, like me.

Carmen's voice sails up to us from the bottom of the stairs.

"La Ma-ya," she calls. "The dinner is waiting for you now."

The automatic garage door makes the floor of the master bedroom hum, which makes no sense, since the garage isn't underneath the master bedroom. It's two floors below the master bedroom and completely on the other side of the house, under the living room, which never hums when the door goes up, but whatever. I've given up trying to figure out the laws of physics in our house. For the three and a half years we've lived here the place has stubbornly operated under its own set of rules, like a resentful teenager refusing to acknowledge a new stepparent's authority. Different pieces of the house break down in unprecedented ways or make noises no one can explain or appear to be working properly only to suddenly reveal themselves to have been humoring us all along. Within our first three months of home ownership, the air conditioner, the dishwasher, and the garage-door opener all quit. I might have wondered what had inspired the mutiny, except that I was too busy trying to keep up with the repairs. Soon afterward, the refrigerator became sluggish, and then a pipe in the septic system disconnected in a horizontal, subterranean rupture that none of the three local contractors we called for estimates recalled ever having seen happen before. After the backhoe rolled away, we drove out of town for a reprieve, during which time a feral male cat clawed through one of our window screens, sprayed every piece of furniture downstairs with urine at four-foot, ankle-high intervals, and held our ten-year-old female cat hostage until we returned.

And did I mention the tarantula? The one the size of a softball I found flexing its hairy black-and-brown legs in the guest bathroom sink one Sunday afternoon? The one we had to figure out how to dispose of on our own after the local fire chief laughed at me when I called the station for help—*another New Yorker comes to town*, you just knew he was thinking—and the man who answered the phone at Animal Control informed me that his office didn't handle animals that were, technically, classified as "pests"?

In the midst of all this chaos, the refrigerator—possibly fed up with not getting the attention it felt it deserved—stepped out of the repair line and fixed itself. Our current problem is with cordless telephones. No matter what make or model I buy, they all go weak in the keypad at number five.

Uzi thinks this is a sign of something larger: that the house and, by extension, the universe are putting us to some kind of test. We need to be open to whatever it's trying to tell us, he says. This is how he thinks. Me, I'm the pragmatist around here. When an appliance breaks down, I don't need to sit around hypothesizing about what it means. I already know what it means. It means I have to be home Tuesday morning between eight and noon for the repairman. The end.

"If everything's breaking down at once, maybe there's a disturbance in the electromagnetic field," Uzi says.

"If everything's breaking down at once, maybe it's because we bought a *lemon of a house*," I tell him.

"Hey. We got a great deal," he reminds me.

That's my man: ethereal yet practical at the same time. When we first started dating, I would describe Uzi to my friends as someone "not of this world." He was a computer software developer who walked on New York City sidewalks with his mind hovering somewhere around mezzanine level. Conversations with him were prone to long pauses and apparent non sequiturs, until I caught on to his habit of reentering a dialogue two or three ideas ahead of the one he'd last articulated, having rushed through the intermediary steps in his mind. It was a little like communicating with someone who can type faster than you can read, but I was up for the challenge. My last boyfriend had been a dashingly handsome writer and amateur comic, the kind of character who marched naked through the apartment in the morning loudly singing "Don't Fence Me In" in a German accent so spot on it made me laugh until I couldn't breathe, but he was also frequently moody and deeply ambivalent about commitment. Or maybe just about commitment to me. Uzi was utterly decisive about moving in together, a little alarmingly so, I thought, only four months after we started dating, but I'd be lying if I said his certainty wasn't part of the attraction. We dated for ten months before we got engaged, with Maya already on the way, and in the flurry of the next six months we moved to California, got married, bought the house, and started preparing for her arrival.

We chose to live in Topanga Canyon because of its natural setting—bordered on three sides by state park and conservancy land and on the fourth by the Pacific Ocean—and its legendary, bohemian aesthetic. This was 1997, and the canyon was still riding on its reputation as a free-love music and art hub of the 1960s and 1970s, a place that Neil Young, the Eagles, and Little Feat had once called home. We arrived just about the time the hippies were entrenched in middle age, and the new generation of middle-class bohemians moving in constituted a burgeoning subculture of "healers." Or maybe the hippies were becoming the healers. Or maybe the hippies had always been healers, but it was now more socially acceptable to use the term and vastly easier, thanks to the Internet, to market oneself as such. As we drove our blue-and-white Rent-It truck up the hill to our new house, the canyon was ripening with acupuncturists and energy workers, rolfers and Vision Quest guides. This could easily have freaked me out, coming as I was from the heart of Manhattan, but it actually felt like a relief. Massage therapists, yoga studios, and crystal stores seemed to be a healthy—and necessary—balance to the supersized egos and rampant materialism I kept colliding against elsewhere in L.A.

We were looking for a sense of community in Topanga. That's what we kept saying: "a sense of community." It was really just another way of saying we were hoping to find a small place where we could belong in a large place where we had almost no family and few good friends. It wasn't hard to find community in Topanga. The town, just twenty minutes from Santa Monica, is still small enough to have only one telephone exchange—455—so that locals need to say only the last four digits when giving out their numbers in town. The general store is 1250; the local veterinarian 1330; like that. About half of our neighbors keep chickens, some have horses, and one has a giant land tortoise roaming his property that occasionally gets loose and ambles across the road. It's like living on a New Age version of Walton's Mountain, with minivans and cell phones. At potluck dinners, people I'd never peg as nontraditional thinkers use terms like "karma" and "the universe" without the acrid taint of irony and freely admit to consulting with astrologers and psychics, offering their phone numbers so I can get a reading, too.

It's tempting to write all this off as southern California cliché, but that would be missing the point. Something larger is going on here, something that may have begun thirty years ago in crucibles such as Woodstock, Sedona, and Topanga but has since started radiating to points far beyond. Over the past three years, while I was scarfing down folic acid and changing wet diapers, a new spiritual revolution was slowly stirring up amid my peers, emerging as a highly individual, soul-based form of spirituality, liberated from both a wrathful God and a benevolent, omnipotent Christ. Despite the unbridled affluence of the late 1990s, or perhaps because of it, people were deeply dissatisfied. They'd begun the decade as devotees at the altar of secular materialism, only to discover that the tasks of acquiring and the responsibilities of having were a hollow substitute for authentic experience, and they were left feeling unmoored. They had everything they could possibly need and in many cases more, yet they were nonetheless ravaged by ennui. They were clinically depressed. When I left New York, nearly everyone I knew was either going on Prozac, coming off Prozac, or trying to sell me on the benefits of Saint-John's-wort. Even my most jaded and argumentative friends, especially after having children, were searching for a convincing set of beliefs to anchor them, yet instead of returning to their religions of origin many were turning inward, developing one-on-one relationships with deities of their own choice and design. For the first time in my adult experience, at parties in New York, Iowa City, even Beverly Hills, I was hearing educated, worldly people talking about their unshakable beliefs in things they could neither prove nor see yet nonetheless believed, with great certainty, to exist.

On the one hand, I can't help thinking this kind of millennial shift grows out of the desperate human need to believe that a kind of master plan exists, that we're not all down here in the dirt floundering around on our ignorant own. Five adult years in the cynic's playground of Manhattan trained me to view all matters of spirituality and faith with a snotty East Coast intellectual's condescension, relegating such beliefs to the province of the uneducated and the deluded, the self-administered salve of the huddled masses. But on the other hand, when I take the time now to listen to some of my neighbors' ideas—such as Milošević's downfall representing an inevitable, cosmic payback for decades of evil—they don't sound all that far-fetched, and it's in these moments that I start to wonder if everyone around me is marching hand in hand toward something profound and transcendent, while I'm getting left behind on the sidewalk, obsessing over the weeds springing up between the cracks.

These are the kind of random thoughts ping-ponging around in my head when Uzi comes bounding up two flights of stairs to our bedroom at 10:37 P.M. I'm already under the covers with a book, feeling slightly peeved. It would be unusual to have him home before ten on a weeknight now, but that doesn't stop me from wishing otherwise.

He comes through the door in his dress clothes and socks. "Hi there," he says, resting his computer bag against his side of the bed.

"Hi," I say. "Remember me?"

"I think so," he says, leaning over to kiss my forehead. "You were the one in the white dress, right?"

"I was the one who planned that whole wedding," I remind him.

Uzi peels off his Oxford shirt and pants and drapes them across a corner of the bed. Then he pulls off his T-shirt, rolls it into a ball, sniffs it, and tosses it in the general direction of the hamper. It lands about a foot away.

"How was your day?" he asks.

"I already ate," I say. I swear, sometimes I don't know why he puts up with me.

"Sorry. Long day," he says.

His office is a bunch of tech and marketing guys optimizing online ad sales. I'm not really sure why this takes up ninety hours a week, but it pays two thirds of our bills so I don't feel I have much right to complain.

"How was your day?" I ask.

"Hmn?" he says. He sounds distracted. Sometimes it takes him a while to get home from work after he gets home from work.

"Your day," I repeat. "How was it?"

He pulls on a pair of sweatpants and a fresh T-shirt and hurls himself onto the bed next to me with a loud, dramatic groan.

"You need to find someone better to hang out with," he says.

"I tried, for a long time. You were the best I could come up with."

He laughs. "Then we're both in big trouble," he says. He leans his head against my shoulder, and I kiss the top of his hair. Exhausted, overworked, hyperbolic: what can I say? He's still my guy.

"How's Maya?" he asks.

"She's fine. I think we've got an imaginary friend in the house, though."

"Hmn. Really?"

"His name is Dodo."

"Like the bird?"

"Apparently."

"That's creative."

"She punched me and blamed it on him."

This gets his attention. He lifts his head. "She punched you? Really?"

I give him my best *yes, really* look.

"Hard?" he asks.

"Not that hard. Hard enough."

"Huh. Well, aren't imaginary friends pretty normal? For kids who don't have siblings?"

"Did you have one?" I ask. Uzi and I are both firstborns, so it would follow.

"I don't think so. If I did, I don't remember. We could ask my mom."

I adore my mother-in-law. She's a nurse and hospital administrator and knows more about the mechanics of the human body than anyone else I've ever met. But Uzi is her oldest child and her only son, which, if you know anything about Jewish families, means he might as well have been born with a crown tattooed across his forehead. According to both of my in-laws, Uzi was a quintessentially perfect, uncomplicated child. I'm guessing that depending on my mother-in-law's opinion of imaginary friends, Uzi either most definitely did not have one or he had the most imaginative one in all of Tel Aviv.

"I had one," I say. Ellen—that was the name of my imaginary friend when I was two and a half. She was a silent, dark-haired girl slightly older than me who held my hand during the day and slept curled up in a space I prepared for her on my closet floor at night. Ellen owned just one article of clothing, a sleeveless, lime green seersucker dress with fuchsia pockets shaped like daisies. Thirty years later, I can still see that dress with more clarity and specificity than I can remember most items from childhood that were real.

"What happened to her?" Uzi asks.

"She disappeared after my sister was born."

He gives me a long, noncommittal stare.

"That's not what I'm trying to get at," I say. I know he's not ready for another child, and if I'm honest about it, neither am I. Fifty-one hours of labor, forty-two stitches, a uterine infection, mastitis, and ten weeks of infant colic—we'd be masochists to do it again.

I pull the comforter up under my chin and stare at the ceiling. There's a small, H-shaped crack above our bed where the previous owner of the house lost his footing in the attic and almost put his shoe through the floor. Every time I look at it, I'm reminded of a joke in the risqué book my parents kept in our downstairs guest bathroom throughout my childhood: "What's the difference between a British girl, a French girl, and an American girl during sex? The British girl says, 'Blimey! I've never had it so good!' The French girl says, '*Mon Dieu*, you are ze best!' The American girl says, 'The ceiling needs repainting.'" Even now, all these years later, that joke still makes me laugh. Because I know that's me, the American girl, always diverting my attention to what needs to be improved.

The crack in our bedroom ceiling isn't bad enough to replaster, but tonight its presence grates on me more than usual. Since dinnertime I've been battling a low-grade uneasiness—just enough to tilt my inner balance slightly askew. The aggression I saw in Maya today worries me, because of the way she knew her behavior was wrong yet seemed unable to control it.

"I'm going to get something to eat," Uzi says. He launches himself out of bed and gets down on all fours to find his house shoes. At the door he pauses and looks back at me with a reassuring smile.

"She's probably just going through a phase," he says.

Sometimes I think the reason our marriage works is because Uzi's natural temperament is to believe that whatever looks bad today will undoubtedly be better tomorrow, therefore making very little worthy of urgent attention. On the one hand, this point of view allows small problems that are likely to resolve on their own to, well, resolve on their own. On the other hand, sometimes it prevents us from giving small problems their due before they turn into big ones. And my maternal instinct is telling me we've got a big problem brewing here. That's because, unlike Uzi's, my natural temperament is to believe that whatever looks bad today has the potential to get much, much worse tomorrow. I'm the queen of identifying the negatives, emphasizing the difficulties, dramatizing the conflict. All very useful skills to have as a writer, although not, I acknowledge, always the easiest qualities to have in a wife.

Still, what's the point of smearing worry all over the bedroom at 11 P.M.? It's not as if we're going to come up with a solution to implement tonight.

"I'm sure you're right," I say, trying to make my voice sound weightless and unconcerned. "In a few days, she'll probably have forgotten all about it."

Ever since Maya emerged from the womb, I've been humbly prostrating myself before the altar of Penelope Leach. Of all the child-rearing experts whose books I've read—and I've read a lot of child-rearing books—I've found Leach's utilitarian, quintessentially British attitude toward problem solving to be the best antidote to my new-mother anxiety. Unlike the relentlessly peppy energy of the *What to Expect* authors or the patronizing charm of T. Berry Brazelton, the grandfatherly pediatrician who appears on the *Today* show, Leach seems to be on board with the idea that new mothers don't need to be treated like idiots, that we might in fact resent being treated like idiots, and that, given proper amounts of information and confidence, we can learn to identify and solve most early-childhood problems on our own. She gets that we don't need someone constantly feeding our obsessive need for detail. What we need is someone who cuts straight to the simplest and most plausible explanation for every new development and then tells us exactly what to do.

I've come to think of Leach as a wise elder, dispensing the kind of straightforward advice my own mother would give me if she were still alive, although the truth is, I don't know what kind of advice my mother would offer. She died of breast cancer in 1981, when she was forty-two and I was still in high school, too early for her to start handing down child-rearing philosophies or directives. Because I'm the oldest of her three children, what little I know about her pregnancies, deliveries, and my early years is pieced together from my baby-book entries, her best friend's stories, and my father's hazy memories, which occasionally mistake my infancy in 1964 with my sister's in 1967 or my brother's in 1971. I like to think that my mother, as a grandmother, would have been eager to share stories about her own early foibles to save me from making the same mistakes thirty years later, but really, who knows? Some of my friends struggle with mothers who can't tone down their criticism, leveraging on their daughters' confusion or ineptitude to soothe their own lingering feelings of inadequacy. Probably my mother, whom I remember as gentle with her opinions, would have stepped back and allowed me to forge my own parenting path. Probably. Maybe? The truth is, I don't know, and sometimes this not knowing makes me feel so sad I can forget how to swallow.

Without a mother to consult on a regular basis, I rely instead on a pastiche of friends and parenting magazines and on Penelope Leach's opinions on everything from expressing breast milk by hand to the psychology of picky eaters. So the day Dodo appears, my inclination is to head into my office after Uzi falls asleep and pull my well-worn copy of Leach's *Your Baby and Child* off the bookshelf.

I settle down cross-legged on the mauve carpet, flip to the book's index, and run my finger down the *I* column.

> *illness, coping with;*
> *imaginative play;*
> *immunization*

That's weird. There's no entry for "imaginary friends." The closest Leach comes to the topic is a paragraph warning parents about trying too hard to take part in a child's imaginary play. "There is only room for one author and that is the child," she writes. "This is her private world which she is making for herself out of the raw material of the real world you show her."

Out of the real world I show her? I've never hit Maya, except for a couple of swats on the forearm to indicate a firm *Get your hand off that now*. I don't even spank the cat.

I slide the book back onto the shelf and pull down *What to Expect During the Toddler Years*. The index promises a short section on imaginary friends, which, when I flip to it, is a list of bland tips for parents that look suspiciously naked without the book's otherwise ubiquitous exclamation points. "Accept and welcome her friend," the authors say. "Let your toddler take the lead." "Don't let your toddler use her friend to escape consequences." "Provide other outlets for your toddler's negative feelings." And "Remember that your child will eventually give up her pretend playmate." An imaginary friend, they add, can give parents valuable insights into a child's state of mind.

Well, *duh*. That's exactly what's worrying me.

Finally, the *What to Expect* authors conclude, if a child "becomes so consumed with, or dependent upon, her imaginary playmate that she doesn't interact with anyone else, or if she seems withdrawn or otherwise unhappy, discuss the situation with her doctor; counseling may be needed."

Counseling? That seems way too premature right now. I scan the bookshelf again.

T. Berry Brazelton's *Touchpoints* advertises itself as "The Essential Reference to Your Child's Emotional and Behavioral Development," and he has plenty to say about imaginary friends. A whole chapter, in fact.

Nearly all three- and four-year-olds develop imaginary friends, Brazelton says (that's a relief), who are "precious" to a child and should be respected by adults around them (okay, easy enough), although most parents feel left out and jealous (really? actually, that sounds a little pathetic). The situation becomes worrisome, Brazelton says, only if a child consistently chooses an imaginary friend over real ones.

And then, this:

> What about a child who uses an imaginary friend to "lie" his way out of a bad situation? This is an extremely common event at these ages. A parent may well wonder whether the child knows the difference between the wish and the reality, for lying at this age so obviously represents wishful thinking.

"An extremely common event at these ages." The sentence has a lilting, lovely sound to it. Extremely common. Event at these ages. I can almost hear Penelope Leach chortling it in a crisp British accent. I reread the sentence, and the little knot beneath my rib cage starts to loosen. If Brazelton knows what he's talking about, which the *Today* show obviously thinks he does, then Maya is experiencing a familiar and transitory event that's easily explained.

Of course. I exhale heavily. Why wouldn't it be? For the past three years, Maya's development has followed a steady, even course, each stage building upon its predecessor and eventually graduating into its successor like a graceful scaffolding. Crawling evolved into walking, which led to running, jumping, and somersaults; single words grew into simple commands, then more complex sentences, eventually turning into mind-bending, existential questions such as "When you were a baby in your mommy's tummy, where was I?" Maturity, it seems to me, inevitably happens to a child when a parent is patient enough to watch and wait and stay out of the way. The hardest part for me is ignoring the urge to intervene.

It's like how at the age of two and a half Maya suddenly started clinging to my legs at the beginning of birthday parties, refusing to leave my side. I would try to peel her off me, encourage her, even bribe her to join the other kids. In a panic, I considered finding her a psychologist, afraid she was going to permanently regress into a timid, socially awkward child. Which wasn't even remotely true. I just didn't yet have the experience to know that what exists in a child's behavior today may not exist next month or even tomorrow. A few months later Maya's party shyness vanished as quickly as it had appeared, just as my friends with older children had told me it would, and I was left feeling humbled and foolish about my reactionary fear.

Give it time, I remind myself. One thing I should have learned in thirty-six years is that few states of being are permanent. Everything changes, eventually. My problem is I lack what my friend Lori calls "the patience." Lori is so calm and unruffled all the time, she's like meditation on feet. When the two of us go anywhere together, it's like a comedy show, one walking slow and steady, the other stumbling to arrive faster. She likes to say that when God handed out the patience, I must have been off somewhere complaining to a supervisor that the line was moving too slowly.

I quietly close Brazelton's book and slip it back onto the shelf. In the next room, Uzi sleeps soundly, secure in the belief that every breakdown is an opportunity for rebuilding and every morning a wake-up call for a new day. Maybe this time he's right. I turn off the office light and go to join my sleeping husband in bed.

chapter two
Los Angeles, California
October 2000

Palisades Park sits tucked away behind Sunset Boulevard, a small pocket of sand and swings surrounded by wide, immaculate neighborhoods of multimillion-dollar homes. My friend Melissa first tipped me off to the park a year ago, and now we try to meet here one Friday a month after our daughters' preschool days end.

I arrive early for our October playdate and lean back into a bench while Maya darts off to the play structure, kicking up small puffs of sand behind her. Two mothers in crisply ironed khaki capri pants and spotless white polo shirts crouch in the shade of the slide, trying to convince their toddlers to share the same blue dump truck. Good luck.

Melissa's redheaded daughter, Colette, comes running across the grassy picnic area and hurls herself elbows first into the sand. Colette has a round moon pie face and bangs that skim the top of her eyebrows. Melissa follows three steps behind, lugging a blue mesh bag filled with sand toys, sunblock, and snacks.

"Hey," she says, collapsing onto the bench beside me. She leans over to give me a quick air kiss near my cheek. "Here you go, kids!" she calls out, tossing the toys one at a time into the sand in front of us. "Remember to share!"

Melissa was a teen actress in the 1980s on a popular TV sitcom, and she still has the perfect skin and dazzling smile of a network star. We met in a prenatal yoga class that morphed into a Friday baby group that lasted for a year. When we get together now, Melissa and I talk mostly about parenting and about what's happening with the other ten women from the group. It's been almost three years since the last baby was born, putting us at the critical juncture when most of the other women are either pregnant with a second child or filing for divorce.

"You heard about Liz," she says.

"Liz? No. What?" Liz was the oldest mom in our group, pregnant with her first child at forty-one, so I'm guessing this isn't second-pregnancy news.

"She and Kurt are splitting up."

"Get out. I had *no idea*."

"Me neither. It just goes to show, I guess."

"How many does that make? Four?"

Melissa silently counts off names on her fingers, touching pinky, ring finger, middle finger, index finger, thumb. "Five."

"Well, there's your fifty percent."

"Still. With the others, like Wendy, I could kind of see it coming, but I thought these guys were okay."

"Me, too." I shrug, a gesture equal parts empathy and surrender. "Marriage is hard," I add.

"Uzi's still working a lot?"

"Pretty much all the time."

"How's it going with Carmen?"

"Good," I say. "We like her a lot."

What I wish I could say is "I like her more than I feel comfortable liking someone who is, technically, an employee instead of a friend." I'd like to add that I understand that it's only by random twists of history and circumstance that I pay Carmen to work from Sunday night to

Thursday night instead of the other way around and also that paying someone half of my income to take care of my child and my house feels lopsided and wrong because for God's sake, I had a child so I could be with her, didn't I? But when writing is as much a part of my identity as motherhood, and when I feel my career receding further into the past with each new book idea I test out and then abandon, I'm not sure what other choice to make.

More than all this, I wish I could tell Melissa that lately I've been worrying, really worrying, that Uzi and I have stepped on the slow track to becoming Couple Number Six. And even worse, that I can't get a good grasp on how I feel about this. Some days I feel certain that meeting Uzi was the best thing that ever happened to me, and other days, with equal passion, I'm convinced I made the biggest mistake of my adult life by getting married. I have no idea if these kind of pendulum swings are normal for married women to have or if they're indicators of real trouble, and I'm afraid to talk about the degree of my ambivalence with anyone, for fear of what I might hear and what it might compel me to do. Nobody knows that lately I've been wondering if being a single parent would be easier than what I am now, which is a kind of weird hybrid, a woman who nominally has a spouse but does 95 percent of the decision making and child raising without him. Sometimes I spin elaborate fantasies about letting go of the husband and the house and the bills as effortlessly as releasing a handful of grass into the wind and renting a two-bedroom apartment where Maya and I can ease back into the simpler, tidier life I had before marriage and parenthood began.

But I'm not going to lay any of this on Melissa, who wasn't expecting such a loaded answer. Our monthly friendship extends only to a certain point and not beyond. That's the way it is for me as a married mother in L.A.: my friends have sifted themselves into four distinct compartments. I have the friends I talk with about writing and teaching; the friends with whom I discuss kids and endlessly obsess about schools; the friends I never move beyond small talk with, because we're married to men who are better friends than we are; and a couple of long-term friends from high school and college who, like me, moved out here as adults and whom I don't want to alarm with pronounce-ments that might end up being nothing more than a temporary blue phase. Melissa's a friend with whom I talk about parenting. Sometimes to great detail and depth, but still a friend with whom I talk only about parenting, and I have the strong feeling that to detour in another direction without warning might strain the unspoken code of our friendship.

I never used to think this way before I moved to California. In New York and the Midwest, where I went to college and graduate school, I could speak with all my friends about everything. Is the sea change a function of geography or of this new chapter of life? Or have marriage, motherhood, and all of the attendant responsibilities somehow reshaped me into someone who's become evasive and obtuse? A year and a half ago, when our baby group had been taking an afternoon walk by the beach with the strollers, Wendy quietly told me that she and her husband, Jeff, weren't doing well. Then she had stolen a sideways glance at me to gauge my response.

"Oh, Uzi and I go in and out, too," I'd breezily assured her. "I think it's pretty normal after you start having kids." But even as I said the words, they felt more like what a hip Los Angeles mama with her hand on the gearshift of adulthood was supposed to say—*Don't worry about it, sister; everything's going to be fine. Soldier on!*—than what I knew I should have said, which was, "Oh no! What's going on?" I hadn't understood how bad off Wendy and Jeff were or how much courage it must have taken for her to send a feeler in my direction. Or how much she must have trusted me to bring it up. I was too focused on my own chronic insecurities in the group of stunning, accomplished, have-it-all Westside-of-L.A. women to hear what Wendy was trying to say. And also, her very simple statement had unleashed a surge of panic in me, making me afraid to hear the grungy details because of what Wendy's marital difficulties might reveal about my own. I remember how she nodded sadly and turned her face away from me, toward the ocean. When I heard, six months later, that she and her daughter had moved back to her parents' house in Arizona, I thought of that walk by the beach and wished I'd had the backbone to get over myself and offer her a sympathetic ear.

It's safer now, for both Melissa and me, to keep the conversation in territory we share, so I carefully select my words to stay within the neutral zone.

"Carmen is a huge help, but it's not like she can be another parent. No matter how much she does or how much I like her, I'm still running the show alone. Know what I mean?"

"So totally you can't even imagine," Melissa says. Her husband works on films as an art director, which takes him out of town for months at a time. It's a common story here among wives of film men—assistant directors, cameramen, gaffers, drivers of the trailers. A whole subculture of women stays parked in Los Angeles raising the children while their husbands log long stretches on location, flying home for anniversary dinners and birthday-party furloughs. Most of the wives, like Melissa, don't seem terribly distressed by the arrangement. I think some of them even secretly like it. When we dot-com wives came along, we were welcomed right into the club.

For the past month, I've been trying to write an essay about this aspect of my marriage, of how Uzi's ninety-hour workweeks have turned me into a de facto single parent. It's titled "The Myth of Co-parenting." You can imagine how big this one's going over in my house. For a couple of weeks I toyed with the idea of turning the essay into a book, to write about other women like myself, the wives of dot-com workers and newly minted attorneys, oil rig workers and military men, women whose husbands either leave town for extended periods of time or come home from work just long enough to grab a few hours of sleep. I was going to call the book *Parent and a Half*, because that's what it feels like we are. My literary agent liked the idea. She thought we might have been able to sell it. But when I mentioned the idea to Uzi and saw the look of hurt surprise on his face, I realized that writing the book would cause more problems in my marriage than a book contract would solve in my professional life. So I put that idea back on the shelf.

Melissa leans back and stretches out her long legs. Her jeans have big, ragged holes in both knees. With her waist-length auburn hair and size-4 frame, she manages to pull this off so it looks chic instead of sloppy.

"Want a juice box?" she asks, pulling a rectangle of apple juice from the mesh bag.

"No, thanks."

We watch Maya and Colette dig a hole in the sand with Colette's plastic shovels. They're going at it with a real sense of purpose. Melissa pokes the little straw into the juice container and takes a few thoughtful sips.

"Are you going to have another?" she asks.

In the sandbox, Maya lifts up her shovel and pours a thin stream of sand onto the top of her head. The timing with Melissa's question is so impeccable it makes me laugh out loud.

"I don't know," I say. "Right now I'm kind of feeling like one is a lot."

Melissa smiles, a big, open smile. "Me, too," she says, and right then we're not a frustrated writer and a former celebrity minding our daughters for a long afternoon or friends limited to single-topic con-versations. We're just two women in their thirties sitting side by side, sharing a laugh on a green bench in the sun. It feels good, so good, to be in the little envelope of this moment. I don't allow myself this often enough, this narrowing of consciousness that tunes out all the back-ground noise—the sound of chapters that aren't getting written or gro-ceries that need to be bought for dinner—to allow for such laser-sharp focus on the present. I sit and let the feeling wash over me, the sense of connection with right here, right now.

Then Colette and Maya start tugging on the same blue shovel, Maya lets out a bloodcurdling scream, and the spell is broken.

"Colette!" Melissa calls out. "Share the big one with Maya!"

"Maya!" I shout across the sand. "You need to share with Colette!"

They both drop the shovel, startled, and go back to digging with pink plastic scoops. "Crisis averted," Melissa says.

For the past few minutes, I've noticed that Maya keeps turning her head to the right, like a nervous tic. I stand up to get a better look. She's saying something to the air next to her. Oh. I sit back down.

"Does Colette have an imaginary friend?" I ask.

Melissa shakes her head no. "Why, does Maya?"

"Yeah. She calls him Dodo. He showed up a couple of weeks ago, and now he goes pretty much everywhere with us."

"Is it a problem?"

"I don't know. She likes to blame him for things. The other day she wouldn't eat any dinner. She tried to convince me that Dodo told her not to eat. And she hits me sometimes and says Dodo made her do it. It's a little creepy, actually."

"Huh. Did you ask Dr. Diane about it?"

Dr. Diane is Melissa's pediatrician. We switched over to her last month after our first doctor became too quick with the prescription pad. I'd heard that Dr. Diane was more naturally inclined and willing to work with parents who didn't want to rely on drugs as a first defense. She'd agreed to do Colette's and Maya's three-year checkups together when I told her that Maya had a tendency to curl up into a ball or clamp her hand over her mouth to block a doctor's access. Melissa had come up with the dual-appointment idea, and it had worked perfectly. Dr. Diane had even commented on how well behaved both girls were.

"I never think of pediatricians for this kind of thing," I tell her. "I always think of them just for medical problems."

"I think they're like jacks-of-all-trades. They have to be, right? What about the preschool teacher? Did you speak with her?"

"No," I say. "But that's a good idea. I'll try to talk to her tomorrow."

Prema, the Montessori Red Room teacher, is half the reason I chose Maya's preschool. The other half is her sister, Helen, the school's director, who teaches the younger kids. Every time I drive up to the school I feel a rush of maternal pride, the satisfaction of knowing that Maya is in a safe, orderly place four days a week from nine to two. When I drop her off in the morning, I can release all my anxiety about her well-being for five hours until Carmen or I pick her up. It's the closest thing to a safety net I've felt so far as a parent.

I wait until aftercare hours have started and Maya is occupied on the backyard play structure with a trio of other kids. Inside the Red Room, I find Prema down on her knees reordering the wooden Montessori learning tools on the low shelves that line the walls. Above her is this month's bulletin board—"Discovering America"—with cardboard cutouts of Christopher Columbus and his ships thumbtacked against a background of triangulated blue construction-paper waves. When she sees me, she stands and gives a big smile.

Prema is Sri Lankan, with long shiny black hair she clips back with a thick barrette and a smile so white and genuine it could stop a parade. Both the students and the parents adore her. Every morning when I drop Maya at school and hug her good-bye at the Red Room door she runs straight for Prema, who scoops her up with a cheerful "Good morning, Mademoiselle!" It would be an uplifting start to anyone's day.

Prema gestures toward one of the squatty round tables for me to take a seat. We settle ourselves into the tiny plastic chairs as best we can. I'm five foot eight, so I sit in a kind of cross-legged slouch with my ankles close to the floor. Prema only comes up to my chin; she fares better with her chair.

"I wanted to talk with you about Maya," I say. "Have you been noticing anything . . . different in her behavior lately?"

Prema purses her lips in thought, and her eyes go wide. She shakes her head. "No," she says. "What kind of things are you talking about?"

"Well, she has an imaginary friend who's pretty active at our house. I'm wondering if he's also coming to school with her."

"Oh." Prema nods in recognition. "You mean Dodo."

"You know about him?"

She laughs. "*Everyone* knows about Dodo."

"Is he getting in the way?"

"No, no." She says this with conviction. "Just if a chair next to her is empty she says it's Dodo's chair. Or sometimes on the playground she introduces the other children to him, that kind of thing. I think maybe some of them will want to have friends of their own like him soon."

"None of the other kids have one? I thought it's supposed to be pretty normal at this age."

"Some kids do. I've seen it before. But in this class so far it's only Maya."

I must look worried, because she adds, "Don't worry. All children grow out of it. Nobody starts kindergarten with an imaginary friend."

This is supposed to make me feel better, but it doesn't really work. It's too easy for me to picture Maya as the kindergarten iconoclast, insisting on an empty little chair permanently positioned next to hers, the teacher calling me at home to discuss a "little problem." It's like a nervous tic I have, this habit of projecting a situation far into the future and imagining the worst possible outcome so I can start guarding against it in advance.

It's a control thing. I know, I know.

"What about during recess? Does she play with the other kids?" I continue.

"Usually," Prema says. "Sometimes she likes to play in the back corner behind the swings by herself."

"With Dodo?"

"I don't know. Do you want me to check tomorrow?"

"That'd be good. And can you let me know if you see anything unexpected, big departures from her regular behavior, that kind of thing, and tell me if she blames Dodo?"

Prema smiles again, but she tips her head slightly and looks a little unsure now, as if she can't quite decide if I'm taking this further than it needs to be taken.

"Yes," she says. "I will definitely let you know."

"Maya?" I ask that night as we're snuggled together in her bed reading *The Red Balloon* for what now has to be the seventeenth time.

"What?"

"At school today, Prema told me you're playing in the back corner of the play yard by yourself. Don't you want to play with the other kids?"

She shrugs. "They play with me sometimes."

"When you go in the back by yourself, are you playing with Dodo?"

"Sometimes yes, sometimes no," she says. She tries to extract a page from underneath my finger to move the story along.

I grip the pages a little harder to keep her focused. "You can tell Mommy the truth," I say.

When Maya started talking two years ago, some of my friends were enrolled in a Mommy and Me program that followed the RIE format, which encouraged mothers of toddlers to speak in clearly enunciated sentences that used descriptive adjectives whenever possible. I tried it for a while, but I was spending so much time alone with Maya that to eject sentences such as "Can Maya please give Mommy the silver spoon that fell onto the big red rug" all day long started making me half insane, and I reverted to talking to her as I'd talk to anyone. Sometimes I still refer to myself as "Mommy," though, a residual quirk I can't seem to shake from that earlier time.

"I don't want to tell the truth," she says. One of the benefits of dropping babyspeak with Maya is that it's given her a vocabulary and syntax much more expansive than most three-year-olds'. The downside is that sometimes she says things that sound so much older than her age, I forget that inside her head, she's only three.

"Maya, is Dodo made up or real?" I ask.

"Maked up," she says.

I exhale a small sigh of relief. "That's what I thought," I tell her.

"Real," she says.

"Wait a minute. You just said he's made up."

She manages to pull the page free and turn it over. The next one is a four-color photo of a young boy racing through the streets of Old Montmartre with a gang of little thugs in hot pursuit.

"I maked him up, so he's real," she says.

Later that night, when I repeat the conversation for Uzi, he laughs out loud.

"You have to admit," he says, "the kid has a point."

He's right: it *is* a legitimate answer, for a three-year-old. Maya doesn't yet understand the distinction between animate and inanimate, between what's "real" and what's not. I can still remember the time in childhood when I hadn't figured it out, either. Until age eight or nine, I still believed wholeheartedly in the existence of fairies and ghosts. Raised on a steady stream of fairy tales and Bible stories, often read to me by my grandmother, I was constantly on the lookout for witches, elves, and booming voices descending from the clouds. The fact that I'd never actually seen or heard such phenomena didn't invalidate their existence. The absence of proof only fed my imagination, allowing me to believe that even more extraordinary possibilities might exist on the other side of an invisible border. It wasn't hard to hold two simultaneous worlds inside my head—one I could see and one I couldn't, but both were equally real to me. As a second-grader I believed—no, I *knew*—that flowers felt pain when I pulled them from the ground, thus requiring a spoken apology, and that my springer spaniel could read my mind. My favorite book when I was nine was Madeleine L'Engle's *A Wrinkle in Time*. The main characters could kithe each other's thoughts, a form of mind communication without words. Sometimes I'd pass time in class by sending mental messages to other students around me—*Raise your hand next time the teacher asks a question* or *Turn around, turn around, turn around*—to see who had the rare gift of ESP.

It didn't hurt that this was an era when American interest in psychic and occult phenomena was at an all time peak. *The Exorcist* was one of the highest-grossing films of the decade, small planes were disappearing over the Bermuda Triangle with unprecedented frequency, and in our kitchen my mother placed a metal spoon in front of the television set to see if Uri Geller could bend it with his mind. My father was a man of simple and straightforward facts, but my mother possessed a secret unconventional streak. "I'm thinking of a number between one and ten. Can you guess what it is?" she'd ask me apropos of nothing in the car, a spontaneous, psychic pop quiz. In 1981, we sat in the paneled-wood basement of our house together to watch the chain-smoking, antagonistic Tom Snyder conduct an hour-long prison interview with the raving mad Charles Manson. I was riveted by the way Manson's rambling, circular nonanswers were punctuated by random moments of unsettling clarity. He would mutter, "How old am I? Forever, since breakfast" in one sentence and then state, "There's only one person you should be scared of, and that's yourself" in another. I didn't know how to reconcile such duality in a single human being. I'd never witnessed it to such a degree before.

"He's a total weirdo" was my assessment at the end.

"He," my mother said, "is an example of a deranged and fascinating mind."

By then I was sixteen, and whatever private connection I had once had to the mystical and unseen had long since shut down. It happened, as I recall, in a series of little deaths. I can still remember the horror—there is no other word for it—I felt at age six, the day I learned that Mr. Rogers's trolley didn't come rolling into his living room on its own volition in response to his call. And the grief I felt upon discovering, at age eight, that the Waltons were not a real family calling out good night to one another in the dark every night with lives that continued, uninterrupted, after the television was turned off. It took me months to adjust to that news. By the time I turned eleven, nearly all of my earlier beliefs had been replaced by the rational certainty of a budding adult. As I remember it, in the fourth grade I was still anthropomorphizing my Snoopy doll and the following year I was rolling my eyes in a Girl Scout meeting when a Seneca woman read us her tribe's creation myth for our badge in Indian Lore. Because, give me a break, *everyone* knew that crows couldn't talk.

Thirteen months after the Manson interview my mother was gone, a death that happened so fast it left all of us spinning without orbits for a very long time. In the first few weeks after she died, the sense of her presence was still so strong I would wake up every morning expecting to see her and have to learn, all over again, that she had died. At night alone in my bedroom, I would try to make contact with her. *Mom, if you're out there,* I would think, *please send me a sign.* If a car drove up our street right then and cast its lights through the window onto the wall above my bed, did that mean she'd heard me? For nearly a year after she died, I spontaneously woke every morning at 2:43 A.M., the exact minute of her death. Did that mean she was trying to send me a message? What was she trying to say? No matter how hard I tried—and I tried hard—I couldn't break through the unseen barrier that kept her from me, and the weeks became months, which became years, and I graduated from high school, and graduated from college, and moved from New York to Chicago to Tennessee to Iowa to New York, fell in love and got a cat and fell in love again and learned how to bake lasagna, all without her knowing any of it, and over time I had to accept she was nowhere at all.

In the nineteen years that followed her death, I became a strict disciple of rational positivist thought, in which scientific rigor—the sacred triad of observation, experimentation, and proof—are the undisputed gold standard for determining what's "real." Yet billions of other people on the globe find a way to integrate religious and spiritual beliefs that defy logical explanation into their mundane, everyday lives. Maybe it's precisely because everyday, domestic life for most of us *is* so mundane that the mystical offers appeal. Which would explain why, when Maya insists that she made up Dodo, therefore he's real, I feel a tiny flicker of hope, for the possibility that I might be wrong when I arrogantly maintain that just because I can't see him, he cannot possibly exist.

I wake just moments before the screaming starts. It's been this way ever since Maya was born, this maternal radar that detects the slightest disturbance in her sleep and wakes me before she utters a sound. My feet are on the floor before Uzi even opens his eyes.

Maya is sitting bolt upright in bed, staring at me wide-eyed when I rush through the door. I take her gently by the shoulders. "It's just a nightmare, sweetie," I say. "Everything's okay."

Outside the bedroom window, the Santa Ana winds wheeze and moan. Someone's garbage pail rakes against the asphalt as it blows across the street.

Maya's breathing comes in fast spurts, and then she screams again. Not in words, just in panicked shrieks.

"It's okay!" I say, a little louder. I put my arms around her and grasp her in a hug, but she squirms away. Uzi stumbles into the room in his boxer shorts, aggressively trying to blink the sleep from his eyes.

"What is it?" he says.

Maya is still staring straight ahead, but she doesn't seem to see us. Maybe she's hallucinating? Does she have a fever? I press my palm against her forehead, then slip my hand around and up under her shirt to feel her back. She's not warm, but there's a thin film of sweat on her skin.

"I think she's having a night terror!" I say, loudly, so Uzi can hear me above the screams. I read about night terrors in one of my child care books, but I can't remember what the author said to do if one occurs.

"What's a night terror?!" Uzi shouts back.

"It's like a nightmare, only worse!"

"Is she awake?" he asks.

"I don't think so."

"Should we try to wake her up?"

You're either supposed to wake up a child during a night terror or not wake up a child during a night terror. I wish I'd paid more attention when I read that page. I didn't urgently need the information, so it didn't stick.

Outside, the wind howls in a bad imitation of Halloween. It's the first night the Santa Anas are blowing this fall, which means fire season has now started. Our brush is cleared within the mandatory two hundred feet of our front door, but still. You never know when a power line is going to come down or some unhinged person is going to toss a match into dry grass just to get a thrill.

A loud, scraping noise followed by a muffled thump outside elicits a momentary pause in Maya's shrieks.

"The porch furniture," Uzi says. "I'll go out and secure it."

The noise was loud enough to startle Maya but not loud enough to shock her into awareness. Waking her myself won't traumatize her, I think, at least no more than whatever's already scaring her. I grip her shoulders a little tighter and give her a few firm shakes. I put my mouth up next to her ear.

"Maya, honey," I say. "Can you wake up for Mommy? You're having a bad dream. Let's try to wake up now. Maya? Can you hear me?" I wiggle her shoulders a little harder, and she wakes with a startle.

"Dodo!" she cries. She clings to my neck. "Dodo was trying to take me away!"

Oh, God. *This?*

"Shh," I tell her, rubbing soft circles on her back. "You're in your bed. I've got you. Nobody's taking you anywhere."

Large sobs shrink to small ones and then to sporadic sniffing. I lay her back down and she rolls over onto her left side and sticks her middle two fingers in her mouth. I curl myself around her back and bury my nose into her freshly washed hair.

"Nobody's taking you *anywhere*," I say again.

When Uzi comes back upstairs, he crawls into her bed from the other side. I start to tell him what Maya just said, but then I stop. We get so little time together like this, the three of us. Every moment of it can't be tainted by conflict. If it is, what else do we have?

"She's gone back to sleep," I tell him.

We lie there in Maya's double bed with her pressed securely between us. Sometimes we hug like this when we're standing. A Maya Sandwich, we call it, which always makes her laugh.

"Should we have done something for her?" Uzi asks. He hates feeling helpless even more than I do.

"I don't know," I say. "I've never seen this before." She's had harmless nightmares where she wakes up shouting, "My sunglasses! My sunglasses!" or crawls into our bed with a drowsy 2 A.M. story about bears in the kitchen, but this kind of terror-stricken screaming, never before. And the part about Dodo trying to take her away? That's a whole new layer of creepiness.

"We need to figure out what's going on here," I say.

"I think we need the opposite," Uzi says. "I think we need a break." He pauses for just the tiniest moment. "To tell you the truth, *I* need a break."

Is he talking about a break from the pressures of parenting or a break from me? Oh, hell, I think he means from me.

As hard as this past year has been for us, as many times as I've thrown my hands in the air—literally—to signify that I've had it with this arrangement, the thought of him leaving makes my heart skid to a stop. I'm supposed to be the one who takes back control of my life by deciding to leave and then, before actually acting on my plan, gets to change my mind. He's not supposed to be the one who leaves *me*.

"You want to move out?" I whisper. My heart lurches back into action, beating so hard I can feel it in my eardrums. Uzi once said he knows I care about him more than I'm willing to let on. I think it's the truest statement he's ever made about me.

"No!" he says, fiercely. "Where are you getting that from? I meant maybe we should take a vacation."

Oh. A *vacation*. He meant a vacation! I'm such an idiot. That's the way my mind works, immediately veering toward panicked thoughts of separation.

A vacation. I smooth back Maya's hair with my right hand, then reach out and stroke the sharp line of Uzi's jaw. Through the dark, I feel him waiting for an answer.

What is it that therapists and 12-steppers like to say? Beware of the environmental cure? Bah. In my worldview, just about anything can be cured by a white sandy beach and a deeply tanned waiter with a tray of frozen margaritas heading my way.

"A vacation," I say, "sounds like an excellent idea."

*   *   *

We haven't been on a family vacation in almost two years, unless you count three weeks last spring at my in-laws' house, which I don't. Since then, I've been campaigning hard to get quality vacation time as a threesome, but we've kept coming up with reasons why we can't leave L.A. Uzi doesn't want to leave his company for more than a few days; or there's a wedding we can't miss; or I have a tight deadline or a class I have to teach. But during the week between Christmas and New Year's, Uzi's company will be closed and my work dries up at that time, which means we're left without a good reason to stay home. And it's early October now, which gives us plenty of time for booking.

Uzi's typical method of vacation planning is to research several ideas simultaneously on the Internet; mull over the options for months; make a final decision a few weeks before our intended departure date; and then get disappointed that airlines and hotels are no longer offering bargain rates. To bypass the kind of bad, bad arguments this invariably leads to between us, I offer to take over the mantle of vacation coordinator this time.

Every vacation we've ever taken before has been on the supereconomy plan, sleeping in friends' guest rooms and maneuvering around frequent-flyer blackout dates. But now we can afford to spend money on a trip for the first time, owing to a small high-tech investment Uzi made that yielded one of those once-in-a-lifetime dot-com returns. Because I'm usually the kind of person who walks around with a detailed, internal list of things to do and places to go, an endless tally of unrealized desires, you'd think a sudden cash influx would prompt me to make a fast, impulsive, and extravagant decision, but it actually results in the opposite. There are so many countries I haven't been to, so many places we've never seen, that I'm paralyzed by all the options.

One morning after I drop Maya at preschool I walk into a Santa Monica travel agency and stare at the brochures on the wall. *Australia and New Zealand.* I went to both countries on a book tour five years ago and vowed to return as soon as I could, but my first four days were spent stumbling around on a perfectly inverted body clock. That would be hell with a three-year-old. *Costa Rica*. I've never been to Central America, but Uzi did a three-week backpacking tour through Guatemala, Costa Rica, and Honduras nine years ago, and he'd rather go somewhere he's never been before. *Japan*. Too expensive. *Peru*. Don't even want to imagine that one with a stroller. *India*. Forget it. Too many vaccines.

Still, I manage to pluck more than a dozen brochures from the wall display. At home that night, I deal them out like poker hands across the top of our bed. *Tahiti. Italia! Costa Azul*. All that taupe sand and blue sky and jaunty yellow typography. Images of peach-and-green Bavarian town houses butt up against photos of svelte women in flowered sarongs striding cheekily toward the camera with huge pink hibiscus flowers tucked behind their ears.

This is how Uzi finds me when he comes home at 10:11 P.M.: sitting cross-legged on top of our bed, encircled by a vibrant array of possibility. An oversized atlas lies open beside me so I can check distances and time-zone increments.

"I'll make it easy for you," Uzi says. He spins around twice and does a little leap in the air next to the bed. "Arf!" he barks, and lands with a loud thump, jamming his index finger onto the atlas's right page.

He barks when he's happy. Also, sometimes just to make me laugh.

"Down, boy," I say. I lift his fingertip and take a look at the small print.

"Burma," I read.

"Myanmar. It's an old atlas."

"Either way," I say. "Try again."

This time, he lands on eastern Guatemala, one of the countries he visited in 1991. He rolls his finger slightly to the right and crosses the border into western Belize.

I lift his hand and give it back to him.

"Like you didn't rig that," I say.

"Who, *me*?"

When Uzi lies, his mouth goes into a flat, unnatural shape, which ruins the deadpan effect he's going for by removing too *much* expression from his face. Whenever I see that look, I press my index finger against the middle of his lips. "Your mouth is doing that thing again," I tell him. It's gotten to the point where I can tell if his mouth has gone flat just from the sound of his voice, which means he can't call the house any more trying to sell me vacuum cleaners or hair-dye products for the cat, as he once almost could. Still, he keeps trying with a kind of persistence and dogged optimism you can't help but admire.

He starts making little, fast panting noises like an excited puppy. I swear, the man is half dog.

"Okay, okay," I say. "I'll check it out."

I don't really mind if Uzi fixed the selection process. In his twenties he worked as a tour and dive guide taking European vacationers to the Red Sea, but since Maya's birth he hasn't gone diving once. Belize has the second largest barrier reef in the world, after Australia's, and I know he's wanted to dive it for a long time. I'm not interested in diving myself—depth scares me, and I don't mean that just as metaphor—but I'm pretty sure I can manage snorkeling. Also, given that I've never been south of Puerto Vallarta, Central America holds a certain intrigue.

After parallel parking and making French toast, research is my third most excellent skill. I feel more at home in a university library than I often do in my own house. For the last three years I lived in New York, I rented the top floor of a brownstone diagonally across Washington Square Park from the NYU library, which made me eligible for a community-access library card that allowed unlimited use of the stacks. When I was working on my first book, I would walk up and down the aisles brushing my fingers against the smooth spines of bound psychology journals in search of the gem of an article that would explain whatever pressing aspect of early mother loss I needed to understand that day. I lingered for hours at long tables highlighting photocopied pages with a fat yellow marker, elbow to elbow with NYU students cramming for Chaucer and thermodynamics exams, all of us enveloped in the cloying forced-air heat while a persistent February wind ravaged the thick glass windows above us. I loved the smell and feel of that library so much—the dull tan scent of aging paper, the constant soft background tap-tap-tap of laptop keys, the aching white glare of the winter sun through the tall windows, casting shadows on the feathery silver treetops of Washington Square Park—that my editor had to order me to stop researching and start writing in order to make my deadline.

The closest research library to me now is at UCLA, a forty-minute drive from the house, but there's Internet access at home now, so that's where I begin. When I type "Belize" into Yahoo!, a long list of travel-planning services, official tourism Web sites, and message boards for travelers and expatriates comes up.

Guatemala, Honduras, Costa Rica, El Salvador, Panama, Nicaragua: I know about the other six Central American countries from twenty years of reading *New York Times* articles about their dictators and civil wars. But Belize? Before I met Uzi, I'd never heard of Belize before. If I'd been hard pressed to locate it, I might have placed it somewhere in Africa, confusing it with Benin, or guessed at an island off the coast of Spain. Now phrases like "most stable democracy in Central America" leap out at me from the Internet and explain why the country hasn't occupied much space lately on the world news page.

Chronologically speaking, Belize hasn't even been Belize for very long. Until 1981 it was British Honduras, before that it was part of Guatemala, and before that it was an area of the great Maya empire that stretched from the Yucatán down to Honduras. Geographically speaking, Belize is small and sparsely populated, with fewer than 300,000 people. Imagine emptying out all of New Jersey and then allowing only residents of Newark back in, and you get an idea of the size and population density of Belize.

As I read more, I learn that because of more than a century of British rule, English is the language of Belize's government and schools, so most people there can speak it even though at home families tend to speak Creole, Spanish, or Maya dialects. The country is divided into six districts, with indigenous Maya and Spanish-speaking mestizos living mainly in the west and south; Creoles in the north; Garifuna, descended from African slaves, along the eastern Caribbean coast; and refugees from the Guatemalan and El Salvadoran wars sprinkled throughout the country. There are also pockets of Mennonite farmers, East Indians, Taiwanese, Lebanese, and young American opt-outs and aging retirees in and around the towns.

I spend the next two nights reading messages from eager tourists and seasoned expatriates on the Belize travel boards. The country seems to offer a perfect fusion of the familiar and the exotic. For Uzi there's the coral reef and the 480-foot-deep Blue Hole made famous by Jacques Cousteau. For Maya there are wild horses, coatimundis, kinkajous, and a blue morpho butterfly farm. For me there's a decent infrastructure and daily English-language newspapers. It seems like the kind of place where anything can happen, but where you can pretty much predict in advance what that's going to be.

On Amazon.com, when I type in "Belize," the typical roster of travel and diving guides comes up. The only two nontravel books offered are *Sastun: My Apprenticeship with a Maya Healer*, a memoir written by Rosita Arvigo, and *Rainforest Remedies: One Hundred Healing Herbs of Belize*, cowritten by the same author. Uzi's fortieth birthday is next week, so I order both books for him, and I add a Fodor's guide to Guatemala and Belize for myself.

And so, with just a few clicks of the computer keys, the choice has been made. We're going to Belize for Christmas.

"You're taking a *three-year-old* to Central America?" Melissa asks when I tell her about our travel plans. Her tone strikes the perfect balance between awestruck and horrified.

"People who moved from there to here bring their kids back all the time," I say.

"But they're *from* there," Melissa says.

"This is how I see it," I say. "Either we bring Maya with us, or we don't go. And not traveling at all for the next five years is not an option."

I try to make the decision sound so easy, so worldly and offhand,

and for that one day it does feel uncomplicated. Until I turn on the computer and discover how hard it's going to be to get us to Belize. Already, the only affordable flights remaining for Christmas week are on Grupo TACA with a layover in Guatemala City. I've never heard of Grupo TACA before, and the only flight it offers from Los Angeles to Belize leaves at 11 P.M. with a connection in Guatemala City at 5:30 A.M., an unkind itinerary for a family if I've ever seen one.

Carmen walks upstairs balancing a load of Maya's clean laundry in a basket on her hip. Carmen flies to Nicaragua every other summer, and her mother travels up from Managua during the alternate years. Possibly one of them has flown TACA before.

I ask her what she knows about TACA. She shudders visibly.

"No TACA," she says firmly. "TACA is El Salvador."

"What's wrong with El Salvador?" I ask.

"You want LACSA. LACSA is the airline of *all* Latin America," she says.

It occurs to me that maybe Carmen doesn't think LACSA is objectively the better airline but that it's the better airline for an American to travel on, specifically an American like me with limited patience for inexplicable, last-minute delays. Uzi has already warned me that traveling in Central America involves chronic miscommunication and interminably long lines and that he's worried I won't be able to handle it.

"I did okay in Sinai," I reminded him. We were there in 1998 on a side trip from Israel, and, considering that we traveled the entire peninsula in a battered 1979 Peugeot with no seat belts or interior door handles, 310,000 kilometers on the odometer, and a Bedouin taxi driver who spoke almost no English, I thought I'd done pretty well.

"True," he said. "But that was only three days. And don't forget the industrial-strength car seat you made me schlep across the desert, even though I knew there were no seat belts over there." The Bedouin driver had looked at the car seat as if it were the wingtip of a UFO.

"You were a good sport about that," I agreed.

I squint at the computer-generated list of airlines flying to Belize.

"LACSA doesn't fly to Belize," I tell Carmen. "We can either take

American through Miami for a thousand ninety per person, forget that, or we can fly Alaska Air, but then we have to lay over in Mexico City *and* San Salvador, and that doesn't make sense at all."

"No El Salvador," Carmen says again. I'm sensing a layer of complexity here I'm never going to be able to understand.

"TACA looks like the only option," I say.

Carmen makes a *whatever you want* kind of face, and I feel an internal tug-of-war starting to rev up. I'm worried about booking these tickets, but I really want to book these tickets, two equivalent impulses fighting for the conqueror's flag.

Let's call the warring factions Me One and Me Two. Me One sides with Carmen: it's too risky to fly on a minor airline; a 5:30 A.M. layover after fewer than six hours of sleep is going to be a disaster; El Salvador is unpredictable, at best—there are so many guns there, probably still guerrillas lurking around. Me Two says *Sister, calm down.* We're talking about the San Salvador airport here, which is probably teeming with security guards, and if you've never heard of TACA, consider that a good thing, since a major air disaster involving that airline would surely have crossed your radar.

Me One says, be a responsible parent, do more research, don't be impulsive or dumb.

Me Two says, look. You keep saying you need to make a change, that your days have become rote and predictable and boring. So? Do something about it. *Book the seats.*

TACA. I say the word out loud. *"TA-CA."* I like the sound of it, forceful and percussive and bold. It sounds like a company that doesn't say no, a company insistent on getting you where you want to go.

"I'm going to buy the tickets," I say.

Carmen, ever the optimist, pats my left shoulder. "All right," she says. "Maybe it will be okay."

chapter three

Los Angeles, California
October–December 2000

Blue is the color of fairy hair, Maya explains, and pink is for unicorn wings. The plastic rectangular pencil box we use for storing Crayolas lies open on the kitchen table. Her rubber baby doll Hursula Zero sits angled between her legs. Its twin, Hursula One, lies facedown on the carpet of the TV room behind us.

When Maya announced the dolls' names a few days ago, Uzi shook his head incredulously. "How does she come up with this stuff?" he asked. But I knew. For Maya's third birthday last week, I'd crouched in a corner of the Montessori Red Room with my camera, trying not to cry, while Maya squeezed a small inflatable globe between her hands and walked three times around a lit candle to signify three full revolutions around the sun. Each time she completed a circle, representing another year of her life, Prema held up a photograph I'd supplied. "This is a picture of Maya when she was zero," she began, showing the class a shot of a newborn in a hospital bassinet. "And this is Maya at age one." By naming both dolls Hursula—which I figure to be a mispronunciation of Ursula, a name she picked up from a *Brave Little Toaster* video—and then discriminating between Zero and One, Maya means to convey that her dolls are sisters, one a newborn and the other a toddler.

It isn't Uzi's personal shortcoming to be oblivious to this type of detail. A fundamental difference between mothers and fathers, I've come to understand, is the sheer volume of information mothers are capable of holding inside their heads. In a college psychology course I once read about how mothers act as emotional containers for their children, offering the child a dumping ground for strong emotions the child can't carry himself, but no one ever told me I would one day become a bottomless reservoir of data as well, a human filing system for the avalanche of small family details to be categorized and cataloged: the dates and times of each month's school field trips and birthday parties; the cell phone numbers of all our emergency contacts; the names of all the stuffed animals in the house; the pediatrician's office hours; where to find the one pair of child's scissors we own and where we've hidden the adult ones; which mothers at the preschool are willing to do playdates at the park and which prefer them at home; which poisons to treat with ipecac and which with activated charcoal.

I have been known to glean a strange sense of power from holding these facts and wielding them before my husband as evidence that I am the more competent parent in our house, the one who knows these things because I am the one paying attention, the one who is consistently around. This is how I sometimes try to right the imbalance between us in my mind, as if to say, "You get to go to an office and interact with other people all day and then come home to a dinner already prepared and a child bathed and in bed, but *I'm* the one who knows where to find the scissors around here, ha!"

And then on some nights, like tonight, I look at Maya drawing at the kitchen table with her crayons, her tongue poking out from between her lips in concentration as she draws, and I realize I'm not the only one in our house who's missing out.

While Maya draws on a sheet of white computer paper, I start paying the stack of monthly bills. Mortgage payment, two car insurances, phone service, long-distance service, electricity, water, gas, gardener, garbage collection, cable TV, cell phone, home owner's insurance, Maya's preschool tuition, and two credit cards. Dear God. When I lived alone in New York I had six bills every month, including health insurance and my student loan. Before that, when I was in graduate school in Iowa, I had exactly three.

"Apples and oranges," Uzi would say. That's the truth.

Maya bends over her drawing, deeply intent on coloring something in. Then her head bobs up triumphantly.

"Guess, Mom," she says.

I peer across the table. Maya's first piece of titled artwork, when she was two, was a series of neat oblong shapes surrounded by wild squiggles. She called it "The Wind Calling a Hot Dog," so this one could be anything. I stare at it closely. From upside down, it looks like a molar wearing a set of Halloween fangs.

"An angry tooth?" I guess.

"Uh-uh."

"A cloud with teeth?"

"No. It's a sh-sh-sh . . ." she says, giving me a prompt.

"A sh-sh . . . shiny tooth?"

"*No.* A sha-sha-shar . . ."

"A shark?"

"Yes!"

I tilt my head sideways. I can see it, sort of.

"Aha, a shark," I say. I give her the thumbs-up sign. "Good job!"

She picks up a black crayon and furiously scribbles another figure on a new page. This time she holds it up for me to see. "Mom. Guess what."

This one looks like a series of fast and sloppy figure eights piled on top of one another. *A Rorschach test,* I think.

"Umm . . . a big mess?" I say.

"No. *Mom!*"

"A storm?"

"*No.*" She pronounces it with an audible, echoey *w* at the end. "Come on, Mom. I will help you. Duh . . . duh . . ."

"Darkness?"

"No. Duh . . . duh . . . doh . . ."

Doh . . . doh . . . oh. *Oh.*

I can't believe I didn't think of this before. All the years I spent in therapists' offices arranging objects in sandboxes, all the articles I've read about getting children to express their feelings through art, and still, it didn't occur to me until right now.

I reach for the sheet of paper. The scrawl is dark and sloppy, shapeless and unrestrained. There's a sort of simple beauty to it, uninhibited and free. But something about it also feels a little sinister. I can't help thinking it's the kind of drawing you'd expect a mental patient to come up with if you asked him to draw the disorder inside his head.

"Dodo?" I say.

She gives me two thumbs-up and a big smile. "Good job," she says.

Dr. Diane's receptionist puts me right through to her, which I wasn't expecting in the middle of the day. I thought I'd get sent to voice mail, so I'd already prepared the message in my head: "Hi, Dr. Diane. This is Hope Edelman, Maya's mother. I wanted to talk with you about an imaginary friend she's got. It feels like it might be more than just a run-of-the-mill kid thing going on here, and I'm a little worried about it. I thought you might have some insights. Can you give me a ring back when you have a chance?" So when a live voice answers after two rings I'm momentarily confused, and I have trouble coming up with actual, coherent sentences.

"Oh! Hi!" I say. "It's Maya's mom . . . Hope. Edelman? We came in about six weeks ago? With Colette?"

"I remember," Dr. Diane says. "What's up?"

"Well, I know this is going to sound strange. And it's probably nothing. But Maya's got an imaginary friend and it's starting to get a little weird."

Damn. Why do I feel the need to back into the conversation like this, to undercut myself right from the start? I always act this way around doctors, or around anyone who I think knows more about a subject than I do and who I therefore expect will dismiss my point of view if I don't chop it down first. But I'm surprised to catch myself doing this with Dr. Diane. She's only a few years older than I am, a kind of Earth-mother hipster doctor with a fresh scrubbed face and two thick blond braids. From the outside, someone would expect her to be intimidated by me and my usually assertive New York attitude, not the other way around.

"What do you mean by 'a little weird'?" she asks.

"Well, she talks to him. A lot. And she blames him for some of her behaviors, especially the negative ones." From where I'm sitting, at the kitchen table, I have an unobstructed view of the range top where Carmen was standing a few days ago, stirring a pot of soup, when Maya ran up and smacked her hard in the butt with Hursula Zero—hard enough for Carmen to stumble forward and almost knock over the pot, which would have spilled boiling liquid on them both. Carmen told me Maya wailed, "Dodo did it! It wasn't me!" as she ran from the room.

I'd sat down with Carmen and nervously explained that Maya was going through a phase. *Just a phase*, I said. It's a phrase I've been carrying around for the past month now like a second wallet, tucking incidents and worries into its ever-expanding folds.

"Ahh," Carmen responded with a nod, her voice downsliding on the musical register from a C to an A. Her mouth formed an expression I realize, only now, was skepticism.

"Sometimes she hits me or her nanny and says it's his fault," I tell Dr. Diane. "But other times she acts completely normal. I don't know. Is it normal to talk all the time to someone who's not there? Is it normal to suddenly start hitting people and blaming someone else? Everyone says it's just a phase, but I've been with this kid every day of her life. I can't explain it better than this, but something about it doesn't feel like just a phase to me."

"How frequent is the hitting?"

"Five times, maybe six. So far it's just at home. But I'm watching her like a hawk now at playdates because I'm so afraid she'll hurt another child. And I'm worried the other kids will think she's strange for talking to someone they can't see."

"How often does she talk to him?"

"Every day." I have a sinking feeling of resignation as I say it. It feels as though the only interval more frequent than "every day" would be "every hour" or "every minute," which would be positively certifiable.

"We just did Maya's three-year checkup, right?"

"Right."

"Well, imaginary friends are developmentally appropriate at this age . . ."

"I know. It's not the existence of the friend that's worrying me. It's the content."

"Anything going on at home that could be making her act out?"

"Her dad's working long hours. But I'm around most of the time. No big changes or upheavals, if that's what you mean."

"Sometimes kids get imaginary friends when there's stress at home. It's their way of creating a situation they can control."

"That makes sense. But it feels more like the friend is controlling *her*."

I hear a soft clicking sound on the other end of the phone, and I picture Dr. Diane tapping the tip of her pen against her desk, wondering if the situation warrants more serious tactics or if I'm just another crazy mom blowing things out of proportion. I'm starting to think maybe I am. A crazy mom. Which scares me even more than Maya's attachment to Dodo, more than I want to admit.

"There might have been mental illness in my family," I say.

"I'm not worried about that," Dr. Diane says. "Tell me, does she talk to this friend in another language?"

"Another language? No. Not that I know of."

"Sometimes that happens. Don't be worried if it does. Is she withdrawing from other kids?"

"I don't think so. Her preschool teacher said sometimes she plays alone, but she's only just started playing with other kids anyway. She was doing that side-by-side play before. Her teacher doesn't seem worried."

"Then I'm not, either. Let's keep an eye on her for a couple of weeks. If you see anything troubling, let me know."

"Like what?"

"If she starts isolating from other kids or starts withdrawing at home."

"You don't think I need to take her to a psychologist?"

"You could. But I don't hear anything that indicates you need to. I wouldn't worry about it. Really. These things almost always disappear on their own."

My friend Sabine has an eight-year-old son named Leo, and Leo is brilliant. I don't mean he's just smart—everyone's kids are smart these days—I mean he's *brilliant*. I've never met a child like him, who can sit at a dinner table of adults and occupy himself for an hour drawing a maze that, upon its completion, no one else can solve. When we play Twenty Questions together, he consistently stumps the adults. I remember Sabine once telling me that when he was younger, Leo had a group of imaginary "cousins." She talked about this as if it were a funny anecdote from the past, but you could tell there had been a time for her when it hadn't been funny at all.

One night after dinner at her house, when we're loading the dishwasher together, I tell her that Maya has an unusual imaginary friend. "I thought you'd be a good person to talk with," I say. "Because of Leo's cousins."

Sabine freezes in position over the sink, holding a blue plate trapped between her yellow dishwashing gloves. "Oh, no," she says. "I feel sorry for you."

"Why?"

"Because it's not so simple a thing."

"What do you mean?"

She turns off the water and leans against the counter, peeling off the yellow rubber gloves. The bay window behind her sink functions as a mirror at night, and I can see my own face staring back at me, waiting for her reply.

"He would talk about having cousins in Texas, and how they always wanted him to visit." She shakes her head. Sabine and her husband, Martin, immigrated to the United States from Germany fifteen years ago, and all of their relatives live back there. In other words, there's no Texas anywhere in their story. "It wasn't even that he talked about them, it was the *way* he talked about them. He would be completely serious about it, as if they were real people. And he would tell me all kinds of details about them, tiny details about their houses and their cars and where the little ones went to school. I would say to myself, 'Where is he getting all this information?' Martin would say, 'Don't be ridiculous, Sabine, it's just his imagination,' but I would say, 'How do you know for sure?' Then one night when I was putting Leo to bed he told me he had decided to visit his cousins tonight, that they were waiting for him, and not to worry if he didn't come back right away. That scared me so much. I mean, at this point I really thought he might be telling me he was going to die. I sat by his bed for two hours after he fell asleep and I kept waking up to check on him all night."

"And he was okay in the morning?"

"He was fine. *He* was, not me. I was the mess."

"And eventually he just grew out of it?"

"Eventually, when he was about six. Maybe five. He was in kindergarten, I remember."

"Great. That's still two years away."

"What kind of friend does Maya have?"

I tell her about Dodo's inaugural appearance in my office, about the aggressive behavior and the blaming, and about my nagging feeling that this isn't something tame and benign. "My friend up the road has a three-year-old son who talks about his 'husbands' all the time," I tell Sabine. "He'll say, 'Can my husbands come to the beach with us?' or 'I'm going to play with my husbands now.' It's a joke in their family, Spencer and his 'husbands.' But I don't find Dodo funny, and I don't think it's because I have a bad sense of humor. I don't see anything to laugh at here."

"It will go away, I think," she says, placing a hand on my arm. "But who knows when? And until then, it might be a very weird time."

The hardest part of planning a surprise party for Uzi is figuring out how to get him to leave work on a Friday before 7 P.M. I finally settle on asking our neighbor Roger, who works at the same company, to offer Uzi a ride to work in the morning and then make up an excuse about having to be home by seven. I leave Roger in charge of the mechanics; I'm in charge of getting everything ready at the house. I buy a helium tank and some balloons and pick up deli platters and a "Happy 40th Uzi" cake I ordered from a nearby market. I know Uzi won't want our friends to feel obligated to buy him presents, so I added slips of paper to the invitations asking guests to make small donations instead. I type up a sheet of paper encouraging them to give to one of three charities I think Uzi would support if he had time to support charities—Doctors Without Borders, the Sierra Club, and the National Wildlife Fund— and prop it up on an entry table. Then I put a little stack of self-addressed stamped envelopes alongside it to expedite the process.

The whole idea is a gamble, since Uzi specifically asked me not to do anything for his birthday, but I have a hard time believing he means it. Isn't his position the one a domestically correct spouse is supposed to adopt? As in "I already have everything I need, honey—you and the kids are enough for me"? I remember my mother's fortieth birthday so clearly, the way she insisted for weeks that she didn't want a surprise party, and how my father, probably relieved to be off the hook, took her request literally. I remember how she walked into the house the evening of her birthday with an expression of demure humbleness on her face and how quickly it was replaced by a look of crushing disappointment when she realized there was no party waiting for her inside. They had a terrible fight that night, my father protesting, "But you told me not to do anything!" and my mother sobbing, "But I didn't really *mean* it!" I vowed I would throw her one for her fiftieth myself, but she didn't make it to fifty, and now I don't want to miss the chance to celebrate Uzi's fortieth. Who knows what'll be in ten years? There are no guarantees, I know.

By 6:30 P.M. our living room is filled with all of our usual party suspects: a dozen or so of the neighbors; Uzi's business partner; my sister and her roommate; Sabine, Martin, and Leo; our Israeli friends from the San Fernando Valley; the members of my writing group; and my three friends from high school and college who live in Los Angeles now, with their spouses and kids. Only after everyone has arrived do I realize I didn't take the parking situation into account. The only place to put all the guests' cars is on our driveway, which means of course Uzi will see them the moment Roger brings him home, which of course is exactly what happens while I'm still running around trying to figure out another place for everyone to put their cars.

It doesn't matter, at least not to Uzi, for whom a surprise at the top of the driveway is just as good as a surprise right inside the front door. We all shout at him in unison when he walks in anyway, mostly for our own satisfaction as well as for the rare photo opportunity of catching him off guard. Maya throws herself at him, and he scoops her up while the guests surround him with backslaps and birthday wishes.

After the initial excitement recedes, he pulls me aside with his arm around my waist. "Thank you," he whispers into my right ear.

"I thought you didn't want a party," I whisper back. I can't help myself.

"I didn't think I did."

What follows are two hours of milling and mingling and laughing and eating and drinking and chasing after small children with plastic plates piled high with finger foods to prevent low-blood-sugar meltdowns. The platters of food evaporate into thin air. I'm in the kitchen refilling the ice bucket when my sister, Michele, wanders in to stuff her plate into the garbage.

"Hey, there. Where's my favorite niece?" she asks.

"She's your only niece," I remind her.

"Right. My only favorite niece."

"Probably in the playroom, communing with the other short people."

My sister is three years younger than I am. She's the head of marketing at a major film studio in L.A. and serves as a classic example of how a kick-ass work ethic, superior people skills, and truckloads of natural smarts can get you so far ahead of the game it makes you wonder why every business school doesn't offer a class in Doing Business Like Michele.

For a brief period of time, we were living parallel lives as single women working full-time jobs. Then I married Uzi and had Maya, Michele got a big promotion at work, and the road forked. Now it feels as if I've become a twenty-first-century version of our mother and Michele's become, well, an even more successful version of who I always thought I'd be.

"How's Maya doing?" Michele asks. She's been getting the blow-by-blow about Dodo for the past month, but we haven't spoken for a few days.

I use my hands to scoop large handfuls of ice from the bag in the freezer into the glass bucket on the counter. "It depends who you ask. My friends say, 'Leave her alone; she'll grow out of it.' The preschool teacher says it's nothing to worry about, she's seen it before. The pediatrician says imaginary friends are 'developmentally appropriate' and then gives me a list of warning signs to look out for. Meanwhile, the kid is having conversations with the air."

"It doesn't sound so bad. I had an imaginary friend. So did you. And we turned out okay." She is nothing if not utterly practical, my sister.

"Speak for yourself, Laurie Bankin," I say. That was the name of her imaginary friend. I can't believe I just remembered that.

Michele laughs. "I don't remember Mommy being worried about it. Maybe you're overreacting."

"Who, me?"

Michele laughs again. "She looked fine when I saw her before," she says.

"That's the thing. She's fine . . . she's fine . . . she's fine, and then all of a sudden she's not fine. Or she's *profoundly* not fine. Sometimes I can get her out of it quickly, and sometimes it hangs on for a while. It's like another force takes over, something that's not even her."

"Maybe it's normal for three-year-olds to act like this."

"What's 'normal'? I mean, were we normal? I thought I was the reincarnation of Laura Ingalls Wilder, you made your G.I. Joe dolls do stealth maneuvers on my Barbies, and Glenn's favorite toy was a stuffed mailman. I don't think I'm qualified to even know what normal looks like."

"Good point," she says.

"Would you call Uzi 'normal'?"

"I'd call Uzi . . . unique."

"That's what I'm saying. If Normal comes to town, it ain't gonna be choosing this house to lodge in."

My friend Deborah wanders into the kitchen, refills her wineglass from the open bottle of Cabernet on the counter, and raises her glass to us in a toast. "Cheers, girls," she says as she heads back into the living room.

"Seriously," I say when Michele and I are alone again. "You know why I'm worried."

"Why?"

"You *know*."

"Grandma?" she asks, and I nod twice.

Michele makes a loud *pfft* noise. "Now I *definitely* think you're overreacting. That's like saying we're both going to have gallbladder problems, just because Dad did. Grandma was Grandma. Maya is Maya. Same family, different stories."

My neighbor Christine takes this moment to lean into the kitchen, carrying her overtired three-year-old on her hip. "If we're going to have cake, now would be a good time," she says. "We're on the brink of a couple of meltdowns out here."

"Right!" I hop into action. Cake. Plates. Forks. I go into the drawer under the microwave for the matches and the candles, which Maya wants to help blow out, except . . . where's Maya? I realize I haven't seen her for at least half an hour.

She's not in the playroom, where a small play table set up with a smiley-face tablecloth, matching paper cups, and plastic utensils is strangely vacant.

She's not in the TV room, where a trio of toddlers is scooping all the picture books from the bookshelf onto the floor.

She's not in the kitchen or in the pantry, her favorite hiding spot. Which means she's either downstairs in Carmen's room—which I check first, without success—or upstairs in her bedroom or mine.

"Maya?" I call out as I climb the stairs. "Honey, are you up here?"

My bedroom door is directly at the top of the stairs. I stick my head inside the open door and look around. "Maya?" I call out. I step back into the hallway, and that's when I notice her bedroom door is closed. I walk over and tap lightly on it four times with my fingernail.

"Maya? Honey, are you in here?" It occurs to me I don't need permission to enter a three-year-old's room. I twist the handle and push open the door.

I see her before she sees me. She's sitting on the floor, cradling a Hursula doll in each arm. "Shakata piman ickter lamod vinyaka?" she asks the empty space in front of her. She nods. "Falafa mingus."

"Maya?" I say.

She looks toward the door, a blank stare. "Nyah!" she shouts in my direction, her mouth curved down into an angry frown, and returns to her play.

My upper body jerks back as if I've just been hit. Sometimes when I pick her up from school she shouts, "No!" and runs away, wanting more time to play, but she's never spit at me like this. Not that I'm even sure I'm an intended target. She's more like a venomous animal, attacking whoever gets close.

I grip the door handle. *"Maya,"* I say again. It's a command this time, not a question.

She turns toward me again, and I watch myself slowly come into focus in her eyes until she sees me, I'm there, and she knows who I am.

"Mom-mee!" she sings out, sweetly. "Dodo doesn't want me to go to the party!"

A whole new kind of panic ripples through me like a cold wind.

I have to get her out of this room.

"You need to go downstairs," I tell her. My voice comes out brittle and too loud. "Do you hear me? I need you to go downstairs. Right now."

A vague look of alarm crosses her face. "Why?"

"It's time for the cake. Go downstairs and find Daddy. Please."

She obediently stands and trots toward the door, then turns to face the empty room and waves good-bye.

"*Maya*," I say. "Go to Daddy. *Now*."

She casts a confused glance over her shoulder when she gets to the top of the stairs.

"I'll be there in a minute, okay?" I say.

Shit. Shit. Outside her bedroom door, I press my back against the wall and slide down to the carpet. Slipping. The floor is slipping away. I rest my arms on my knees and then my forehead on my arms. This is my position of surrender. I assumed it against the side of a black Trans Am in a humid, nighttime parking lot when I was sixteen, surrounded by a cluster of theatrically sympathetic friends after the first boy I ever loved had just told me he'd slept with Lisa Kaminsky—who was six inches shorter than me and a whole year younger—when I was away at summer camp. And again, the following year, next to Michele in the orange carpeted corridor of Good Samaritan Hospital, across the hall from our mother's semiprivate room while a parade of relatives shuffled past us to say their final good-byes.

It was the same position I assumed throughout my twenties when I picked up the phone late at night to the sound of my grandmother's pleas. What had I eaten for dinner? Something from the supermarket? I had to be more careful. Didn't I know? The government had a plot to poison our family's food. She'd heard it on the radio. We had to speak quietly. The FBI was tapping the phone. Just yesterday, workers from the phone company were on her street in a cherry picker, messing with her line.

"Grandma," I would say, trying to keep my voice measured and controlled. "Voices are *not* talking to you from your television." When that didn't work, I would try a different tactic. "Tell them they have to be quiet," I'd say. "Tell them your granddaughter said to leave you alone."

I loved my grandmother fiercely, protectively, wholly. When she started losing her hold on reason, it unraveled something inside of me, too. It wasn't just losing her, which was bad enough, but also the discovery that such a thing could happen to such an energetic, creative mind. Yet there was also something slightly thrilling about witnessing the descent, like the wonder of discovering a tenth planet that contains a life-form never before seen by man. Who knew such an alternate universe could exist simultaneously with our own?

I maked him up, so he's real.

I press my eyebrows hard into my forearm. Beneath the floor, party voices buzz in a steady, comforting drone. For a brief, irrational moment I think about firing off an email to the authors of the *What to Expect* series, demanding a checklist for something urgent and real. *What to Expect When Your Child Can Hear Voices*, I thought. *What to Expect When You're Afraid Your Child Is Going Nuts.* Item number one: Has your child's behavior recently undergone a dramatic change? Item number two: Is there a history of mental illness in your family? Item number three: Are you scared?

Oh, God. I hope, even more than I've hoped for myself and my siblings over the years, that such a condition isn't hereditary. This is my real fear, the one that Prema and Dr. Diane and even Uzi, who knows about my grandmother, don't know I harbor: that whatever triggered my grandmother's state could have worked its way down through three generations of DNA into my daughter's blood. Could such a thing even be possible, or am I succumbing to hysteria myself? Truly, I don't know.

My grandmother was lovingly eccentric for as long as I can remember, deeply committed to her family, yet also prone to episodes of obsessive worry and regret over family matters. She also had a kind of eerie prescience, with theories about the number thirteen, the color black, and processed meats that sounded like random, hysterical ravings during my childhood yet, years later, showed up in Kabbalistic teachings and on the nightly news. This made me come to think of her, after she died, as an underappreciated seer. Tribal cultures believe those who can hear voices are healers, receiving messages from another world. How do I know my grandmother wasn't similarly gifted, in her own way? Still, we lived in suburban New York, not the rain forests of the Amazon, and in our setting her troubles during my late-teen years departed significantly from the norm. Yet I adored her in spite of it and because of it, exactly the way a granddaughter can, and became increasingly protective and defensive toward her as the years progressed. When she passed away at age ninety, just a few months before I became pregnant with Maya, I experienced the loss as a terrible blow.

It's impossible for me not to wonder how far back in time my grandmother's condition reached. Were its seeds already germinating in the 1950s, when my mother was applying lipstick for her first date? Tackling long division in 1948? Taking her first steps in 1939? Or do I have to reach even further back to the time before my mother's birth, to an immigrant apartment in Newark, New Jersey, in the year 1912, where a Polish-born mother of five sets aside her seamstress work and walks to the stove while a father bends over his worn bible in silent concentration? She stirs the chicken stock, lost in thoughts of Tanya Levitsky's wedding dress. He dreams of the Sabbath, his single day off. Both of them are blissfully unaware of what has begun to tick away in the mind of their generous, lighthearted, copper-headed girl.

After the last guests drive away, Uzi walks through the house with a black plastic garbage bag collecting errant napkins and cups, and I carry Maya up to her bed. She curls up against my chest and plugs her second and third fingers into her mouth. I kiss her forehead. "Good night, Maya Bear," I say.

She clings to my neck for one last hug. "Good night, Mommy," she says. There's no sign of the disorientation I saw in her room two hours ago, no evidence she even remembers what happened.

I lay her down gently on the bed and tuck her Pooh comforter around her waist. "Best kid in the world," I whisper into her ear.

"Best mommy in the world," she murmurs back. She's asleep almost before I get to the door. 10:07 P.M.

I take the cordless phone into the TV room and dial the number of my friend Sarah, a therapist in Manhattan. Sarah lives in a big, rambling, comfortably cluttered West End Avenue apartment with her thirteen-year-old son. She usually stays up reading long after midnight, which means she's one of my few New York friends I can call this late.

"Maya just turned three, right?" Sarah asks. "She's right around the age where she's starting to have negative impulses she doesn't know how to handle. She can't take them out on you—that's too threatening. So she creates an imaginary character she can project her negative feelings onto. It's called splitting. That way it's not really her who's misbehaving. Make sense?"

"Why would she want to take it out on me?"

"She doesn't want to. That's the point. How long has this been going on?"

"About two months. Maybe I'm working too hard?"

"*Are* you working too hard?"

"Not really. What I mean is maybe I'm working too much."

"You're not working too much," Sarah says. Her voice grows both softer and harder at the same time. Sarah is fourteen years older than me. We both lost our mothers to cancer in our teens, but she also lost her husband in her early forties and raised their son alone. Sometimes it feels as if she has a lot of compassion for me and not a lot of compassion for me at the same time.

"She was talking to him in gobbledygook tonight," I say. "It didn't sound like any language I'd ever heard before."

"Maybe she's trying to speak Hebrew like Uzi?"

"She can speak real Hebrew. Her last babysitter was Israeli. Do you think I'm overreacting?" Meaning, am I creating a drama where none exists? It wouldn't be the first time. Or the tenth.

"Overreacting? I don't like that word. If you're worried, you're reacting to something that's real to you."

If the phone had a cord, I'd be winding it tight around my finger. I pick up one of Maya's stuffed bunnies from the floor and start rubbing the inside of its ear instead. I'm afraid to say what I want to say, but then I go ahead and say it anyway.

"You know about my grandmother," I say.

"Don't even go there. That's not part of this."

"How do you know?"

"Because I know," Sarah says.

"I feel like I'm starting to unravel. Really starting to unravel."

"You're not starting to unravel."

"Why do you get to have such certainty about what's going on in my life?"

"Because I'm on the outside, which gives me perspective. You're on the inside, which gives you myopia. Listen, Maya's a smart kid. Why don't you try to reason with her? Try saying, 'Dodo hasn't been behaving very nicely lately. Why don't we send him home to his mom for a while?' and see what happens."

"What if she completely freaks out?"

"Then she freaks out. We try something else."

The next day, after I pick up Maya from preschool, I edge into the slow lane on Pacific Coast Highway. I take my time adjusting the rearview mirror until she fits snugly in the center of its parentheses. Then I turn down the volume on the Wee Sing tape and check for messages on my cell phone. When I run out of distractions to create, I count to five inside my head. Then I say it.

"Hey, Maya. I've been thinking. Dodo really hasn't been behaving so nicely lately. Maybe we should send him home to his mom for a while. Maybe he needs a time-out."

"Nuh-*uh*," Maya says. She sucks up the last bit of juice from her juice box, a noisy, draining sound. "Anyway, he doesn't have a mom."

"He doesn't have a mom? How can that be?"

"None of the Dodos have moms," she explains. "They live alone on the big, cold island. They just protect themselves."

None of the Dodos?

I glance at my daughter in the mirror, at her messy dark curls and little fingernails and impossibly tiny white teeth, and I feel a rush of love so strong it makes my cheekbones ache.

"Maya," I say, carefully measuring out each word. "Exactly how many Dodos are there?"

"There are many," she says. "There are boy Dodos and girl Dodos. And good Dodos and bad Dodos." She chews on her straw thoughtfully. "Of course, mine's a boy."

"And he's a bad one?"

"Sometimes. Sometimes he's good."

"And you can see these Dodos?"

In the rearview mirror, she nods. "I see them all," she says, clearly enunciating each word, and I feel a sudden downward lurch in my chest, like an elevator missing a floor.

That night, Uzi and I lie on the couch with my feet in his lap, the History Channel broadcasting black-and-white footage into the toy-cluttered TV room.

"How worried do you think we should be?" I ask.

I know how worried *I* am, but I'm trying to gauge whether I should sink into it or try harder to reel myself back in. I'm counting on him to haul me out. Because if I just sink into it, I've got the feeling we're talking bottomless lake.

"About what?" he asks. I'm right. He hasn't been paying attention.

"The Dodos. They're, like, *multiplying*."

He widens his eyes and raises his shoulders slightly. I know this look. It's neither dismissive nor disinterested, but it neatly relinquishes ownership of the problem. "Who, *me*? I leave these things up to you," it says. Sometimes it seems as if Uzi believes that problems ignored for long enough eventually vanish through a secret magic only wives know how to perform. I'm thinking I need to get myself one of those wives.

"I don't know," he says. "Who can we ask?"

"I talked with Sarah. She thinks Maya's splitting her ego in half to push all the negative stuff onto someone else. She said it's pretty common for kids this age."

"That makes sense," he says, without sounding convinced. For as long as I've known him, Uzi has harbored a mistrust of therapists, maintaining that most of them go into the practice of fixing other people because they need to be fixed themselves. Judging by some of the therapists I've known over the years, I can't say he's completely wrong.

I pull my knees to my chest and hold them there. A grainy Third Reich unit marches in formation across the television screen. I nudge Uzi's thigh with the ball of my foot.

"I need you to take this seriously," I say.

He points the clicker at the television and the screen goes dark on a German ticker-tape parade. "Okay," he says. "I'm listening."

"Something just doesn't feel right about Dodo," I say. It feels oddly appropriate to talk about him as if he's a real person. "It's like he has a hold on her. You know?"

Uzi squeezes his temples with his left hand. He looks so tired. How have I not noticed how tired he looks before? In our wedding pictures taken three and a half years ago—before he started his company, before the crippling workweeks began—his face was uniformly smooth, his hair still a continuous shade of brown. Those images look like air-brushed versions of the real Uzi now. I reach over and lightly rest my fingertips against his cheek.

"I'm sorry," I tell him. "I shouldn't have said it like that."

I should have been, I don't know, less dramatic? More upbeat? Less blunt? I don't even know how to act anymore. It's one way with Uzi, another way with Maya, and a third way with Carmen. Somewhere in me, I have to believe, is a woman still capable of identifying her own convictions and acting upon them, but we're going to need a formal reintroduction here.

"It's all right," Uzi says. "Actually, I've been thinking the same thing myself."

If my husband—my paragon of underreaction, the one person I count on to consistently assure me that everything will be fine even when all signs point otherwise—if my husband is expressing worry, it means that by anyone else's standards something is seriously, verging on catastrophically, wrong.

"I didn't think you'd noticed," I say.

He looks at me like I've just sucker punched him with a one-two combination I'd promised never to use.

"Of course I've noticed," he says. "Of *course* I have."

The TV room is where he finds me late at night on November 26, clutching the remote control bar with the cat snuggled on my lap as I obsessively flip back and forth between CNN, ABC, and NBC.

"What?" he says, stopping short at the threshold when he sees my face.

When I look up at him, I feel like a child who's been waiting all day for her mother to get home, only to burst into tears upon seeing her.

"They're stealing the election," I say. He's been in his work cocoon all day and probably hasn't heard. "Those bastards are stealing the election."

Uzi flops down on the couch beside me. He's one of a hundred million Americans who believe there's no difference between the presidential candidates this year and that all politicians are part of a broken system. Still, if he ever gets tired of listening to his lefty wife's rants about the Florida recount, he doesn't let on.

"What happened?" he asks.

"Katherine Harris just certified the Florida vote and gave it to Bush. Palm Beach County finished counting two hours after the deadline, so their votes weren't included." West Palm Beach is where my grandparents spent their winters, and I feel a kindred sense of outrage on behalf of the whole county. Plus, I have friends and relatives down there who've been working around the clock recounting ballots by hand. "Bush just announced his transition team is moving ahead," I say.

"I'm sorry," Uzi says.

I lean my head against his shoulder. For nineteen days, the country has been in president-elect limbo, and I've been taking it hard. I was the child who took the Pledge of Allegiance seriously every morning in grade school, careful to enunciate clearly with my hand placed properly over my heart, and the adolescent who automatically teared up at the start of every Yankees and Mets game when we all rose and sang "The Star-Spangled Banner." National pride has always been a larger part of my identity than regionalism or religion, and my sense of civic duty never wavered, even during the seeming illogic of the Reagan years.

But this? I'm aware that in a democratic system, the tides shift back and forth between leaders who represent your ideals and leaders who don't. But handing an election to the Republican candidate over 537 disputed votes in the state where the Republican secretary of state is the co-chair of his campaign? Where his *brother* is the governor? I can't wait to see what history books say about this in another thirty years.

Upstairs, Maya screams in her sleep. Another night terror. The cat leaps off my lap, digging her back claws into my thighs as she goes, and darts under the kitchen table to hide. The blinds on the window behind me choose this exact moment to come loose from their left inside mount and crash down against the back of the couch, narrowly missing the top of my head.

There is just so much I can take, and this is not included.

I am starting to crack. I really think I am. Starting. To crack, that is.

"I'll go to her," Uzi says. "You stay here." He rushes upstairs, leaving me with the cognitive dissonance that has become CNN.

Carmen is the one who finally comes up with a plan. Carmen, a child of rural Nicaragua, a believer in all things magical, a frequent client of an East L.A. *curandero*, who she claims cleanses her spirit with herbal baths and the *veladoras* she lights every night. The trunk of her Toyota clinks loudly with grocery bags full of the empty glass cylinders adorned with portraits of Jesus, the Virgin Mary, and various patron saints. When she spends the night with us, fragrant smoke wafts out from underneath the guest room door.

"Mrs. Hope," Carmen says one evening in the kitchen, after I've just turned off the computer, "I am thinking. It is time to get rid of El Dodo."

"Really?" I say and immediately wince. It's embarrassing, how much raw eagerness can be compressed into just one word. "You think so?" I add, which doesn't sound much better.

Carmen switches off the flame beneath a pot of rice and turns to face me. Her voice is weighted with certainty. "He is too much in the way."

I feel a slight ascension of relief. Maybe the equation really is that simple, after all. Dodo is in the way. He needs to be removed. Carmen has a plan. I set my water tumbler down on the counter. Glass onto granite. Things that are solid.

"Okay," I say. "What do we do?"

"First, we need an egg." Carmen walks to the refrigerator and removes an egg from the molded rack inside the door. She conceals it at thigh level and slips it furtively into my hand, even though no one else is in the room.

"You take this egg," she says. "You rub it all over Maya. Up the arms and down the arms. Up the legs and down the legs. Like this." Carmen swipes her left hand up her right arm and down her left leg to demonstrate. Her fingernails are painted a careful, frosted blue. "Then you bring the egg back to me. I take it outside and throw it into nature. Also, I say a prayer in Spanish."

I look at the egg. It looks . . . like an egg.

"Just out of curiosity," I say. "What, exactly, does the egg do?"

"It takes the bad spirit from the body."

"You think she has a spirit attached to her?"

"Of course!" She sounds surprised that I could have missed something so obvious. "What else is El Dodo?"

To Carmen, life is a collection of unambiguous polarities: good and evil, earthly and spiritual, right and wrong. At first I mistook her stubborn certainty for simplicity. Only over time have I come to recognize it as an enviable form of clarity. What would it take to think as Carmen does, to believe so unequivocally in the supernatural power of an ordinary piece of food? But really, what alternative do I have? A psychological diagnosis means God knows what kind of tests and medications. A spirit seems infinitely more manageable. A spirit, as Carmen explains it, can be effectively removed. One thing, out of all the things that feel broken, I might be able to fix.

I close my eyes and feel the egg lying cool and hard against my palm. I rub my thumb across its smooth, unblemished shell. *Egg*, I think. *Egg*.

I can make a choice, I realize: mental illness or spirit. I choose spirit.

I find Maya in her room, dressed like Tinker Bell and trying to manipulate a blue evening gown onto an unrelenting Barbie doll. "Hi, sweetie!" I say, with extra exclamation points. "I've got something really fun for us to do!"

"What?" Maya looks up, already suspicious.

"See this egg? I'm going to run it up and down your arms and legs, like this." I demonstrate on my forearm.

"Why?"

"Because Carmen says so. It'll just go up and down, up and down. It feels really good." I stroke the egg against the side of Maya's thigh.

She giggles. "It's cold!" she squeals. A brief surge of interest ignites her eyes. "Okay," she agrees.

Afterward, I dutifully return the egg to Carmen, who cradles it carefully in her hands and heads for the ravine at the bottom of the driveway. When she returns, she swipes her palms together noisily, twice, as if to say, "That's that!" Then she takes a handful of week-old basil from the refrigerator and explains I need to squeeze it into Maya's bathwater, taking care to pour it over the top of her head.

Once you've agreed to drag an egg up and down your child's limbs to remove an evil spirit, bathing her in basil isn't much of a leap. Not only do I fail to feel ridiculous doing it, I try hard to do it right.

"Now things get easier around here, I know it," Carmen nods as she supervises the bath. "These are *very* powerful actions. *Very* powerful."

It is not a complete failure. Maya doesn't mention Dodo for two full days. In his absence, I'm filled with an uncharacteristic levity. For the first time in months, I write five pages in a day. I clean out the drawers in the master bathroom vanity, organizing all the little items into tidy, individual plastic cells. In a fit of inspiration, I find a Belizean travel agent named Carolyn on one of the Internet travel boards and call her to start booking hotel rooms for our trip.

But on the third morning, as we're driving to school, Maya calls out "Hel-*lo*?" from the backseat in a tone reminiscent of thirteen-year-olds at the Sherman Oaks Galleria mall. "Can we get another *car seat* back here?"

"Another car seat? What for?"

She makes a little, impatient noise in the back of her throat. "For *Dodo*," she says. And just like that he's back, as if he'd taken only a short detour before boomeranging back to his rightful place.

"El Dodo is more tough than we know," Carmen concludes gravely.

"Do you want me to find you a local referral?" Sarah asks.

"Maybe we need to find a shaman in Belize," Uzi says.

The prospect of an otherworldly explanation for Dodo seems if not actually to please my husband, then at least to engage his interest in the removal process. Such a connection would support his belief that a simultaneous, unseen dimension exists alongside the one we experience every day. Ever since he started reading *Sastun* and learning about the author's apprenticeship with Don Elijio Panti, the last great Maya healer of Belize, he's been eager to find a shaman for us to see there.

Uzi believes in determinism. He believes in reincarnation and karma and a number of other intangible concepts that make me squint one eye and retract my head three inches when they come up in conversation. For a short time in the 1980s I believed in such ideas, or at least tried to believe in them, until three years of graduate school followed by five years in New York wrung the last of those impulses out of me. But my husband: my husband believes with a certainty, with a calm and unwavering sureness I can't poke a hole in, regardless of how hard I try.

This is a way of explaining why Uzi's face, when I tell him about Carmen and the egg, registers mild bewilderment—not because of the act itself, which he thinks was a good idea and worth trying, but because he's surprised I agreed to go along with it. He didn't think I'd be open to such ideas. "Open"—that's the word he uses, as in, I'm not being "open" enough. As if I stubbornly and deliberately walk around with an aperture that's too small.

"Open to what?" I ask. Shamanism? New ideas? *His* ideas?

"Everything," he says. "You need to have more trust."

"In what?"

"In the universe."

Oh. That word, again.

I hadn't expected any of this from Uzi when we married. I'd always thought of myself as the more susceptible partner, the one whose innumerable anxieties would make me more likely to embrace the unconventional if it offered reassurance, however fleeting that might be. But over the past few months I've started to think of myself as the more grounded partner, the one left juggling all the practical, earthly minutiae of family life while my husband spends what little free time he has reading books about the power of consciousness and alternative healing. It's as if I've suddenly become the capital letters in this enterprise— bold, solid, and assertive—while Uzi drifts around in italics: lovely and loopy; slightly off center; constantly reaching for more.

In late October, he befriended a group of people who call them-selves Pranic Healers and claim an ability to clear negative energy fields. On weekends they come over and sit around our kitchen table, drinking herbal tea and waving their hands in the air. Once when they were visiting I had a bad case of hiccups. One of the women told me to stick a silver knife into a glass of water and drink it down. The metal would act as a conductor for the energy that's all around us, she explained, which would calm down the spasms in my diaphragm. I fig-ured I didn't have anything to lose by trying. Also, I didn't want to appear rude by refusing. I was the only one in the room who was sur-prised when it worked.

When Uzi's father, an M.D., came to visit in early November, he agreed to let the Pranic Healers work on him. He was in the early stages of Parkinson's disease, already having trouble with his balance, and well aware of where his condition was heading. They sat him in a chair in the middle of the TV room and hovered around him silently for nearly a half hour with their hands facing him in midair. When they finished, he stood up and walked in a straight, steady line for the first time in months. The effects lasted for several hours. That one was harder to explain.

"What do you believe in?" Uzi asked me one night.

"I'm a card-carrying member of the Church of the Senses," I said. "I have to see to believe."

"No, I'm serious," he said. "What do you believe in? Really believe in?"

To parse out what I truly believe in from what I once used to believe in and what I wish I could believe in—it's a harder task than one might think. As a child I believed wholly in an omnipotent and power-ful God, the God of my illustrated Bible books, so awesome His name was shrouded in euphemism, written as G–d or spoken, in my Hebrew school class, as Ha Shem, "The Name." The one to whom I sent silent prayers to keep my family safe and to whom I apologized every night for all my perceived eleven-year-old sins: cursing, talking back to my parents, bullying my younger sister. "I'm sorry, I'm sorry, I'm sorry," I would mentally recite twenty times in bed every night, just to have a couple extra in the bank in case I slipped the next morning and accidentally thought, "Goddamn." But it became impossible, at seventeen, to continue supplicating to a divinity that stood by silently as cancer tore through the body of a forty-one-year-old woman who'd never hurt anyone and took her life in sixteen months, leaving three school-age children and a husband who had little idea of how to raise them alone.

And yet . . . and yet . . . there has to be *something* out there larger than ourselves, no?

Call it my fall from innocence or even my fall from grace. From the night of July 12, 1981, onward, I've never entirely let go of the belief that some kind of higher power might exist, but I stopped wanting a personal association with one that would allow such suffering to unfold. If God, or whatever entity was behind it all, didn't have time to protect my family, then I wasn't going to waste my precious time on Him. Or Her. Or It.

The truth is, I'm not sure what I believe in now. My current spiritual life resembles a religious Greatest Hits collection, patching together the highlights of Buddhism, Hinduism, Judeo-Christian theology, Jungian psychology, and practical street smarts, and my loyalty to even this fluctuates according to whim. Depending on my mood, I think either that the Pranic Healers are onto something really big or that they're full of shit.

"What do you believe in?" my husband asked.

Surely I must believe in something, the question implied.

What do I believe in?

Well. I believe in the sound of a lone acoustic guitar strumming in the back of a smoky bar. I believe in the scent of night-blooming jasmine. I believe in the look of calm wonder I saw on my daughter's wet face right after she was pulled from my body and placed on my chest. I believe in the miracle of radio and the way it pulls music right out of the air. I believe cats can smile. I believe, especially from the back window of a taxi speeding across the Triboro Bridge from La Guardia late at night, that New York is the most magnificent city in the world. I believe that I will get back there, somehow, one day.

"I believe in the possibility of everything," I told my husband. "But I can't place my trust in anything without visible proof." I've never been lacking in imagination. It's taking things on faith that gives me a harder time.

"What do *you* believe in?" I asked him. Turnaround seems only fair.

He did a one-shoulder shrug, a little "Well, it's really very simple" kind of gesture. He doesn't have the kind of inner conflict about this that I do, which is probably why I keep trying to provoke it in him, to justify my own cynicism.

"I believe the world is governed by polarities and paradoxes," he told me, "some that we can see, and some that we can't. Some we know about, and some we can't even imagine yet. We think polarities are there to create divergences, but really they exist to create dynamicity. And that's only a piece of it. To think we already know all there is to know or that we can see all there is to see, that's just our egos speaking. That's arrogance speaking. We know only a tiny speck of what there is to learn."

"Whoa," I said. "I'm way too much of an empiricist to go for that."

"That's the problem," Uzi said. "After a certain point, you've got to let go of rational thinking and just believe."

Most of the time, I let comments like this float right on by.

"If it makes sense to you," I tell him.

"If it makes you happy," I say.

But late at night after Uzi falls asleep and early in the morning before he wakes, in the gray hours when my thoughts are my own, I lie next to him and place my hand against his spine to feel his steady, even breathing. And I worry.

Which is more frightening, I wonder: that my husband is forming a belief system based on the strength of other people's convictions or that he really believes the things he says?

"Half the people we know are spiritually stubbed out," Uzi says when I voice my concern. "I'm learning new things every day. What's the harm in that?"

But I know about the potential for harm from my own explorations, years before I met Uzi, when I felt lost and lonely and somehow got the idea that a makeshift combination of Adult Children of Alcoholics meetings, weekly services at the Unity Church, and crystals of various colors and sizes left outside to absorb the energy of the sun could heal me. I know firsthand about the unrestricted enthusiasm of the seeker and about the feelings of despair that often fuel it. And I know that the reason one goes searching is not necessarily to find something new but to get away from what currently exists.

I've seen the expressions on people's faces when I mention how many late nights Uzi puts in at the office. I hear the way my voice gets just a little too adamant, trying just a little too hard to convince people, when I insist, "He'd never do that." What I don't say is that I'm afraid I'm already losing him to something far less concrete than another woman or a demanding job.

"He's thanking his *food*," I tell Sarah on the phone late one night in early December.

"He's what?" From behind Sarah comes the sound of a receding siren and then several car horns bleating on West End Avenue. Sounds that to me signify *home*.

"When he sits down to eat, he closes his eyes for a few seconds and gets this beatific look on his face. He holds his hands up over the plate like he's trying to press the air down. The other day I asked him what he was doing. He said he's thanking the animals and plants that sacrificed their lives for his meal and thanking the food for nourishing his body."

"Actually, that sounds kind of nice," Sarah says.

"Sarah!"

"Right," Sarah says, recovering quickly. "So it's making you uncomfortable. It's not normal behavior for him."

"It's not normal behavior, period." I leave out the part where I sit on my own hands when I see Uzi doing this, as my form of silent protest. I'm not so sure that's normal behavior, either.

"What does Maya say when he does it?"

"Nothing. She doesn't even notice."

"Maybe that's a good thing."

When I sit quietly and remember to breathe, I know that Sarah is right. Praying over food—it's a small thing, after all. Billions of people do it around the world, probably millions in Los Angeles, for all I know. My own family did it every Friday night for my first seventeen years, reciting Hebrew prayers over bread and wine before the Sabbath meal. It was my mother's idea, she of the Orthodox Jewish upbringing, and it was a good plan for us all, establishing a ritual both predictable and consistent in a family otherwise inclined to spill over into chaos. After she died my father tried to keep Friday-night dinners going, but it was too hard for him to cook a three-course meal after an eight-hour workday and an hour-long commute from the city back to the suburbs. He started picking up a mushroom pizza or a bucket of Kentucky Fried Chicken on the way home instead. It didn't feel respectful to say prayers over that, so we stopped with the wine, too. Within just a few months the idea of Friday-night dinners became an exotic and inaccessible memory, like an immigrant's dim recollection of having once lived with purpose in a distant land. Maybe this is what bothers me most about Uzi's mealtime prayers, the idea that he's found a way back to an idealized version of home without me, instead of working harder with me to create one of our own.

Maya's cough tows me out of sleep, pulling me from an airplane with auditorium seating where my college boyfriend is introducing me to his new wife, to a master bedroom in southern California where my husband slowly rolls toward me and opens his eyes.

"Oh, no," he says.

We recognize the cough even in our semiconscious state, the seal-like bark of it, like repeated, determined attempts from a broken trumpet. I know when I press my hand against Maya's back her skin will be burning hot. I push back the covers and rouse myself out of bed.

"I'll start the shower," Uzi says. This is the fifth time we've woken like this in three years. By now we've got the system down.

The first night of croup is always the worst. Maya and I will be sitting in the bathroom for the next half hour, running a hot shower to let the steam open her airways. I know what to expect afterward: three days of high fever and the seal-bark cough, followed by three days of no fever with a rough, gravelly cough and a terrifically sore throat, followed by two days of lethargy before she's strong enough to resume a normal schedule again. Eight days, from beginning to end.

In college, I had a roommate from Greenville, Mississippi, who, at times of unexpected distress, would plant her hands on her hips and ruefully announce, "Well, doesn't *this* just suck big, green donkey dicks?" This qualifies as a donkey-dick moment, if I've ever had one.

Ten minutes later, sitting on the closed toilet seat with Maya dozing against my chest, the small bathroom filling with a diaphanous steam, I start running numbers in my head. Today is December 13. Eight days from now brings us to December 21. Our flight to Belize leaves the night of the twenty-second. It's enough time for the virus to run its course and still allow us to make the trip. Barely.

Except this time my math is off. Six days later, Maya's still coughing the seal-bark cough and running a low-grade fever of 100.5°. Dr. Diane doesn't recommend treating a fever lower than 101, so we're doing cold compresses and drinking lots of fluid. I've already tried all the remedies—*Aconitum, Hepar sulphuris,* and *Spongia*—that my homeopathic M.D. recommends, and they don't seem to be doing a thing. I call Dr. Diane's office and get squeezed in for an appointment later in the day.

Dr. Diane is in Santa Monica, five blocks from Uzi's office, and I promise Maya we'll visit Daddy afterward if she's a good girl for the doctor. Our last pediatrician called this "offering an incentive." I call it what it is—a bribe—but I'm not beyond trying it to extract cooperation.

And in doctors' offices, I have to. Ever since she was a year old, Maya has had a rabid aversion to anyone in the service or professional industry touching her. After her first dental exam, the pediatric dentist used the word "combative." The last hairdresser we tried just tossed her shears onto the Formica countertop and muttered, "Jesus *Christ.*" I've been doing Maya's haircuts myself for the past year.

Dr. Diane walks into the examining room clutching Maya's file to the chest of her white lab coat. "So, how are we doing today?" she asks.

"Hi, Dr. Diane!" I say, a little too cheerfully. Maya immediately clamps her hand over her mouth.

"Dr. Diane's just going to look down your throat," I say. "And in your ears, to make sure they're okay for flying in a plane. It's only going to take a minute, and then we'll go visit Daddy."

Maya shifts her hands to cover both ears and pulls her lips in so tight they disappear.

"Remember how we came with Colette last time?" I remind the doctor. "This is why."

"It's all right," Dr. Diane says. She sounds neither bothered nor impressed by Maya's display.

"Okay, Maya," she says. "We're going to use this to look inside your ears." She holds up the otoscope for Maya to examine and turns it from side to side. Maya couldn't be less interested.

"Do you want to look in my ears first? Or your mom's?"

"That's a good idea," I chirp. "Do you want to look in my ears first, Maya?"

Maya shakes her head no with a controlled, jerking motion. Left. Right. Left. Right. "No!" she shouts. "Dodo says no!"

"Dodo?" Dr. Diane asks.

"That's the imaginary friend I told you about," I say.

She backs up a step and skims Maya's chart. "Did she do this before the friend?"

"She's done this forever," I say. "You should see her at the dentist." Then I add, just so she doesn't start getting any ideas, "She's never been touched by anyone against her will, not as far as I know." *Unless you count a doctor in our first pediatric group*, I think, who pinned Maya down when she was a year and a half old to scrape wax out of her ear canals, causing her to erupt in a violent screaming and kicking fit, which is another reason why Dr. Diane is our pediatrician now.

"Where are you going on vacation?" she asks.

"Belize," I say. "Central America."

Dr. Diane goes on a volunteer mission every year to vaccinate kids in Honduras, which is probably the reason why, instead of looking at me askance for taking a preschooler to Belize, she nods and says, "Nice. You'll like it there." Then she adds, "If you want to take her on an airplane, I really need to check her ears."

"I don't know if she'll let you."

"How important is it to you to make this trip?"

"Pretty important," I admit. I feel a small *unk* inside my ribs as I say it, that little pinch of guilt—what kind of mother prioritizes a vacation over her child's health? *A mother who badly needs the vacation*, I think. *A mother for whom the word* nonrefundable *induces panic*. I try to calm myself with the reminder that Maya's not so terribly sick. Uncomfortably sick, yes, persistently sick, yes, but not distressingly sick.

"Okay, Maya," the doctor says. "We're going to look in your mom's ears first." She points the otoscope toward me, and I obediently tip my head to the side. I can feel the instrument hovering outside my ear canal as the doctor pretends to investigate.

"Hmm, looks pretty good," she says. "Okay, your turn, Maya."

Maya shakes her head forcefully from side to side. Dr. Diane catches my eye and motions her eyebrows toward Maya. I get the message.

At moments like these, my carefully crafted child-rearing philosophies—respect the child, treat the child the way you'd want to be treated, don't break the child's spirit—completely evaporate, replaced so fast by a kind of chop-chop, utilitarian functionality it makes me wonder if I've only been fooling myself with the rhetoric all along. In one swift motion I hug Maya tight, pinning her arms against her sides, and Dr. Diane rushes in, holding the crown of Maya's head steady with one hand and peering into her right ear, then shifting around behind me to sneak a peek into her left. It's over so fast that by the time Maya realizes what we're doing, it's finished.

"Looks clear," Dr. Diane says, snapping the black tip off the otoscope.

I let go of Maya's arms. Her hands immediately fly up to her ears again.

Clear ears. I wasn't expecting that. I'd thought a diagnosis of clogged ears would make the decision to cancel the trip easy, but this news instead adds a new layer of uncertainty. Does this mean we can take Maya to Belize without worry? Or does the news that one body part passed the test nonetheless mean that another might flare up in a remote Central American town?

"What do you think?" I ask Dr. Diane. "Should we go?"

She lifts her shoulders in a *Who can say?* kind of gesture. "It's a virus, and a virus has to run its course. Either she'll get better up here, or she'll get better down there. It's really your call."

"No offense," I say. "But that's not very helpful."

She smiles, a little.

"If you were me?" I ask.

"If I were you, I'd go. I don't think there's good enough reason to cancel."

I nod. I'm about to thank her, but my attention is suddenly diverted to a burst of activity on my left where . . . what? Maya is *punching the wall.*

"Maya!" I say. "What are you *doing*?"

She hurls herself at the pale green wall next to the sink, smashing her fists against the drywall. Her face is a deep red and twisted into an angry grimace. "I want to break this house!" she screams, rearing both fists back for another direct hit. "I want to break this house!"

I lunge to keep her from knocking the glass jars full of Q-tips and tongue depressors onto the floor. I've seen her combative before, but never this violent or out of control. Dr. Diane looks as surprised as I feel. I turn my head toward her as I try to restrain Maya. *You're the child expert in the room*, I'm hoping my pleading look conveys. *So, can you take charge? Like, now.*

"O-kay," Dr. Diane says. "Let's get her out of here." She opens the door and motions me across the hall. I scoop up Maya, still screaming, and follow the doctor into another room, more sparsely furnished, with puffy yellow-striped fabric on the walls. Something about the way it looks makes me want to press my fingertips into it, so I do. Cushioning.

Cushioning? Is it? Oh, my God. Padded walls.

"Why don't you wait in here until she calms down?" Dr. Diane says. She hands me a prescription before backing out the door. "Cough medicine," she says. "It'll get you over the hump. Also, it'll help her sleep." She knows we don't like giving Maya prescription drugs, but there's no point reminding her about that now. I take the slip of paper.

"I'll be right down the hall if you need me," she says, and then she's gone.

I get it. She needs to keep us sequestered. Other patients are waiting, who can't be allowed to see this.

Maya hurls herself at the wall, bounces off, and, undeterred, tries again. I sit on the mauve swivel chair and stare at her. This is so far beyond a donkey-dick moment I don't even know what to call it.

I am terrified of these times, I mean truly terrified, when the only barrier separating my daughter from potential danger is uncertain, imperfect me. At these moments a woman's maternal limitations are tested to the max—can she summon the strength to stay in control, or will the pressure of the responsibility cause her to shrink back or fall apart?

I can't fall apart. I can't fall apart. *I can't fall apart.* Because right now, I'm the present, reliable parent in this picture.

I lift my head. "Maya," I say. "You have to stop this. *Right now.*" I grab her by the arm. "*Enough,*" I say.

To my true surprise, she swallows the next scream with a hiccup, and the outburst slows down to loud sobs. Was she only waiting for me to exert control? I grip both her shoulders and look straight into her eyes. I don't feel nearly as calm as I sound, but my voice comes out steady and firm.

"You can control this," I tell her. I have to believe she can. "You *can*. You can make whatever it is stop right now."

In another ten minutes she's recovered enough to reenter civilization, and then I get her out the door so fast I don't even stop at the front desk to make my co-pay. I get her onto the sidewalk and into the weak December sun. My hands won't stop trembling. I don't know how I'm going to calm down enough to drive us home.

Uzi is at his office, just five blocks away. *Please*, I think. *Please don't be in a meeting.* I fumble for my cell phone and dial his office number.

"It's me," I say when he answers, and then, before he can even respond, "Are you in a meeting?" The knowledge that he probably is, and that he shouldn't be interrupted, makes me start to cry.

"It's okay," he says, which means he's in a meeting. "What happened?"

"It's Maya," I say. "She went ballistic at the doctor's office. She was screaming, punching the walls, completely out of control. I've never seen it that bad before."

"Where is she?"

"Right here. On the sidewalk next to me."

I look at Maya, who's now sitting on the low concrete wall in front of the building. She smiles up at me obediently.

"She looks fine now. But I don't think I'm okay to drive." Tears and snot are running down my face, and I don't even care. "We're right outside the doctor's office. Eleventh between Broadway and Arizona. Can you come?"

There's a slight pause at the other end of the line, just long enough for me to regret having asked.

"I'll try," he says.

He'll try.

I snap the cell phone shut and toss it back into my purse. He'll *try*? I don't even know what to say to that. How about "I'll *try* to take Maya to the doctor next time she's sick." Or "I'll *try* to remember to feed her every day."

"Daddy's coming?" Maya asks.

"I don't know." I sit beside her on the concrete wall in front of a cluster of red geraniums and wipe my nose with the back of my hand. She plucks a petal off one of the flowers and lets it drop to the sidewalk. When I don't object, she does it again. And again. A woman walking by gives us a sideways stare. Normally I'd tell Maya to stop, but right now I can't rally the social conscience to care.

He'll *try*. It would be so easy to take Maya's hand right now and start walking northeast. Brentwood is only a mile away, with its long strip of condo complexes and low apartment buildings off Montana Avenue. We could rent an apartment there that opens onto a courtyard with a swimming pool. I could push her to Starbucks every morning in her stroller. I would paint her bedroom mauve, the same color it is now, and we'd get a little dog—a Lhasa apso, or maybe one of those sniffy little pugs—and name him Ernie. In the evening we'd watch television before bedtime and go to sleep together, without waiting for someone else to eventually come through the door.

"Daddy," Maya says, and points in the direction of his office.

I see him coming from all the way down the street, less than an inch high in the distance. He's wearing a royal blue dress shirt and black pants and his head is bobbing, well, a little strangely, and he's getting too big too fast, and that's when I realize he's running.

His breath comes out in short, shallow bursts when he reaches us. "Hi," he exhales, reaching out to cup the side of my head. "I got here as fast as I could," and in that moment I forgive him for everything.

In a few hours, after I calm down, I'll have the good sense to wonder why it is that when Uzi says, "I'll try," he means he'll try but I hear him saying, "I won't." Right now I'm just so relieved to see him I can't do much of anything except cry harder.

"Dad-dee," Maya coos, raising her arms to be lifted.

He picks her up and kisses her cheek. "What's up with you, Maya?" he asks.

She giggles and smooths down his wayward curls with both hands. "Nothing," she says.

It figures that the moment he arrives she reverts to the picture of normalcy, making my phone call seem, frankly, like an enormous over-reaction.

"I'm not making it up," I say, "I swear." I hold my hand in the air so Uzi can see it still trembling.

"I believe you," he says. He kisses the side of my face. I tuck my head into his shoulder. This is how it should be, the three of us a single unit, bound together by compassion and desire, not by dependence and convenience.

"It's going to be okay," Uzi whispers against my cheek.

"Promise?"

"I promise." He tightens his grip around my waist. "I promise. We'll find a shaman in Belize."

When I was a child I played a cheap carnival game that involved dropping a penny into a large bucket of water, aiming for a smaller bucket on the bottom. The penny sinking down into the water: that's what it feels like inside my chest right now.

I back away from Uzi so fast it's as if he wasn't ever holding me at all.

"A *shaman?*" I say.

"What?" he says. "It's just an idea."

I hear Sarah's calm, measured voice telling me, "Remember to breathe."

"Please, try to be open to it," Uzi says.

I press the heels of my hands into my forehead. *I'm losing him*, I think.

Remember to breathe.

I take a deep breath in and let the air out. A shaman.

I can't believe I'm doing this.

"All right," I say.

Breathe, I remind myself after I've quieted down enough to drive home, with Maya coughing in the backseat and Dodo strapped invisibly into place beside her.

Breathe, I remind myself the next morning, as I stand on line at the pharmacy to pick up Maya's prescription to pack into my carry-on bag, just in case.

Breathe. It shouldn't be that hard to do. It's an involuntary act, after all. But when my thoughts begin to spiral out of control, when what I see lying ahead of me is a child who can't get well and a husband whose judgment about her condition is clouded by a belief in its supernatural origin, I feel utterly depleted. The only idea that can energize me is the thought of boarding the plane to Belize. Belize, with its lush jungle and its soft Caribbean lilt; Belize, with its promises of red and blue saltwater coral and powdery white sand. Belize, where my husband believes a man can lift a dark spirit from a child like a flock of crows rising into the sky. When I close my eyes and think of our trip, I feel something small and still bright burning deep inside me. It sustains me through the last cold, rainy days before our departure. Then Maya packs a suitcase for herself and Dodo, Carmen lights a Jesus candle for our safe return, and TACA lifts us into the air.

chapter four
Guatemala City, Guatemala
December 23, 2000

Don Elijio Panti, the last great Maya shaman of Belize, had few blood relatives to whom he could pass down his knowledge. His only child, a daughter, died while giving birth, and his surviving grandchildren at first had little interest in learning the traditional healing ways.

"Listen to this," Uzi says. He leans across Maya's airplane seat so I can hear him above the jet engines. "'People don't want to appear "backward" by associating with healers. Many prefer the methods of Western doctors in white lab coats, who dole out expensive synthetic drugs—some culled from the very plants and herbs growing in their own native soil. Christian missionaries have also made people feel ashamed of traditional healing by labeling it the devil's work.'"

He's reading out loud from *Sastun*, Rosita Arvigo's memoir of studying traditional healing with Panti when she was in her early forties and he was close to ninety. Arvigo had moved from Chicago to Belize with her husband and daughter in the early 1980s with a plan to cultivate a piece of the jungle and create a healing center there, until they discovered the rain-forest environment to be more challenging than they'd expected. Whatever vegetation they cut back quickly returned as new growth, and the healing herbs they'd brought from Chicago grew moldy in the constant dampness. Just when they were about to give up and return to the United States, Arvigo met an old Maya man with a remarkable ability to heal even the most complicated physical and spiritual ailments. He was an aging shaman who needed to pass on his knowledge. She was an herbalist and naprapath, trained to manipulate joints, muscles, and ligaments to treat disease and relieve pain, who needed a local teacher. Their pairing resulted, after his death in 1996 at the age of 103, in an American-born woman of Iranian and Italian heritage becoming one of the best-known healers in Belize.

A few weeks ago, Uzi asked Carolyn the travel agent if she could get Maya an appointment with Dr. Arvigo. "Really?" Carolyn had said, sounding surprised. She must have pegged us for the kind of clients who wanted only snorkeling trips and tours to Maya ruins. "I'll try," she offered. A few days later she called back with a 1 P.M. appointment for December 23. Which is—or rather was—four hours ago.

A good question right now might be why, at 1 P.M. today, we were boarding a plane at LAX instead of sitting at Dr. Arvigo's farm in western Belize. Another good question might be why, at 5 P.M., we're now sitting 30,000 feet above Mexico when we should have landed in Belize eight hours ago. The answer to both of these questions would have to be that I was too damn stubborn to listen to Carmen. Instead of heeding her words of caution, I went ahead and booked us on what might possibly be the most disorganized airline in the hemisphere.

We arrived at LAX at 8:15 last night, a good two and a half hours before our scheduled departure time, to find the line at the TACA counter stretching across the international terminal before winding back around a corner. There had to be at least a hundred and fifty people ahead of us, many of them balancing enormous towers of baggage on top of the airport's puny metal luggage carts. Tremendous suitcases teetered precipitously on top of dishwashers and electric clothes dryers in their original boxes. I couldn't imagine how all those items were going to make it onto one plane. Apparently, neither could the TACA ticket agents. Whenever I walked ahead to check for small signs of progress, the two beleaguered agents on duty were either furiously punching numbers into the keypads on their phones or instructing families to unpack their suitcases and repack them differently to redistribute the weight. They were utterly disinterested in the plights of those of us near the end of the line. I couldn't help noticing that everyone in the front half of the line was Latino and everyone in the back half Caucasian. Clearly, the Central Americans were onto something about this airline that anyone else was learning the hard way.

About every ten minutes I jogged around the corner, then jogged back with the same progress report: none. I felt like one of the pedestrians at crosswalks who keep pressing the "Walk" button every five or ten seconds until the light changes. It doesn't make the signal change any faster, but it gives you something to do with all that pent-up nervous energy.

"Nobody cares how long the line is," I reported to Uzi after my third reconnaissance mission. "And nobody ahead of us is complaining, which is just plain weird."

"That's what I mean about Central American travel," Uzi said.

"They'll have to hold the plane for this many people."

"I wouldn't count on it."

Maya tugged on my pants leg, a gentle, jerking motion. When I looked down, I saw she was crying.

"What's wrong, sweetie?" I asked, squatting beside her.

"Dodo called me poopy," she sobbed.

She was wearing a pull-up, which she still needs at night. Maybe this was her way of letting me know she'd had an accident?

"Do you need to be changed?"

"No."

I motioned for her to lean forward, pulled her waistband back to inspect the inside of her pull-up, and patted her back reassuringly when I was done. "You're not poopy. Dodo's wrong. Tell Dodo *he's* the poopy one," I said.

Seven years of higher education, two university degrees, and these are the kinds of conversations it all amounts to. Astonishing.

Maya shook her head fiercely. "He won't stop bothering me," she said.

"Then let's send him back to the cold island."

"Bad Dodo doesn't live on the island. He lives in a toilet."

"A toilet?" I said.

"An orange toilet," she confirmed.

"So . . . that means we can flush him down."

"No!" she cried, horrified.

"Do you think he'll listen to me if I tell him to go home?"

"He doesn't like mothers."

"Well, I don't know what to tell you, Maya," I said, pushing myself up to standing. The line, the conversation, the hour—it was all pushing me beyond mortal limits of exasperation. "I can't see Dodo, and I can't hear him. So I don't know how to get him to leave you alone."

She crossed her arms with emphasis and sank down in the stroller in a defiant pout, pressing her knees together hard.

"You're mean," she announced.

"I am mean," I agreed. And tired. And cranky. Very, very cranky. "I'm a mean, mean mother. Bad, mean mother, that's me."

"Huh?" Uzi looked up. He'd been playing with the address book on his cell phone and chosen that moment to resurface.

"Bad Dodo called Maya poopy," I said, to bring him up to date. "Bad Dodo lives in an orange toilet."

Uzi blinked at me, then laughed. It *was* funny. I guess.

"I'm going to let you have this one." I patted him on the shoulder and added in my best *Mission: Impossible* voice, "Good luck, Jim," as I walked away.

All the stores in the international terminal were either already closed or in the process of closing by 10 P.M. I squeezed into a Hudson News and bought a pack of Trident bubble gum and a bottle of water just before the manager pulled down the metal gate. Then I took a quick walk around the terminal, comparing other airlines' lines to ours. British Airways had a flight leaving for London at 11:35 P.M., and its line didn't even extend beyond its roped maze.

When I returned to Uzi and Maya, they were only about ten paces closer to the ticket counter. Maya had fallen into a doze again, with Hursulas Zero and One tucked tightly under her arms. Uzi had struck up a conversation with the woman on line behind us. I started pulling underwear and T-shirts from our backpacks and stuffing them into my carry-on bag.

"What are you doing?" Uzi asked. Maya opened her eyes with a blank expression, registered we were still there, and closed them again.

"I'm not optimistic about the bag situation," I said. "With this level of chaos, we'll wind up in Belize while our luggage vacations in El Salvador." I pulled out my makeup case and more underwear for everyone.

"Good idea," Uzi said.

It turned out to be, since at 11 P.M., when our flight lifted off for Guatemala City, we were still a good dozen people away from the ticketing desk. When we finally reached the counter, the agent judiciously avoided eye contact while informing us that there were no more flights to Guatemala City until tomorrow.

"Tomorrow?" I said. "That's the best you can do?"

She shrugged, as if to say, *not my problem*, and clicked away at the computer keyboard at waist level.

I slammed my hand flat onto the counter. "I should have listened to Carmen!" I shouted at no one in particular. "She *told* us not to take this airline!"

The agent looked up just long enough to send me a withering glare. "You're free to find a seat on any other flight going out tonight," she snapped.

"Do any other airlines have flights going to Belize tonight?"

"I wouldn't know that," she said.

"It's not my job to find a seat on another airline. It's your job to find us seats on *this* airline."

"Hey, hey," Uzi interrupted, but it was unclear who he was talking to. Me, I think.

In the end, our bags were checked through to Belize, and we were told to return for an 8 A.M. flight. A plane would be brought in for us. From where, no one could say.

"Unbelievable," I muttered as we pushed the stroller away from the counter. Maya, who'd woken up during the argument, was sitting up straight, cradling a doll in each arm. Her cheeks were hot and pink, which wasn't a good sign. "They have to bring a special plane in for all the people they couldn't manage to accommodate? What, does an empty plane just sit out there on the tarmac all day, waiting for the next TACA screwup?"

I didn't have to see the expression on Uzi's face to know what he was thinking. Central American travel: difficult. Hope's attitude: difficult squared.

"I know, I know," I conceded. "You warned me."

We had no car to drive home in, since we'd taken a shuttle to the airport, and we had to be back at 6 A.M. anyway to check in for the flight, so we opted for the nearest hotel with free shuttle service and a vacant room: the Sheraton Gateway. If I could have calmed down, I might have seen this as the first step in our family's rollicking Christmas adventure, a colorful story to tell once we finally landed in Belize—*so you see, Carmen was right!*—but I wasn't able to shape the story that way, especially not after I woke Maya in the morning. After only four and a half hours of sleep, she was pale and coughing harshly, though her spirits still seemed good. I sat cross-legged on the hotel bed, wondering out loud if we should return to the airport or play it safe and call a car service to take us home, effectively ending the trip before it began.

"What does your intuition say?" Uzi asked.

I closed my eyes and tried to intuit a message. All I felt was an ache in my lower back from sitting cross-legged on a too-soft bed.

"My intuition tells me to let someone else decide," I said.

I was starting to feel like a contestant in some kind of cosmic reality show, presented with obstacle after obstacle to test how badly I wanted to go to Belize and how much I was willing to compromise to get there. I considered calling Carolyn to ask if we had any hope of a refund if we canceled the hotel reservations on such short notice. I'd have to call her anyway, to let her know we weren't landing in Belize as scheduled and that we weren't going to make the appointment with Dr. Arvigo at one.

If we gave up and went back home, we'd have to forfeit the cost of the plane tickets, for sure. I remembered Dr. Diane saying "Either she'll get better down there, or she'll get better up here" with a calm certainty I wished I could share.

Uzi stared at me expectantly. To make it to the airport for a flight at eight, we would have to leave exactly . . . now.

I looked at Maya, who was drawing swirly shapes on the little pad of hotel paper with the free Sheraton pen.

"How you feeling, Maya?" I asked.

"Okay," she said.

If we went home, I'd be stuck sitting inside with Maya until she recovered fully. Carmen was visiting her father in Miami and Uzi would go to work every day, even if the office was closed. In Belize, at least the three of us would be together. But in Los Angeles, we'd have Dr. Diane if Maya's condition worsened. But maybe in Belize we'd find someone who'd help us differently. If we gave up and took a cab back to Topanga, we'd be relinquishing that chance.

Giving up. That's how it would have felt.

I looked at my watch: 5:45 A.M.

"We'd better get to the airport," I said.

We made it to the departure gate at 6:30 A.M., but we didn't board the promised flight at eight. Or at nine or at ten. By eleven, "a plane we'll bring in for you" was starting to sound suspiciously like "a plane we have to locate." By noon, it was sounding like "a plane Boeing has to build." While Uzi sat in a molded plastic chair, calmly reading *Sastun*, and Maya drew pictures on loose sheets of computer paper, everyone else who'd missed the flight to Guatemala the night before—and there were enough of us to reveal that the airline had committed a gross

overbooking error—hovered restlessly near the departure gate, period-
ically calling out to anyone in a TACA jacket until, just about when half
of us were truly about to give up, a plane materialized at the end of the
jetway and we were hustled on board with what qualified, to that point,
as unprecedented corporate efficiency and speed.

Uzi and I settled into our seats with Maya between us. He took the
window, as always, leaving the aisle for me. My fear of heights and, by
extension, my fear of flying is a trait I inherited from my mother. She
gamely flew on family vacations, unwilling to limit herself or us to
road-trip distances, but she would clench the armrests with white
knuckles for much of the time and always bought insurance at airport
kiosks adjacent to our departure gates. Before I married Uzi, I flew frequently for work, once logging seventeen cities in three weeks on a
book tour, and the only way I could cope was to book aisle seats, close
my eyes on takeoff and landing, and never, never look down.

After clicking Maya's seat belt closed, I took a drawing pad and
some crayons from my carry-on bag and arranged them on her tray
table, then pressed my hand against her forehead. Warm but not hot. I
looked down at the tickets that had been reissued last night. Our new
flight to Belize was now scheduled to leave Guatemala City at . . . oh,
never mind. We weren't going to make that one, either.

A perfect definition of powerless, I thought, *is being stuck in a metal tube
hurtling through the lower atmosphere with no control over where you're
going, when you'll get there, or what will happen when you arrive.*

"I guess we'll just have to figure it out in Guatemala," I told Uzi.

He smiled and kissed the side of my head.

"That's the spirit," he said.

The flight from Los Angeles to Guatemala City takes four and a half
hours. After the plane reaches cruising altitude, I lift the armrest
between my seat and Maya's so she can lie on my lap. She sticks the
index and middle finger of her right hand into her mouth and promptly
falls asleep.

Uzi takes *Sastun* from my carry-on bag and opens to where he left off at the airport.

"Here's more," he says, leaning a little closer over Maya's sleeping form. "'People do not understand the healer and often mistrust us.' That's Don Elijio talking to Rosita. 'When we heal what the doctors cannot, the doctors call us *brujos*, witches, and whisper lies about us. They say we work with the devil. It is a lonely life, I warn you.'" He raises his eyebrows a little and lets out a tiny puff of air. "It's a miracle any shamans are left anywhere with that attitude around," he says.

Shaman. Whenever I hear the word, I can't help thinking of the first time I heard it spoken outside a classroom, by a man I knew in Iowa City in the early 1990s. Burt was a middle-aged drug counselor and a graduate student in religion who had a beautiful Abyssinian kitten named Six that I took in whenever Burt left town. One day when Burt came to pick up Six from my house, he casually mentioned he was a shaman. He pronounced it "shay-man" instead of "shah-man," as I'd always heard it spoken before. I must have looked confused because he added, "You know, a healer."

I knew what a shaman was. It was the pronunciation that had thrown me and also the idea that a white man could assume the job. In college I'd minored in cultural anthropology and taken an introductory class with Napoleon Chagnon, the scientist who'd made first contact with the Yanomamo Indians of the Amazon in the 1960s. Yanomamo shamans, as we read in Chagnon's book, *Yanomamo*, are the tribe's spiritual leaders who unify the natural and spirit worlds. The class consisted mostly of lectures and reading, punctuated by occasional film footage of Chagnon in a jungle village. In one, he wore only black bicycle shorts and Converse high-tops as he squatted in a circle of Yanomamo men blowing hallucinogenic drugs into each other's nostrils through thin pipes the length of golf clubs. Before long, everyone's nose was running green. The entire lecture hall of freshmen and sophomores thought this was hilarious.

But a white man as a shaman? It felt like a vocational oxymoron, an appropriation that had gone a step too far into comedy, like an Amish electrician or a Buddhist drill sergeant. Also, I never knew if Burt really was a drug counselor—or a graduate student, for that matter, or maybe a compulsive liar. You'd think that a true shaman would at least know how to pronounce the word like anyone else.

A year later I met Arthur in a café on campus. Arthur was a big, lumbering guy with a round face, large plastic-rimmed glasses, and black hair down to his ass who trudged around campus in a blue windbreaker and baggy jeans. He was getting a master's degree in sociology and spent weekends back home on the Mesquakie lands an hour west of Iowa City, where he was apprenticing with his tribe's medicine man. I was consistently sick that winter with one ailment after another, and Arthur kept suggesting I come home with him for a weekend. "I'll do a sweat for you," he offered. The invitation may or may not have been sexual—I couldn't tell with Arthur—but I never accepted it. I couldn't get past the glasses. They were huge and octagonal with pale gold plastic frames, the kind that belonged on a secretary or schoolteacher circa 1982. I don't know what I was expecting from a medicine man, but the glasses weren't it. It was terribly shallow of me, I knew, but the glasses destroyed whatever mystical aura I needed to place around Arthur to take him seriously as a healer.

Uzi opens *Sastun* wide to a series of black-and-white photos in the center of the book. The first photo shows a pair of weathered hands displaying a small clay pot and a smooth marble. *Don Elijio holding his sastun*, the caption reads. A *sastun*, the book says, is a Maya shaman's divination tool. Uzi turns the page. "Look," he says. "That's him. Don Elijio." In another picture, a jockey-sized, dark-skinned man tends to a village woman and her infant at a small wooden table that holds a kerosene lamp, a thermos, and a small bouquet of dried leaves. He's wearing a baseball cap, aviator sunglasses, and a soiled windbreaker. He's so small he looks almost miniature.

"He looks like a very short golfer," I say.

"He was ninety-something in that photo."

"He doesn't look it."

"Didn't," Uzi corrects me. "He's dead."

He points to a small photo on the adjacent page. This one is of a woman leaning out the passenger window of a car. "That's Rosita Arvigo," he says. "The author." I take the book from his hands for a closer look. She comes across as refreshingly normal, nothing exotic or spooky about her at all. The outer edges of her eyes curl down just slightly, and her smile looks natural and content. Her hair is short, dark, and windblown. Although the face doesn't bear much resemblance, I can't help noticing she has the same hairstyle my mother used to wear, shorter on the sides than on the top.

Another photo shows Don Elijio with an enormous white sack gathering leaves in the jungle. The body of the sack rests on his back, and the shoulder strap is looped across his forehead to leave his hands and arms free for the picking. It looks like an ingenious method. In addition to my carry-on bag, I'm traveling with a small, embroidered purse with a long shoulder strap to hold our passports, my driver's license, money, Chapstick, and two credit cards. It's about the size of a paperback book. I toss it between my back and the seat and loop the strap around my forehead to see what it feels like to wear a satchel that way. The answer is, not much. The bag is too light to make an impact. I noodle around in the carry-on bag at my feet and pull out a juice box, a pack of cards, and a travel hairbrush, stuff them into my purse, and sit up straight. There. Not bad, actually.

"What are you *doing*?" Uzi asks. From the expression on his face, I can tell how strange I must look to anyone outside the boundaries of my own mind.

I point to the photo in the book. "I'm trying it out."

To my husband's great credit, all he says after a short pause is "Oh." Then he resumes his reading.

Maya stirs in her sleep, and Hursula One rolls from the seat to the floor.

"Can you get Hursula One?" I ask Uzi.

He leans over to retrieve the doll, inspects it, and tucks her back under Maya's arm.

"How do you tell who's who?" he asks.

Hursula One is technically Water Baby, who came in a bathing suit with her own plastic tub and bar of plastic soap. Hursula Zero is a hand-me-down from our seven-year-old neighbor. She looks identical to Hursula One from a distance, but up close you can tell she's a slightly older model of the same doll, molded from a more pliable rubber.

"Zero is the bendy one," I say.

I run my fingers through Maya's front curls, and my palm passes across the top of her head. I put my hand under the back of her shirt, against bare skin, to be sure.

"Oh, no," I say. "She's got a fever."

Uzi presses his hand against her forehead. "You're sure?"

"I'm sure. Feel her back."

"How much?"

I spread my fingers wide against her spine and let the heat radiate against my hand.

"Hundred and one? Hundred and two? Definitely more than a hundred."

He releases a big exhale. "Well, not much we can do about it now," he says.

In the backpack I checked at the ticket counter I have a children's homeopathic kit, first-aid supplies, and a small pharmacy of natural supplements I've been taking since a bout I had with Lyme disease last year. I packed it carefully, making sure I'd have everything we'd need, but none of it does me any good now, since our bags are likely to be on their way to Tegucigalpa. In the carry-on bag at my feet I have a travel tube of Dramamine, baby wipes, and Maya's prescription cough syrup, which we haven't yet needed to use. I dig deeper into the bag. Two juice boxes. Goldfish crackers. Plenty of extra underwear. I keep digging until my fingers close around a fat cylinder of chewable Children's Tylenol. Good. I'll give her one when she wakes up.

I gaze past Uzi out the window at an expanse of unbroken sky, and unbroken sky, and unbroken sky, which makes me feel queasy knowing we're up so high, and at some point I must have closed my eyes, because when I open them again the flight attendants are asking us to return our seat backs to the upright position and Uzi is motioning for me to look out the window where a large conical peak protrudes from the ground like a perfect gray triangle. A volcano. Guatemala. We're here.

The entry hall of La Aurora International Airport holds more people than any structure designed for the purpose of transport should be allowed to contain. Seven years from now, it will be expanded to include eighteen more gates, a five-hundred-car parking structure, and a glass-fronted second concourse, but tonight we're making our way through the original 1968 terminal, and the place is a human beehive. Thousands of travelers swarm in all directions simultaneously. Guatemalan families lean out and over the gallery railing that rings the two-story entrance hall, scanning and waving energetically at the crowd below. I look up into a densely packed audience of young men with jet black hair, elderly women wrapped in dark shawls, and toddlers in frilly white party dresses. Their shouts create a vibration so strong it makes the surface of my skin hum.

I hold my carry-on bag tight against my side and stick close to Uzi to keep from getting separated. Inside my bag are our new tickets, TACA's third, pathetic attempt, which now include a 7:30 A.M. flight to San Salvador with a 10 A.M. connection to Belize.

"Try to think positive," Uzi suggests over his shoulder as he deftly steers Maya's stroller through the throng. "We're getting to see all these other countries for free."

It's hard to tell if he's testing out sarcasm or just being his relentlessly optimistic self. I can't see his face to get a read. I'm pressed tightly against his back as our little clump of TACA discontents, eight in number, tries to follow the officious airline representative to the hotel shuttle outside. We can manage only a few steps at a time, in unison. It's like being part of a biological process.

Our group of connecting fliers consists of the three of us; a pretty, thirtyish woman traveling to El Salvador with her two school-age sons;

a slightly older Honduran woman moving back home after two years in Los Angeles; and a middle-aged, bearded man who doesn't say a word the entire ride to the hotel. Where he's from and where he's going is anybody's guess. The airport is only about four miles from Guatemala City, but the streets are crowded and the pace is slow. Dusk is settling as we ride into the city, and the small, crowded *tiendas* and parking lots we pass on the outskirts of town are all suffused with shades of gray.

The whole way into the city, Maya coughs. She coughs low and deep, as if she's juggling handfuls of gravel in her chest, and she coughs harsh and violent, as if trying to rid herself of the whole noxious mess.

Every time she coughs my own throat constricts, an involuntary, anxious response. I remember how little tolerance my father had for illness when I was a child, how we had to hide the telltale sounds of stuffy noses or laryngitis from him or else find ourselves in the spotlight of his withering glare or, worse, cringing at his shouts of "Goddammit!" every time we coughed, and how this still makes me, even thirty years later, automatically want to apologize every time I feel a chest cold coming on. Family car trips were interminable because there was nowhere to hide. I spent long stretches on the New York State Thruway holding my breath in the backseat to suppress a cough. Now it's my child who's sick, and I feel a kind of desperate rage bubbling just beneath my surface, wanting to explode in a demand that I regain control. And I understand now that it was not anger but anxiety, and a helplessness he couldn't handle upon seeing his children suffer, that made my father act the way he did.

"Does it hurt when you cough?" I ask Maya. She nods. "Does your throat hurt, too?" She nods again.

"Poor thing," the woman with the two sons says, casting a sympathetic glance at Maya. Her name is Maria, and she's a bank teller in Reno. She's taking her sons to see her family in El Salvador for the holidays. I learned all this back at the airport, when we stood around for two hours while TACA figured out what to do with us once they realized they had no more flights leaving for San Salvador or Belize tonight.

"She didn't get much sleep last night," I explain. "And it looks like she won't get much tonight, either."

"My older one used to get bronchitis all the time," Maria says. Her son looks back at me and nods in agreement. He's nine, his brother's seven, and it's impossible not to notice how well behaved they are. At the airport when we were waiting for the new tickets, they occupied themselves by giving each other rides on the luggage cart, and when their mother calmly asked them to stop they immediately stopped, without stalling or objecting. Then they waited quietly for another half hour, until the airline representative who'd been assigned the sorry task of rebooking us organized everyone's tickets, hotel vouchers, and meal coupons. The boys were tired—how could they not be? they'd spent all of last night at LAX—but they never complained. It was almost freakish, how good these kids were.

"What's your secret?" I asked Maria.

She shrugged, but I could tell she was pleased I'd asked. "I'm lucky," she said. "They're just easy kids."

Still, I'm convinced there has to be some kind of special ingredient, something concrete, that a mother does or doesn't do to turn out such golden kids. At the same time, I'm aware of the random mystery of temperament. It's hard not to notice how babies who are docile infants tend to grow up into calm, good-natured children and the ones who are the most active babies keep their parents hopping all the way through grade school. I'm a little dismayed about where that leaves us. Maya came out of the womb red-faced and screaming and cried non-stop for her first ten weeks. "Calm" and "easy" have never been words used to describe her, though "exceptional," "creative," and "precocious" have. These may be adjectives other mothers hope for, but I wouldn't mind a day or two of "uncomplicated" every week.

Uzi and Maya play "I Spy" through the shuttle's back window—"I spy a red car, I spy the letter *w*"—while I open my Fodor's guide. We'll be in Guatemala City for only nine hours, but that's the research bug in me. I need to know as much as I can about any place I visit, even if I'm just passing through.

Here it is, on page 89:

> The capital is a big, busy, and—let's face it—ugly city, hardly a reason to visit Guatemala. It's almost unavoidable, however, since traveling to the rest of the country usually means passing through. Though the city as a whole isn't terribly attractive, it has some of the country's best and most varied restaurants and hotels, several excellent museums, occasional cultural events, a healthy nightlife, and all the amenities of the modern world that you might miss while exploring the less-developed regions.

> A sprawling metropolis divided into 21 zones, this city of more than 2.5 million may seem intimidating when you first see a map. But travelers have few reasons to stray from four central zones, which makes Guatemala City—or Guate, as the locals call it—much easier to manage. These areas can be grouped into two units: the old city, which centers on Zona Uno (Zone 1), and the new city, to the south, which comprises Zonas Nueve y Diez (Zones 9 and 10) and stretches up into Zona Cuatro (Zone 4). A sort of transition area between new and old, Zona 4 is dirty, tacky, and best bypassed.

I put my finger in the book as a placeholder and look up toward the driver.

"*En qué zona está el hotel?*" I ask.

"*Qué?*"

"*En qué zona . . . a qué zona vamos?*" It's been eight years since I last sat in a Spanish classroom, and in fifteen years of on-again, off-again studies I had teachers from so many different countries—Mexico, Chile, Spain—with so many different accents I can't even imagine what I must sound like to a native speaker. Probably like an undereducated mutt.

"*A Zona Nueve,*" he says.

"*Gracias.*"

I look down at the city map in my book. Well, that makes sense. Zona 9 is the southernmost part of the city, closest to the airport. At least we won't have a long drive back in the morning.

"*Y el nombre del hotel?*" I ask.

"*Princesa Reforma.*"

"*Toda.*"

Uzi gives me a funny look, and I realize I've just said "thank you" in Hebrew. That's what happens when you speak two foreign languages, neither of them well: words from one spontaneously pop up in the middle of conversations in the other. It's as if the "non-English" language center of the brain loses the ability to discriminate when it's under pressure to perform.

I flip ahead a few pages to 99, where Fodor's reviews the Princesa Reforma Hotel. "This comfortable hotel in a stately former residence is a wonderful alternative to the modern lodgings that dominate the new city," the paragraph reads. "You enter the grounds through iron gates, and both the classical statue at the center of the circular driveway and the manicured lawns and gardens enhance the beauty of the white mansion before you." TACA's putting us up in a former mansion? That's hard to believe, but then there's this: "Just beyond the reception area is a comfortable lounge with a fireplace. The restaurant is in the former courtyard; its cast-iron chairs are surrounded by stout pillars and arches and the greenery of dangling philodendrons against white walls. Rooms have tile floors and white walls hung with Guatemalan art, and are furnished with antiques and reproductions."

It sounds beautiful. Then again, guidebooks always make things sound better than they are. Isn't that part of their job? But when we pull up at the hotel, it's clear that Fodor's wasn't exaggerating. A doorman in a tailored black suit steps into the perfectly landscaped courtyard to greet us. It's like being bumped straight up from steerage to deluxe first class. The lobby is all cherry-stained wood and polished toffee marble, with a four-story atrium towering overhead. My pink-and-orange-striped cotton pants and royal blue T-shirt are several wardrobe levels beneath what this place is used to seeing, but everyone treats us graciously. It's a welcome relief after interacting with exasperated airline representatives for the past twenty-four hours.

Upstairs, our room is impeccable, with soft white sheets tucked tight around the king-size bed, beige marble tiling in the bathroom, and green-and-white-striped wallpaper on the walls. I toss myself backward onto the mattress in a big, dramatic display of exhaustion. The ceiling is painted a soft, unblemished white.

I want to stay here forever.

"I want to stay here *forever*," I announce.

Maya lifts herself from her stroller and looks at the bed as if she wants to jump on it. The Tylenol has brought her fever down far enough to return some of her spunk, but not quite that much. She settles for climbing onto the bed and bouncing on her knees next to me.

"I like it here," she says. "Dodo likes it here, too."

"If you want, we can stay an extra night," Uzi says.

It's not a bad idea, but that would mean reentering the TACA ticketing vortex. Plus, what about Belize? When I called Carolyn from the Guatemala City airport a few hours ago, she assured me that the owner of the jungle resort would meet us at the Belize City airport tomorrow morning. The trip could proceed from there as planned, she said, with the exception of seeing Dr. Arvigo. She had bad news about Dr. Arvigo, she said. With Christmas Eve and Christmas now upon us, there weren't any more appointments with her available during our stay. I hadn't known whether to feel disappointed or relieved.

"What I'd really like is a hot bath," I confess. I haven't showered since the afternoon we left our house, which was . . . was it only a day and a half ago? It feels as if at least twice that amount of time has elapsed.

Maya lets out a cough, a long, sustained one, and I rub her back until she's finished.

"Why don't you take a bath?" Uzi says. "I can bring her down to the lobby and see if the restaurant's open."

We haven't eaten dinner, and it's almost 9 P.M. Guatemala time. I really should go down with them. We have to be back on the shuttle in eight hours. Through the open bathroom door, I catch a glimpse of fluffy white towels and brightly lit mirrors. It might be the last hot bath I see for another week. Will fifteen minutes really make that much of a difference?

"I'll take a fast one," I say.

After the door closes softly behind them, the room plunges into a sudden, enveloping silence. When I was a child, I believed that silence had a sound I could hear, a sparkly, low-level crackle like billions of atoms exploding at once. I would listen to it at night when I lay in bed and wonder if I were listening to tiny messages from outer space that needed to be decoded. I haven't heard this kind of silence for a long time, the kind that's unbroken by a child calling for me, or NPR news in the background, or a husband's soft midnight sighs. The silence that surrounds me now is more like an even frequency, or a vibration, which makes me think of the Pranic Healers, which makes me think of how Uzi wants to find a shaman for Maya in Belize, which makes me feel like I really do need that long, hot bath.

The bathtub has old-fashioned white porcelain knobs shaped like fat Xes—*C* and *F,* for *caliente* and *fría*—that feel chunky and substantial in my hand. I squeeze the tiny bottle of hotel shampoo into the stream of running water until the foam starts to build. Three mirrored walls surround the tub, and they immediately start fogging. With a soft white towel I clear a spot on the back wall just large enough to encircle my face.

Whoa. After two nights of travel, the reflection in the mirror looks more than a little disheveled. My hair has gone completely wacky in the Central American humidity. My bangs have shriveled up into unruly commas. I didn't bother putting on makeup this morning in the Sheraton, and my skin looks washed out and flat.

I rummage through my makeup case for a mascara wand, take a few swipes, do the same with a blusher brush, then push a headband up and over my forehead. Better. With my hair smoothed back I look more like myself: the same straight nose as always, the same small brown eyes, the same lightly freckled skin. The same little arched wrinkles above both eyebrows that appeared almost exactly when I turned thirty-five, the ones the bangs are supposed to hide. The same tiny horizontal scar under my chin from where I fell on the concrete next to the swimming pool at our apartment building when I was three. Hello, me.

The tub is steaming. I fold my clothing carefully and place the items next to the sink, then lower myself into the water in degrees. Stretched out and submerged up to my shoulders, I breathe in, breathe out, breathe in, breathe out. I feel myself reentering myself again as the tension from the day starts to slough off like an extra, unnecessary skin. The effect is slowly intoxicating, in the way that the first few sips of bourbon take the edge off almost any anxiety and the next few make anxiety seem like . . . anxiety? A quaint and distant memory.

I trace circles with my big toe in the fogged-up wall at the foot of the tub. In the discs left behind, I catch fractional images of myself as I move my legs: a piece of knee here, a corner of thigh over there. I unwrap the bar of hotel soap, dip it in the water, and start soaping up my arms. By this time tomorrow, will we have located a shaman in Belize? The thought is both intriguing and repellent at the same time.

Here's the thing about me and shamanism: no matter how hard I try, I can't make myself believe in it. As much as I like the concept of a mortal journeying into the spirit world for answers and bringing them back to this world for execution, embracing the idea as fact feels as if I'm betraying a commitment to basic common sense. Yet a small, insistent corner of my personality wants to believe, badly needs to believe, in the prospect of such magical phenomena, and I don't know how to reconcile this duality. How is it possible to simultaneously discredit an idea and hold forth hope in its existence?

Uzi knows about my ambivalence, and it frustrates him. He points to the two days after Carmen and the egg, when Dodo was strangely absent from our house. He points to the many sections in *Sastun* where Don Elijio penetrates the veil between the physical and spiritual worlds to cure his patients of everything from migraines to paralysis and evil spirits. One woman was brought to his doorstep drooling and growling, having been unable to sleep or eat for two weeks, and he returned her to a normal state in nine days through a combination of teas, prayers, and incense.

"How much more proof do you need?" Uzi asks.

"More than that," I say. To believe as he does, I'd have to witness the acts myself. But this is what I'm wondering now: if my skepticism automatically renders me ineligible. Some philosophers say that the belief systems we bring into a situation become amplified and reflected back at us, causing us to create for ourselves more and more of the same. If you enter a situation from a position of disbelief, do you generate more, thereby denying yourself the chance to witness something profound? And if you do observe something extraordinary, is the strength of your resistance directly related to how vehemently you'll try to attribute the results to coincidence or imagination?

Thinking along those same lines, if you want something badly enough, does that mean you'll nearly always find meaning in events that aren't truly meaningful? It seems to me that Uzi and I . . .

Footsteps skitter across the room outside, and the handle on the locked bathroom door jiggles impatiently.

"Mom!" Maya shouts.

Well, that was short-lived. Just enough time to remind me I have a brain still capable of rumination.

"I'll be there in a minute!" I call back.

"Sorry," Uzi says. I can tell from the slight echo in his voice that he's standing right up against the door. "She really wants you."

"I'll be there in a minute!" I say, a little louder this time. Their voices jerk me back from the edge of relaxation so fast it's like a fire alarm piercing my sleep. That's how quickly I snap back into mommy mode.

Reluctantly, I lift myself from the tub. The bubbles cling to my stomach and legs like a fizzy frosting. I reach for a fluffy white towel and wipe them away.

"Mom!" Maya pounds on the door four times and jiggles the knob again. "Is it a minute yet?"

* * *

The restaurant in the lobby stays open late to serve us dinner when they see we have three hungry children in our group of seven. We sit at a long rectangular table with Maria, her boys, and Rosa from Honduras. Maya sticks Hursula Zero in an empty ice bucket in the center of the starched white tablecloth and lays Hursula One across her lap. She tucks her white Keds under her butt to raise herself to table level. Thank God she doesn't ask for an extra chair for Dodo. I don't know what Maria or her boys would make of that, and I don't feel like having to explain it to another mother, who may or may not understand why I'd feel compelled to ask the waiter for the chair.

"Let's take a picture," Uzi says. "Do you have the camera?"

I reach into the bag under my chair and pull out the 35-millimeter Minolta we bought last year in New York. Uzi knows all about the nuances of lighting and perspective; ergo, he takes way better photos than I do. I'm a basic point-and-shoot kind of photographer, with a primary interest in quantity. When we travel, I want to catalog all the details of a culture's everyday life: the shape of the buses, the color of the breakfast dishes, the local traffic signs, food labels, postal workers' uniforms. I don't really care whether any of it looks perfect in four-color, because I'm scribbling random field notes to fill in the gaps. That's the anthropology minor in me. I'd much rather spend an afternoon wandering the back streets of a town, snapping quick, staccato shots of everything I see, than going to a museum or taking a guided tour of anything. Uzi is all about artistic quality. He adheres to the set-up-and-calibrate-and-shoot-and-shoot-and-shoot method of photography, figuring if he takes enough photos of the same frame it greatly ups his chances of getting the perfect shot. This is still in the years before digital cameras, so whenever I get a roll of film developed it's likely to contain twelve completely different, poorly lit shots I've taken of items inside restaurants and grocery stores plus twelve of his shots of the same street corner from only slightly different angles. But I'll be damned if at least one of them isn't pretty near perfect.

So I'm surprised tonight when Uzi adjusts the camera to fit everyone at the table in its viewfinder at the proper aperture and then hands it over to the waiter. He quickly slips back into his seat beside me to be in the photo, too.

"*La niña,*" the waiter says, making a circle in the air with his forefinger. Maya has her back to the camera, and he wants her to turn around.

"Maya," I ask, "can you turn around for the picture?" I say it anyway, knowing it's a futile request. For the past few months, Maya has adamantly turned away from any camera pointed in her direction, stubbornly willing to show only the back of her head.

"It's okay," I tell the waiter when Maya ignores me. "You can go ahead. *Puede continuar, por favor.*"

Years later, I will look at this picture and all the sensory details of the moment will come rushing back: the feel of the roughly starched white tablecloth beneath my forearms, the tingling of newly clean skin after the bath, the slight pounding behind my forehead from jet lag and the hours of lost sleep. But at the time, sitting at the table, I am aware only of the feeling of Maria's eyes on me, kind and concerned, and of my own swift desire for Maya to act more like Maria's sons, amiable and obedient, a child who turns to the camera when her mother asks her to with a blinding smile that says, "Hello world! I'm so happy to be me!" and then of the fast kick of guilt that comes from wanting my daughter to be anything other than what she is.

Uzi and Rosa are talking about Honduras, a country he traveled throughout in 1991. He likes to tell the story of an afternoon he spent on Utila, an island off the Caribbean coast, where he was invited to attend a wedding between a local woman and an American man. During the ceremony, which was performed in a dialect of Anglo-American-Carib English—"pirate English," Uzi calls it—the minister asked the bride to promise to be obedient to her husband. In the local twang, each syllable was carefully pronounced: o-be-di-*ent.* Sometimes when Uzi thinks I'm being unreasonable, he reminds me, "Womah! In Honduras you would be o-be-di-*ent.*"

Rosa finds Uzi's story hilarious. "Utila has its own way," she says with a laugh.

"I wish I could be more obedient, for his sake," I tell her. "But I'm just not the type."

"Pfft," she says, swatting the air with her hand. "In Honduras, women are not obedient. Men had better do what a woman says, or else."

"That's my kind of country. Uzi, why are we wasting time with Belize? Let's go to Honduras. I'll be obedient on Utila, but on the mainland it's my show."

"Sure," he says agreeably.

The crazy thing is, when Uzi says "sure" to Honduras, he really does mean "sure." While I'm always trying to minimize enormous changes at the last minute, Uzi doesn't get ruffled by them. If I called TACA right now to switch our tickets to Honduras, he'd readjust without resentment or complaint. He'd probably even applaud me for acting spontaneously, for once.

The waiter walks over with plates of tortillas, eggs, rice, and beans, all food we hope Maya will like. She hasn't eaten since we left Los Angeles, and she has to be hungry, but she shakes her head after only a bite of each, claiming it all hurts her throat on the way down.

We offer her sliced banana. We offer the soft, mushed-up insides of dinner rolls smeared with salted butter, which she normally loves. The waiter, picking up on our plight, brings a side plate of avocado and cucumber. Maya manages to get a few cucumber slices down.

"Drink more water," Uzi urges.

She picks up her water glass with both hands, but in the middle of a sip she starts to cough. "Oops," I say, as the water sprays across the table. I set down my fork to lightly pat her back, an automatic reflex, but it doesn't help. She coughs and coughs and coughs, and then I get that she's coughing so hard she can't catch her breath. Everyone around the table falls silent. Maya huddles over in her chair, clasps both hands to her chest and presses. The image is more terrifying than I could have imagined, a child trying to fix her little body herself in the simplest, crudest way she can. The fear rushes up into my throat. What can I do? What do I do? I remember from somewhere that if a person is coughing, they're still getting air, and the best thing to do is to let them keep coughing. I put my arms around Maya and hold her lightly, just so she registers that I'm there. When the coughing finally stops she takes a few ragged inhales, and I look up at Uzi.

"We've got to give her the cough medicine," I say. "This can't go on. I'll take her upstairs while you get the bill."

At the mention of medicine, Maya goes rigid. Carrying her up to the room when she's imitating a forty-pound stiff plank is exactly as difficult as it sounds. "No medicine!" she shrieks, as the elevator doors close. "No medicine!" she hollers again, as they slide open. Inside the hotel room, she breaks loose and scrambles across the mattress, squeezing herself into the slim margin between the bed and the wall.

If anything makes Chop-Chop Mom appear on the scene, it's this type of behavior at this kind of time. When I have a critical task at hand and control starts slipping away, I shut down and become a machine of functionality, with no room for emotion or inner debate. Only a few minutes ago I was balanced on the edge of despair, but this display sends me careening into business mode so fast you can practically smell the burning rubber.

I get the medicine bottle from the carry-on bag, wedge my arms into the narrow space against the wall, and drag Maya up onto the bed. "Let's go, Maya," I say. She doesn't resist, but she's not helping, either. I prop her up into a semisitting position and pin her there with my legs. "Just a teaspoon. It's going to help your cough." *Please, God,* I think.

"No!" She swats my hand away, and the teaspoon flies across the room. It hurtles past Uzi's face as he opens the door.

"*What!*" he says.

"Yes! Uzi, the spoon. There's an eyedropper in the bag, too. Hurry."

"Okay, okay, calm down," he says.

Maya presses both hands against her mouth. I pour a perfect teaspoon full of liquid into the spoon Uzi hands me and give the bottle to him.

"You have to take it," I tell Maya. "Let's go."

She closes her eyes and whips her head from side to side. Well, at least Uzi is getting to witness it this time.

"Hold her hands back," I instruct him.

He hesitates, unsure. "I don't know," he says. "I don't think we're going about this the right way."

"We don't have another way," I say, trying to control Maya's thrashing with my free arm. "If we can't stop the cough, she's going to be up all night and tomorrow she'll be even worse. How much worse are we going to let it get?"

"Okay," he says, but I can tell he doesn't like the idea.

There's no way I can get the spoon anywhere close to Maya without spilling its contents. "I have to try the eyedropper," I say.

"No!" Maya screams. "Dodo says no!"

"What?" Uzi drops her hands and raises his in a *what the hell?* kind of gesture.

I grab the eyedropper and use it to suck up the medicine from the teaspoon in my hand.

"No medicine!" Maya shouts. "Dodo says no medicine! Dodo doesn't want me to get better!" She flops onto her stomach and starts clawing at the sheets to crawl away.

"I don't care what Dodo says!" I shout back. I've had far more than enough of this Dodo business. I grab Maya, flip her onto her back, and pin her down with my knees. I'm really losing it now. "*I'm* the mother, and *I* say you have to take your medicine!"

She opens her mouth to shout again, and I squeeze her cheeks with one hand, forcing the eyedropper into the side of her mouth with the other. She flings her head to the side, refusing to swallow. The ruby liquid gurgles back up her throat and runs out of her cheek and onto the bed, staining a puddle into the white sheets.

"No!" she gasps. "Dodo. Says. No!"

"Mommy says *yes*!" I shout back.

"Don't do this," Uzi says.

I quickly measure another teaspoon into the eyedropper, stuff it into the corner of her mouth, and squeeze, but my timing is terrible. It goes in just as she's inhaling and she starts gagging and coughing. The syrup spews all over the sheets, scattering crimson droplets that look like spattered blood. Bloodstains on a white bedsheet. My daughter. Oh my God. I've let this go way too far.

"*Hope*," Uzi says, his voice just stern enough to sound like the warning it is. "Stop it."

I roll Maya to her side and wait for her to catch her breath, and the shame comes rushing in so fast it feels like nausea. Lying there, she's just this tiny thing, and looming above her, I'm so big. Yet in that moment of struggle, she felt so powerful, a force that had to be wrestled and contained.

"Dodo," she sobs, trying to regulate her breathing. "Dodo-o-o."

I flip around to the side of the bed and face the wall. I should have stopped when I felt the rush of violence coming on. I know now how a parent can snap and do real damage to a child without ever intending to. It can happen that fast. What great stroke of luck just stopped it from happening here? I know Uzi would have stopped me, but even more, I have to believe I would have retained enough presence of mind to have stopped myself. I have to believe that.

Uzi comforts Maya on the mattress beside me, but I can't turn around. I don't want them to see me. I can't even look at myself.

After a while, I feel Uzi's hand on my shoulder and I reach up to grasp it. He intertwines his fingers with mine and kisses my ear. "It's okay," he says, softly massaging my shoulder, and then, "We should try to get some sleep."

Later, with Maya bathed and kissed abundantly and apologies offered all around, we lie in bed with her sleeping between us and I reach out and place my hand against his cheek.

"I'm sorry," I say.

"It's okay," he says, stroking my arm. How he can still love me after what he just witnessed is one of the great miracles of my life.

"I feel like I'm going crazy."

"I know," he says.

"Do you think I'm going crazy?"

"No," he says.

"No, you don't think so or no, you don't want me to know that you think so?"

"No, I don't think so," he says. "But I think we're both under a lot of stress right now."

"This was supposed to be our vacation."

He lets out a little laugh that says, *Yeah, right.*

"Maybe things will slow down soon," I say. I don't really believe it, but this is the line we use to comfort each other whenever the pace starts moving too fast. Saying it puts forth the hope that simplification is possible, and that in itself makes us feel better. The problem is, for the past three and a half years, ever since we bought the house, moved out to California, planned a wedding in nine weeks, and gave birth to Maya, the pace hasn't slowed down, ever, not even a little.

I wrap my right arm around Maya and clasp Uzi's hand in mine.

"Good night, my prince," I say.

He kisses my knuckles. "Good night."

I close my eyes and pull Maya a little closer. A few months ago on public radio, I heard an interview with an expert on the Maya calendar. He was talking about the concept of time acceleration, a phenomenon some present-day researchers believe is encoded in the complex astronomical and mathematical systems the ancient Maya used to measure time. The Maya, who thought of time as cyclical, he said, identified nine creation cycles of consciousness, which they called the Nine Underworlds. The first one started 16.4 billion years ago with cellular development, the second began about 40 million years ago and tracked mammalian evolution, the third saw the establishment of family systems, and so on and so forth all the way up to the Ninth and final underworld, the Universal, which will start in 2011. When that one ends, a new form of human consciousness is expected to emerge and the Maya master calendar will be reset to zero.

You have to imagine all the Nine Underworlds, the man said, starting at different points in time but nonetheless running concurrently. Imagine them stacked on top of each other like a wedding cake, or a pyramid, so that each time a new underworld starts it's layered on top of the others, which serve as its foundation. And imagine each layer of the pyramid divided into thirteen equal slices, representing alternating periods of light and darkness that bring either progress and creativity or chaos and destruction to the earth.

You might say, *huh?* That's what I was thinking in my car. But here's the part of the radio interview that grabbed me and kept me sitting for half an hour in a café parking lot to hear it in its entirety. We use a base-ten system for calculating time, but the Maya used a vigesimal system, meaning base-twenty math. According to their calculations, each of the Nine Underworlds lasts for exactly one twentieth the time of the one it's built upon. For example, as the man on the radio explained it, the Seventh Underworld, which started in 1755, is 256 years long. The Eighth Underworld, the one we're in now, started on January 5, 1999, and will last for less than thirteen years—which is one twentieth of 256. The ninth and final underworld starts in February 2011 and will last for only 263 days. This is why, the man said, it took 15 billion years for cells to develop but only about a dozen for the Internet to take hold. Because the shifts between periods of light and dark happen twenty times faster in each new underworld, the amount of change that used to take place in a lifetime now occurs in a single year. If it feels as if time is speeding up, the man said, that's because it is.

All this time, I've believed that the chronic shortage of time I experience is my own doing, that I've been trying to pack too much activity into each day. But now I've started wondering if what I'm feeling is the nature of time itself in this new millennium. Maybe I'm going to have to learn to swim faster instead of endlessly waiting for the current around me to slow down.

chapter five
Cayo District, Belize
December 24, 2000

S ome people actively pray for a miracle, others are content to patiently wait for one to occur, and still others, like myself, are more likely to write off extraordinary happenings as coincidence. For this reason, I find myself at a loss to explain exactly how, when I am certain all hope of reunion is lost, we step into the small, air conditioned Belize City airport and pass through the rapid stamp-stamp-stamp of passport control to find our three pieces of luggage standing in a perfect, upright row alongside the single baggage carousel, as if they have been patiently waiting there all morning for us to arrive.

BIENVENIDO A BELICE, said the black print letters on the exterior of the terminal when we descended a set of silver stairs from the plane and stepped onto the airport's single airstrip, and it does feel like a generous welcome.

"All *right*!" I shout, punching the air in triumph. It feels good to smile. Even Maya cracks a small grin from her stroller when she sees her Scooby-Doo suitcase again. Boosted by our unexpected good luck, we hand over our customs forms and stroll through the half-empty airport terminal and out into the sudden sunlight. I shade my eyes with my right hand and look out upon a half-dozen taxi drivers in flowered tropical shirts and Panama hats lounging against their front fenders, smoking hand-rolled cigarettes. No one looks in a hurry to get a fare.

We pull our bags over to a bench to wait for Victor Tut, the jungle resort owner who Carolyn the travel agent has said will meet us here. We've been sitting for only a few minutes when we hear someone shouting loudly from across the street. A man on the other side is standing next to a white van, waving both arms expansively over his head.

"Ai-ya!" he calls. He jogs across the road, grabs hold of my backpack with one hand, and slaps Uzi on the shoulder with his other. "Finally! It's you!"

A sturdy, weathered man in a baseball cap and a short-sleeved, plaid, button-down shirt, Victor picks up Maya's suitcase and my backpack and hustles the bags across the street. "You made it!" he calls over his shoulder. "We weren't sure!" We don't have much choice but to follow Victor, so we do.

"So here you are, in our little country," Victor says, sliding open the van's side door for Maya and me to climb in. "Not big like yours, but nice still. We like it."

Smaller than California, yes, but it's going to take us two hours to drive clear across the country to Victor's resort near the Guatemalan border, which, after the past thirty-seven hours of travel, makes Belize big enough for me.

Uzi takes the passenger seat up front, and Victor steers the van away from the curb. "Anything you need here, you ask Victor," he says as we pass underneath a huge green arch announcing, this time in English, WELCOME TO BELIZE. "Even for your daughter, we have my little grandson, an automatic friend."

We drive past a field of low trees and horses and then a strip of scrappy houses and stores. A boxy white industrial building bears a sign for the Maya Belize Cement Company.

"Look, Maya!" I point out. "There's your name!" She lifts her head and nods, then lies back down.

"She has croup," I explain to Victor. "She got it pretty bad this time."

Victor shakes his head. "I don't know it," he says.

"Maybe you call it something different here," I say.

"Maybe."

Small, ramshackle wooden homes painted in bright shades of green, yellow, and blue and *tiendas* plastered with soft-drink ads dot the sides of the road. On our left we pass a tiny white shed with a black hand-painted sign—HIGH WAY BARBER—and then we speed by the neon green Everyday Market on the right.

"Is it true there are only two paved roads in the country?" I ask Victor. I read this somewhere, but the information must have been dated. The road we're on is missing a center stripe but otherwise rides fine.

"You want paved roads?" Victor asks.

"Not really. I was just wondering."

"This one is paved," he says. "But not all the others. How is the little one doing back there?"

As if on cue, Maya starts coughing vigorously, causing Victor to glance back with concern.

"Ay, *reina*," he says. Then to me, "You know what is *reina*?"

"Queen?"

"Very good. You speak Spanish?"

"A little."

"*Un poquito?*"

"*Muy poquito*," I clarify. I hold my thumb and forefinger about an inch apart to show exactly how much.

Victor smiles in the rearview mirror. "Good. Then you know. That little one is like a queen."

We ride in comfortable silence for a few minutes as the van leaves the outskirts of Belize City. For many years Belize City was the capital of British Honduras, until Halloween Day 1961, when Hurricane Hattie came roaring out of the Caribbean and decimated the city. To avoid a repeat, the government packed itself up in 1970 and relocated fifty miles inland to Belmopan, but nobody wanted to follow. Thirty years later, Belize City remains the economic and social nucleus of the country, while Belmopan, the new capital in the center of the country, exists mainly for the few thousand civil servants who report to work there every day.

We're traveling along the two-lane Western Highway all the way out to the Cayo District, to the twin cities of San Ignacio and Santa Elena. Victor's family-run resort is just south of San Ignacio, on the banks of the Macal River. The Macal flows north to connect with the Mopan River from the west and forms the Belize River, which comes all the way out here and spills into the Caribbean. From the time of the ancient Maya Empire until just recently, this internal network was the country's main artery for communication and trade, and nearly half of Belize's population still lives along its route.

Along the roadside, wood-plank shacks advertise pork and beans for sale. We slow down to cruise across a narrow bridge outside the village of Burrell Boom. Farther down the road we bear right around a traffic circle, where a boy of seven or eight stands on the shoulder lifting a giant dead lizard above his head.

"See the iguana?" Victor asks.

"He's selling it?" I say.

"Oh, sure," Victor says. "For the meat. We call it 'Bamboo Chicken.'"

Maya lifts her head. "Where's the iguana?" she asks, but it's already behind us.

"We'll see another one, baby," I promise her, smoothing back her hair. She clutches the Hursulas tightly to her chest and nods.

About every twentieth structure is a storefront whose windows open to glimpses of cold drinks and canned food, a throwback, I imagine, to a time when few people owned cars and local commerce was the only way to buy goods. Most of the homes are built on stilts, even though there's no water in sight. When I ask Victor why, he says it's to improve airflow and reduce indoor heat in the summer. "Also, it's good against too much water," he explains. This road flooded badly just two months ago, during Hurricane Keith, and everything on ground level was lost. What we're seeing now is what survived the flood. I think about this as we pass a pale blue cinder-block house with JESUS LOVES ME stenciled in small black letters on its side. Then Uzi turns to Victor.

"We were wondering," he says, "if you know of any shamans in Cayo."

He means to be straightforward and efficient, wasting neither words nor time, but the question rushes out abruptly and without context. I check Victor's profile for a flicker of annoyance, expecting to hear the dismissive stock answer he uses with all Americans who ask this, but his tanned, creased face remains unchanged as he drums his forefingers against the top of the steering wheel. He seems to be considering the question.

"You mean a bush doctor?" he asks.

"I guess so," Uzi says. "We want to bring our daughter to one."

"There was one famous one. He lived in San Antonio, not too far from us."

"Elijio Panti?" Uzi asks. "We read about him."

"Mmm. He trained some people before he died. I know of one in San Antonio. You want to go when?"

"Today?"

"Hoo!" Victor laughs. "Okay. Maybe today."

"Maybe we should call first," I suggest. "See if he has an appointment open?"

Victor shakes his head. "No phone. You just go. Okay. We'll try today."

Uzi looks back at me and raises his eyebrows. *See how easy this is?* his expression says. I raise my eyebrows in return and rest my hand on Maya's back. She's fallen asleep again. Easy. So far.

I stare out the window and watch the scenery stream by. A young black man in military fatigues hitchhikes by the side of the road, his face shading from hopeful to dispassionate as we speed by. Two girls in white party dresses play hopscotch in front of a low aqua house. Along the shoulder, a bearded man in a blue Cinzano biking outfit jogs with what looks, bizarrely, like a plastic birthday cake in his hands. The houses here all seem cut from the same mold: wooden, rectangular, and single-story, about half on stilts, with a lone electrical cord extending from the corner of a corrugated tin roof to a pole on the street. Each house makes a colorful statement. Sky blue, mint green, canary yellow, pink, peach, and aquamarine repeat themselves every mile.

We pass a few empty schools, nondescript cement-block buildings with overgrown basketball courts that feature faded Sprite ads on the backboards. Old yellow school buses sit parked in adjacent yards, bearing the names of the American school districts where they originated in bold, black letters along their sides: NEPTUNE CITY, NEW JERSEY; BAYTOWN, TEXAS; LINCOLN COMMUNITY SCHOOLS. The school system here must purchase the used buses when U.S. school districts upgrade their fleets. Speaking of schools, it's Tuesday morning—where are all the students?

"No school today?" I ask Victor.

"Christmas Eve, a holiday." Oh. Right. I'm losing track of days.

Victor turns on the radio, and reggae music eases its way to the backseat. A light rain drops tiny dots onto the windshield. The song is hypnotic, soothing, generically Bob Marley–esque. Uzi rests his right foot on the dashboard as we pass Belmopan, the capital, distinguishable only by a lonely intersection north of town where a cement bus shelter hugs a corner across the street from what looks like an empty fairground. At some point Victor waves his right hand toward the passenger window, gesturing north. "Mennonites," he says. I must be dozing because I'm only able to utter a woozy "Mm-hm," which makes Uzi and Victor laugh, and then the jungle starts closing in.

The Crystal Paradise Resort is a neat cluster of two-room cabanas on a slight rise above the Macal River. The tall, square sign at the entrance reads, "Crystal Paradise, The Adventure Continues. Belizean Hospitality." We turn off Cristo Rey Road and head down a long gravel driveway framed by lush, ornamental trees and palm fronds that arc overhead. As Victor swivels the van into a parking area off to the right, he mentions that he and his six sons thatched all the roofs on the property themselves. At lunch, I stare up at the thousands of dry beige palm fronds uniformly woven together above our heads in the open-air dining hall. It looks like a tremendous amount of work.

The meal is rice, beans, chicken, and plantains, served family style in the dining hall. Because Maya is still refusing all food except cucumbers, Victor's wife, Teresa, cuts one into slices she arranges in a circle in a shallow glass dish. Carolyn the travel agent, who grew up in Cayo, told me we'd like the family that owns and runs the resort. "They have a very large number of children," she said. "Ten, I believe."

We're seated at a rectangular wooden table with an enthusiastically blond, deeply tanned woman and her fifteen-year-old son, a strapping barefoot, bare-chested boy in board shorts who wears mirrored aviator sunglasses throughout the meal. I notice that the woman holds her hands over her plate of food before she eats, just like Uzi. She looks as if she spent the first forty years of her life on a surfboard. Her son looks lost without one.

We start exchanging names. The son is Kevin. Uzi is Uzi.

"Like the gun?" Kevin asks. Every American, and I do mean every American, who meets Uzi when we travel feels compelled to ask this question.

"The gun was invented by an Israeli," I explain. "The gun's named after a person, not the other way around." The inventor's name was actually Uziel, but people aren't usually interested in this detail. My husband wasn't named after a gun: that's all they want to know.

"What's your name, sweetie?" the woman asks Maya.

"Maya," Maya whispers.

"Maya," I say a little louder, to make sure the woman heard.

"Maya!" the woman repeats. "That's a good name for here."

It's a good name for an American, but it's actually a funny name for here. Belizeans would never name a child Maya. It would be like an American naming a child "Latino" or "Swede."

"It's a popular name in Israel," I say, which is true. We were looking for a name that would work in both our cultures, and we also wanted to name Maya after my mother, Marcia, which by Jewish tradition meant we needed a name starting with *M*. By the end of my eighth month of pregnancy, we'd narrowed it down to Maya or Melanie. Then we took a final prebaby vacation up the California coast. One night we stayed in downtown San Francisco in a hotel just outside the gates to Chinatown. As we were getting ready for dinner in our hotel room, we were going back and forth about the name. Maya or Melanie? Melanie or Maya?

When we went downstairs to eat, we stepped out of the hotel onto the sidewalk, and, right there, right in front of the hotel, was a newspaper vending machine with the name *MAYA* spray painted on the side in huge black graffiti letters. Had it been there when we walked into the hotel? We didn't know. Either way, even to me, this was a sign too blatant to ignore.

"I'm Hope," I say to keep the introductions going around the table.

"Another good name," the blond woman observes.

Her name is Shanti or Shakti or something similar that can't possibly be her real name, and she claims to be a psychic. She lives in Santa Cruz, California, she tells us, and she'd never heard of Belize until a few weeks ago when she looked online for last-minute package deals and found this one at a deep discount. It occurs to me that if you were really a psychic, you'd know in advance where you were going to spend your winter vacation, but I keep this observation to myself.

At the end of the meal, Maya rests her head on the table and Uzi wanders over to the wooden bookshelf in the corner. It's a backpacker's library, filled with well-thumbed paperbacks left behind by prior guests and a few encyclopedias about the flora and fauna of Belize. He returns with a photographic book of Central American butterflies for Maya and a frayed copy of *Many Masters, Many Lives* for himself.

"That's a classic," the psychic says, eyeing the cover.

I read it ten years ago, during my brief New Age phase, and I remember the broad strokes. A psychiatrist noticed that some of his patients, while under hypnosis, spoke about details from other cultures and eras they couldn't possibly have known about in their present-day lives. He decided they must have been accessing material from lives that preceded this one and offered some compelling examples to support his argument. But still. People read books, watch films, exercise their imaginations, respond to suggestion. It can't be that impossible to fool a psychiatrist, especially one on the lookout for every shred of evidence to support his nascent theory.

I stroke Maya's hair and try to coax a piece of bread into her mouth. She shakes her head forcefully. I put the bread back on the plate.

"She's sick?" Shakti asks Uzi.

"She's got croup," he says. "And an imaginary friend. We're taking her to a shaman this afternoon."

"That's cool," Shakti says.

Behind us in the kitchen, Teresa shouts something in Spanish and a small boy in rubber flip-flops runs laughing from the kitchen, clutching a banana to his chest.

"Mom," Maya whispers, her cheek pressed against the tabletop.

"Hmm?"

"I see a boy here."

"Victor's grandson."

"I wish I could play with him."

"I know, sweetie. Maybe in a few days." I lift her head carefully and hold a glass of water to her lips. Uzi and the psychic are talking about reincarnation and spirit guides, and, despite the content, I feel a small pang of regret for being shut out of the conversation. Despite my long-standing conviction that I've never been a fourth-century Chinese peasant or Mary Queen of Scots, Uzi and the psychic are laughing amicably and I don't want to appear unfriendly. Also, I can't stop myself from acting overly solicitous around alternatively minded people, as if I'm trying to overcompensate for my skepticism by trying too hard to pander to their beliefs.

When Uzi ducks under the table to retrieve his fork, I turn to the psychic. "That's really interesting," I say. "So these spirit guides you're talking about—are they like voices inside your head?"

"Actually, that sounds a little schizophrenic," says the woman.

"So . . . it's more like an awareness?"

"You could say that." She shrugs, though not dismissively. "It's not that easy to explain."

After lunch, Uzi lies cradled in a blue-and-yellow scoop of Maya hammock on our cabana porch reading the past-lives book while Maya naps in our room. I sit at the top of the cabana's wide cement steps, occasionally rubbing my thumbs against the smooth red polish on my toenails. Our cabana is a duplex, with two private rooms side by side, and the psychic and her son have been occupying the other for the past three days. They lounge deeply in the wooden Adirondack deck chairs, blissed out on dark bottles of Belizean beer. She's telling us about a dream she had early this morning, a complicated story involving a shaman and a feather and a bell.

"Dude," the son keeps saying. "Oh, *dude*."

As her story draws to a close, the psychic lifts her beer bottle toward Uzi in a simulated toast. Is it just my imagination, or did she deliberately pivot her breasts in his direction? Yes, he's handsome—at least *I* think so—but come on. Is his wife not sitting six feet away?

"Isn't it funny," she says to Uzi, "how you can travel all the way down here and wind up sharing a cabana with someone who lives down the road from you at home?"

It wasn't my imagination.

"Topanga's not really 'down the road' from Santa Cruz," I interrupt before Uzi has a chance to answer. It's more like a six-hour drive. And I'd like to add that we're not exactly sharing a cabana either, but Uzi shoots me a look that says, *cool it*, so I cut it off there.

It's only two o'clock. The afternoon is barely inching along. On the lawn in front of the cabana a gray horse nibbles on the grass next to a bougainvillea tree exploding with hot pink flowers. Through the screen door behind me, I hear Maya coughing in her sleep.

"Maybe I can get some medicine down her while she's sleeping," I say.

Uzi looks up, reluctantly. "Maybe wait till after?" he suggests.

"We've *been* waiting," I say. I stand up and rub my damp palms once, twice against my striped cotton pants.

"He'll be here soon," Uzi says and slowly turns a page.

I sigh, deeply and dramatically, and head for our room, pulling the wooden door shut behind me with a gentle wheezing sound. The air inside abruptly thins, and the ceramic tile sends a sudden chill up through the soles of my bare feet. Everything about the hut's interior is designed to minimize heat, from the slatted hardwood blinds to the white ceiling fan that orbits lazily day and night. I look up at the thatched roof and register that the room has no ceiling: the fan hangs suspended from a horizontal wooden pole that runs right from one side of the sloping roof to the other. When I look up, I'm staring directly at the tightly thatched rows of dried palm fronds. I think this is the most strange and marvelous hotel room I've ever stayed in.

Maya lies wrapped in an orange Guatemalan blanket on the twin bed, her mop of dark curls poking out from beneath its fringed border. I crouch next to her and rest my chin on the mattress. Her forehead is pink and smooth, unpuckered by daytime worries. I press my palm against it. She still has a fever. I decide against trying the cough medicine. Better to let her have unbroken sleep.

I smooth the blanket around her shoulders and tuck the Hursulas in neatly alongside her. Maya's tongue moves slightly between her lips a few times, as if she's sucking an invisible thumb, then stops.

I once read that being a mother is analogous to the moments in open-heart surgery when the patient's blood circulates outside his body. How can I explain that feeling to friends who don't yet have children or even to Uzi? From the moment Maya arrived, my world shrank to the small parameters of my daughter's body. The morning she was born I held her in my arms as the sun rose over the hospital in Van Nuys. Just two hours old, she was the cleanest page I could imagine. There was so much potential packed into her little frame. It was an idea nearly overpowering in its beauty and its grace. I pressed my lips against her warm forehead. My daughter. She would be the happy one, the one who laughed easily and often, forgave quickly, and always remembered the punch lines to jokes. The one who'd know the security and trust that can come only from growing up in an intact, loving family. She would be the one for whom everything went right.

A scraping, scuffing sound comes from the cabana's front porch, and I think perhaps Victor has arrived for us. But when I walk outside there is just Uzi, only Uzi, reading and rocking himself in the hammock with one foot anchored on the tile floor, his dark, wavy hair bent in concentration over his book. When he hears the screen door open, he looks up and smiles at me impulsively, a gaze lavish with contentment and devotion, and just as impulsively, my heart leaps forward to meet it.

"You're beautiful," he says.

"You haven't seen me for ten minutes. You've probably forgotten what I look like." After four years, he still can make me blush.

"That's true, number one," he says. "Number two, you *are* beautiful."

He reaches a hand toward me, fingers splayed wide for maximum contact. I reach for it and intertwine my fingers with his. He has the most beautiful hands, just slightly larger than mine, with slender fingers and neatly trimmed nails. He normally doesn't wear a wedding ring, doesn't like the feel of metal on his body, but today he's wearing the hematite band Maya helped me pick out for him at the crystal shop in Topanga a few months ago.

"How's she doing?" he asks.

"Sleeping."

"Fever?"

"About the same." I scan the empty porch. "Where's Shanti?" I ask.

"Shakti."

"Shakti," I repeat.

"She went to find Victor. She wants to go with us to the shaman."

"Oh, God. He should sell tickets."

Uzi looks at me for a long moment, and releases my hand.

"I don't see what the problem is," he says. "She's just trying to be friendly."

"A little too friendly, if you ask me."

"What's that supposed to mean?"

"What it sounds like."

He sighs loudly and turns back to his book. After a moment he says, "She thinks you have a lot of fear."

"She said that?"

He nods at the pages.

"How would she know?"

He shrugs. "Just from watching you, I guess."

"What I have is none of her business," I say, although in a voice much punier than normal.

I'm not sure which bothers me more: the fact that my husband is discussing me with a middle-aged blonde in a tank top two sizes too small who's known me for all of twelve minutes, or that this Shakti woman is able to see through me so fast. Not that it takes a psychic to divine that I'm edgy right now; anyone with retinas can see that. But what I thought I keep well hidden is that this isn't a temporary condition. I'm scared *all the time* these days, of breast cancer and carjackers and phone calls in the middle of the night, of wildfires and choking and tornados, of rats and AIDS and airplane turbulence and mean-spirited book reviews. Uzi says I have the most extreme startle response of anyone he's ever met. Sometimes when I'm standing in the bathroom with my back to the door and he walks into the room without warning, my whole body jerks and I literally scream from fright. It worries him, a lot.

It worries *me* that he might be discussing these things with Shakti.

"PS, I'm not even convinced she's a psychic," I say. Uzi sighs.

Well, I'm *not*. It seems to me that an authentic psychic wouldn't feel the need to introduce herself as one. Wouldn't a real psychic just humbly *do* paranormal things in the course of an ordinary day and let that serve as her calling card? Like my high school psychology teacher, Mr. Gelman, who looked like a mini Albert Einstein. You'd never know it from his lectures on Pavlov or Skinner, but he could hold a piece of your jewelry in his hand at the end of class and spout random and specific details about your life that nobody else could possibly know. And what about the Psychic Twins, whom my friend Jeff encouraged me to see four years ago, just before Uzi and I became engaged? Terry and Linda were exact replicas of each other, both about five foot ten and stick thin, with long, wavy red hair parted in the middle. They sat shoulder to shoulder on the couch in their Culver City apartment, dressed in matching purple velvet skirts and long-sleeved red blouses, scribbling madly on individual yellow legal pads throughout the session.

It didn't look as if they were doing much, but then they started talking. They told me I wasn't going to get breast cancer anytime soon—that was a relief—and that my father would live for at least a few more years, which has turned out to be true. They said I'd have a daughter in 2001 who'd be a dancer, but this was 1997 and they missed that I was already pregnant with Maya, something I didn't even know yet myself. They told me my soul mate had salt-and-pepper hair and wire-rimmed glasses and worked as an attorney. When I asked if they could in any way be confusing him with the man I was currently dating, even though he had brown hair and 20/10 vision and worked in high tech, they scribbled a few more sentences on the legal pads, shook their heads in unison, and then immediately perked up.

"But remember," the twin on the right reminded me, "you can always change your destiny!"

I wasn't terribly worried by the soul mate comment. The idea that there's one, singular person crafted as my perfect spiritual complement whom I need to find to feel complete—I've never bought into that one. The way I've always thought of it, the landscape of human connections is more like a giant city divided into subdivisions. Every subdivision has its own set of streets, every street is lined with houses, every house is full of rooms, and every room has a couple of tables. You can feel it when you meet someone for the first time who lives in your spiritual neighborhood, and you know when someone comes from your house. Those to whom you feel an automatic, magnetic attraction are the ones sitting at your table. I've had two or three relationships with men at my table, and the attempts were all glorious disasters. (I've never understood the appeal of dating someone who can finish your sentences. That kind of thing makes me positively nuts.) Uzi and I, I'm pretty sure we're from the same street. That's about as much proximity as I seem able to manage in a romance.

Me and Shakti, I can tell we're not even from the same town.

I look up as Victor's son Everald joins us on the porch. He's one of the older children in the family, maybe twenty-five or thirty, with a thin mustache and close-cut brown hair. We've heard that one of the sons is an expert on local plants; is it him? No, that's Jeronie, the eldest, Everald tells us, although he knows a lot himself, just from growing up here. Do we have plans tomorrow night, for Christmas? he asks. There'll be a party in the dining hall with a marimba band, local music, we should come.

"We'll have to see how Maya's doing," I tell him, and he nods.

Car keys jangle from the side lawn, signaling Victor's approach. I look over to see Shakti trailing a few steps behind him with an expression of wry disappointment crimping her mouth to one side.

"Oh well," she calls ahead to Uzi. "I guess it wasn't meant to be."

chapter six
San Antonio Village, Belize
December 24, 2000

The bush doctor lives in a Monopoly house, squat and square and green. It sits perpendicular to the road, about fifty feet from the encroaching jungle's rim. Victor's van rolls to a stop alongside a small, thatched-roof roundhouse that seems to function as the house's storage shed or as a makeshift barn. Inside, empty milk crates sit stacked next to open barrels of chicken feed.

Victor leans three times on the horn, each one an arresting blast that tears through the placid jungle air. *Are. You. There?* Maya cringes and coughs quietly, a loose, rumbling sound like distant thunder.

"It's okay, baby," I say, kissing the top of her head.

Six minutes ago, at the entrance to San Antonio Village—called Tanah, or "Our Home," in Yucatec Mayan—Victor pulled the van up to a small yellow shed that looked like a child's playhouse moonlighting as a tiny general store. A red Coca-Cola placard was posted above the open door, next to a single flap-down window that revealed a glimpse of canned food and paper towels shelved inside.

Two teenage girls in halter tops and cutoff shorts sat in lawn chairs on the grass in front, minding a pair of toddlers. Victor exchanged a few sentences with one of them, then returned to the driver's seat.

"I asked for directions to the bush doctor I know, but they said there's another the people trust more," he said as he steered us off the grass lawn and back onto the road. The girls waved a cheery good-bye as we pulled away. "Over here, to the left," Victor added.

We headed up a slight hill and past a blue house, then a purple one. House paint is a luxury people don't scrimp on here, even when they can afford to cover only the front. Nearly every house we pass is a bright splash of color against the constant green backdrop of fields and trees.

Inside the village, evenly spaced wooden homes and small general stores house and supply the more than two thousand Maya Indians who live here. Chickens peck their way across the roads, and laundry sways gently on taut clotheslines in neatly kept yards. There is a visible sense of egalitarianism here; no one home appears larger or more ostentatious than any other. A hand-painted sign near the middle of town welcomes visitors to the home of Don Elijio Panti, great Maya healer of Belize. His original wooden house and traditional Maya pole-stick hut, where dozens of cars once lined up on treatment days, have been preserved as a small museum his grandson runs.

Before the Spanish conquistadors arrived in Belize in the sixteenth century, a million Maya lived in the region, but so many died from diseases carried over from Europe and in wars over land that today only about twenty thousand Maya—roughly a tenth of the country's total population—live in Belize, and many of them migrated in from elsewhere. The Kekchi group of Maya migrated from the highlands of Guatemala when their land was usurped for coffee plantations; the Mopan Maya, who live mostly in the southern region, were forced out from Belize and into Guatemala by the British in the late 1700s and returned a hundred years later; and the Yucatecans came in the nineteenth and early twentieth centuries, fleeing race wars in Mexico's Yucatán peninsula. The primary language in San Antonio is Yucatec, a tongue so complicated—with numerous pronouns, complicated prefixes and suffixes, and extremely specific delineations of time—it prompted one renowned anthropologist to proclaim it easy to learn only if you're a Maya toddler.

Victor parks the van about a hundred feet from the pale green wooden cabin. "Ai-ya!" he shouts, sliding from the front seat onto the damp grass. I squint at the house in front of us. It's built of odd-sized wood scraps that appear to have been nailed together like a patchwork quilt. A faded sage green paint covers the front of the house and wraps partway around the side. The planks around the front door are stained ankle high with mud, and pale blue curtains hang in two windows that have neither panes nor screens. The house has no discernible front path or driveway, only grass on all four sides. If not for the single electrical wire stretching from the corner of its tin roof to a pole by the road, the house would look as if it had dropped straight down from the sky.

A small group of children are playing tag in the yard to our left, running circles around a fire burning high in an old oil drum. When they hear Victor's shout, a boy of about nine or ten skids to a stop, jams two fingers into his mouth, and whistles loudly. The chickens at his feet scatter in frantic disorder.

There's still time left for me to say no to this, but not much. I don't know what to do. I scan the yard for a marker that might indicate "trusted healer": a line of solemn customers outside the front door waiting to be ushered in or perhaps an orderly row of glass jars filled with dried herbs on a windowsill, like the ones that covered the wall of a voodoo store I once stumbled upon in the French Quarter of New Orleans. Instead, I see a sand pile ringed with stones with a dog sleeping on its side in the center and a row of empty, upright pink, green, and white plastic ten-gallon buckets on the grass. And then, while I'm wondering what use a healer might have for so many buckets, the bush doctor appears from around the back corner of his house.

What do I expect a Maya shaman to look like? Certainly not like its caricature, no bare-chested man with a headdress and heavy ornamental jewelry prancing around in a rapturous, rhythmic trance. And certainly not someone as ordinary as Burt the drug counselor in Iowa City. I'm waiting, I suppose, for someone who looks familiar yet not too familiar, authentic but not too authentic, indigenous but not uncomfortably anachronistic. Too much exotica will strain my credulity, but too little will have the same effect on me.

I'm expecting *something*. Something other than this short man with a black bowl haircut and dirty jeans, his knee-high Wellington boots spattered with chicken shit and mud, who ambles toward us across the muddy lawn.

"Is that him?" I whisper to Uzi.

"I think so," he whispers back.

The man pulls off a work glove and shakes Victor's hand. He looks harmless enough. They start talking, but I can latch onto only every tenth word. I hear a few Spanish numbers and other clipped sounds that don't resemble any language I've heard before. The word *curas*, with a question mark, coming from Victor, and a nod from the man.

"I think they're talking in a mix of Mayan and Spanish," I say.

"I'd better go out there," Uzi says, opening the passenger door. Maya lifts herself off my lap, clutching Hursula One tight against her chest.

"Are we getting out?" she asks weakly.

"In a minute," I say.

I watch Uzi carefully pick his way across the grass in his flat, open sandals. He joins the men by the side of the road, and there are nods and handshakes all around. Then I see Uzi gesturing with his hands on either side of his mouth, to signify a cough. The bush doctor stares.

I knock on the glass. "It's not just that!" I shout.

Uzi looks up at me blankly. *"What?"* he mouths.

"It's not just that!" I shout louder, making Maya flinch. They still can't hear me. I lift her off my lap and shift her onto the gray passenger bench.

"I'll be right back," I say. "Wait here for Mommy."

On the grass, the men are trying to communicate in a mix of

English, Spanish, and pantomime. The conversation is so fractured, I can't tell where I'm entering it.

"He wants you to tell him," Victor says.

Spanish is the second language for most residents of San Antonio, English usually the third. I'll take my chances with Spanish. *"Habla español?"* I ask the bush doctor.

He smiles and nods. His eyes are so black it's as if the pupils have completely overtaken the irises. His skin is the exact color of cinnamon.

"Nuestra hija está enferma," I begin. *"Por dos semanas."* I hold up two fingers and pause.

"Sí," the bush doctor says.

"Ella tiene . . . Victor, *como se dice* 'she's coughing'?" I pound my chest and make a loud, hacking sound for emphasis.

"Está tosiendo."

"Ella está tosiendo mal, muy mal," I begin. From behind me there comes the soft booming noise of Maya pounding on the van window with both hands. *"Mom!"* she shouts. Her voice comes to us from a great distance. I give her the one-minute sign.

"Y ella no quiere tocar su . . . *medicino? Mi esposo piensa que* . . . *es posible?* . . . *un espíritu mal* . . ." My voice goes wobbly, and I look toward the van again. Hursula One's rubber face is pressed against the glass alongside Maya's at an unnatural angle, frozen in its perpetual rosebud smile. *"Mi hija* . . ." I say, and then I can't get any further. I wasn't expecting that to happen.

"Ah." The small man nods. *"Necesita una cura.* Okay."

"Una cura," I repeat. *"Sí."*

I press the tip of my sneaker into the soft lawn and watch the water seep out of the soil. The edges of Uzi's sandals are already ringed with orange mud. Maya watches us through the window as Victor and the bush doctor talk some more. Maybe they're trying to negotiate a price?

Victor angles his head toward the van window but keeps his eyes on me. "He wants to know about the doll," he says.

"*Mom!*" Maya screeches, pounding on the window again with both hands. I start moving in her direction.

"The doll?" I ask over my shoulder. "I don't know. It's just a doll. She's had it for three months, maybe. *Tres meses?*"

They consult again in low voices.

"Three days I see," the man says, in English. "And the baby a bath."

I'm not sure what he means. "Okay," I say.

"All right," Victor says. "You go with him to the house. I'll wait here."

There are moments in a mother's life when answers appear with precise and stunning clarity, but there are many more, I've come to recognize, when the swell of momentum carries you along. All your Mommy & Me friends start putting their children to bed in their cribs, and the parenting magazines warn about the dangers of the family bed, so you leave your infant crying alone in her crib at night even though you spend half the night crying over it, too. Or the pediatrician officiously hands you a prescription and the receptionist directs you to the pharmacy downstairs and you hand the slip of paper over to the clerk in the white lab coat, without stopping to think you might have a choice. In San Antonio Village, Victor says go in the house, and the bush doctor motions for us to follow, so I do.

"We're going into the man's house now," I tell Maya, lifting her from the van's seat. She wraps her legs around my waist and tries to pull me back down. All we've told her is that we're going to see Victor's friend. If we use the word "doctor" with her, we'll never get her out of the van.

"I don't want to," she says.

"It'll only be for a few minutes," I lie and then add, as if it will sweeten the deal, "Mom and Dad need to talk with him. Let's leave Hursula in the van."

The cabin's front door is barely six feet high. Uzi has to duck about an inch to have safe clearance, and behind him, I instinctively dip my head when I enter. Inside, we blink against the sudden darkness. Only the outlines of objects are discernible at first. Then a soiled blue-and-white hammock stretched across the back of the room takes shape and, in front of it, a simple wooden table. My left knee bumps against a low, shallow bench against the wall, painted pale blue and covered with an orange cloth. Other than the hammock, it's the only place to sit, so we sit. I arrange Maya on my lap, her back against my chest. Directly across from us at eye level a small color television fits snugly into a wall alcove. Four young Latino dancers in white go-go pantsuits sing and gyrate on the screen with the volume turned all the way down, giving the impression of a high-intensity lip sync.

"I am sorry," the man says, sweeping his arm outward in a grand arc. "My house . . ."

"It's okay," Uzi says, gently.

Underneath the television, a plastic milk crate holds an overflowing pile of worn, white women's dress shoes. Is a wife in the back room? Do children live here, too? I scan the room for evidence, but the cultural markers I'm accustomed to seeing—primary-colored Fisher-Price toys, plastic sippy cups, a finger painting with a name and date printed in the bottom right corner—aren't the clues to look for here. *Huaraches*, I think, illogically, and my mind fastens on the image of little woven sandals. I look around the floor for a pair of tiny huaraches. None.

The bush doctor hoists a black nylon duffel bag onto the table and starts rummaging through it. I look around the room some more. Portraits of religious figures are thumbtacked to three of the walls. The pale linoleum on the floor has worn through in some spots to reveal packed dirt.

Goddamn it. Descendants of the most brilliant astronomers and mathematicians the planet has known, opening the twenty-first century in improvised wooden shacks with packed-dirt floors. Where's the justice here?

It's the story of what happens everywhere after the white men come in and take what they need, but the regularity of that story doesn't make me feel any better to be sitting in this cabin with my pale, lightly freckled skin—me, who came strolling into the jungle with my sick child to leverage on another culture's knowledge, soon to fly back to my house in California with newly installed hardwood on the master bedroom floor. *I am sorry . . . my house . . .* The bush doctor felt the need to apologize because we force him to look at his house through American eyes, or his idea of American eyes, and through them he finds it lacking. No wonder half the world hates us. I look down at my hands and feel relieved to have left my engagement ring at home. I'd feel disgusted with myself if I were wearing it now.

Maya swivels around in my lap and presses her stomach against mine, her cheek resting on my chest. I check to see if she's starting to doze off. She's not. She's watching the bush doctor very closely, but she's calm. That's a good sign.

Uzi nudges my shoulder and points next to the front door, where a handwritten poster is thumbtacked to the wall.

MAYAN · TRADITION

I am a Mayan Indian and life long resident of San Antonio, I was trained in the art of Mayan Medicine by the late shaman healer Don ELIJO PANTI I can offer guided bush walking to see and where appropriate pick medicinal herbs to make your own remedies

TREATMENTS

Herbalism   Massage   Cupping
Pricking   Spirit Reading
   Spirit   Prayer   Cleansing
please bring camera your souvenire will
be knowledge & the medicine you make
Orencio Canto
San Antonio

"Did you bring the camera?" Uzi whispers.

It's in the backpack at my feet. "No," I whisper back.

Ovencio Canto. So that's his name. I look back at the sign and notice a laminated card hanging just above it, a type of ID. I scoot over a little on the bench and squint at it. Across the top it reads LICENSED BUSH DOCTOR/MEDICINE and beneath this there's a small color passport photo of the bush doctor, his name, address, birthday, and signature. I do some quick math and realize he's forty-four. I would have guessed at least ten years younger.

Uzi nudges me with his elbow again to pull my attention back to the room, where Canto pulls a stubby, cloudy plastic vial from the black duffel bag on the table.

"It is to put . . ." he says, motioning with large circles in front of his chest, ". . . *tres veces* . . ."

"We put that on her chest three times?" I ask.

"*Sí.*"

"Three times a day or three times total?"

"*Sí.* Also, we take leafs for a bath. Now I take . . ." he says, crouching down at Maya's side, balancing back on the heels of his muddy Wellingtons, ". . . the *bebé* hand to pray . . ." He takes Maya's left hand between his forefinger and his thumb, and that's when the room explodes.

"No!" Maya shouts, snatching her hand back and pinning it against her side. "I don't want him to touch me!"

"Maya," I say. "It's all right. He's just going to hold your hand. He's not going to hurt you." I try to sound soothing, but something critical gets lost in the effort and my voice comes out sounding tight and curt, which has exactly the opposite effect of calming her down.

"*No-o-o!*" she howls, jamming her body into a stiff line. This is her pose of abject resistance. When she was an infant she would go straight as a plank like this whenever I tried to put her into the car seat. Uzi and I used to call it "doing the board."

Maya kicks at Canto's chest, making contact, and he falls backward onto his hands.

"*Maya!*" Uzi admonishes her. She clamps her hands tight over her ears and screams, one staccato shriek followed by another, and another, and another, with barely a pause for breath.

I look at Canto apologetically. "*Lo siento,*" I say, raising my voice loud enough to be heard over Maya's screaming. "This is part of the problem."

He shifts forward into a crouch, resting his elbows on his knees. "*Bebé,*" he croons to Maya. "*Bebé.* I want to hold your hand."

"No!" Maya screams. She releases her ears and tucks her arms around her chest, her hands clenched in tight little fists. "No! No! No! No!"

"Maybe you should . . ." I start.

"*Maya,*" Uzi interrupts me. "Come on." He's losing patience. So might I, if I hadn't seen her behave like this a half-dozen times before. With the exception of that one time in Dr. Diane's office, I've learned that once it's begun, there's nothing I can do to make it end. Except keep throwing ten minutes at it, and ten minutes, and ten minutes, until she's done.

Canto's hands dangle helplessly between his knees. "*Bebé, bebé,*" he murmurs. He's either remarkably calm or ridiculously passive, I can't tell which. Either way, he doesn't seem to be attaching any importance to the kicking or the noise.

"All right," Uzi says. "Let's get on with this." He reaches out and forcibly peels Maya's right arm away from her side.

It happens so fast. My husband . . . my daughter . . . and then Canto has her wrist gripped firmly between both of his hands, his right thumb pressing against her pulse point as he starts whispering rapidly in Mayan.

Maya immediately falls still. For a moment, it seems that his touch has calmed her. Can that really be? After months of the 24/7 Dodo show, all we had to do was land in Belize, inquire about a shaman, be taken to one the same day, and have him touch Maya to have her cured? I have just enough time to feel a small, irrational lunge of hope in that direction, and then Maya's body jerks violently, once, twice, and the silence splinters into a flailing kaleidoscope of arms and legs and an unearthly howl.

She lashes out with her free arm, but when I try to grab hold of it a leg breaks free, and when I try to restrain the leg the arm pops out again and takes a swing at the air beside her. I don't have enough limbs to contain her. I shift my weight to the right, then sway back against the wall, trying to stay steady on the bench. Fifteen years ago, in a New Orleans bar, I drank three rum-and-Cokes and tried to ride a mechanical bull. That was easier than this. *Hold on to her,* I think. *Don't let go.* But trying to hang on to her is like trying to hug a speeding windmill.

The screams that emerge from her now are inhuman, worse than in the hair salon, worse than in Dr. Diane's office, worse than anything I've ever heard coming from a child anywhere before. If we were out in public in Los Angeles, a dozen people would be fumbling for their cell phones, frantically trying to dial 911.

She tips her head back and lets out another howl. I kiss the smooth white skin on her exposed throat. "It's okay, baby," I whisper. Over Maya's shoulder, I catch a glimpse of the Latin dancers in blue majorette costumes arranging themselves into a human pyramid on the TV. To my right, just beyond the open door, the oil drum sends flames six feet into the air. Can this day possibly get any more surreal?

"It's okay," I whisper. My voice is shaking as if I'm shivering. "It's okay. It's okay."

The bush doctor is still whispering rapidly with Maya's wrist in his grasp. "I don't want him—to touch me!" she gasps, thrashing against my hold. "I don't—want him—to touch—me!" Her chest is so congested, she has to gasp for each breath of air.

She has to be stopped before she hurts someone. Or suffocates.

Am I the only one thinking in these terms? Hello, there's a mother over here who's freaking out. Guys? *Guys?*

But the men are acting so normal. And Victor's not running inside to find the source of all the noise. Maybe the scene isn't as dramatic or as loud as it seems to me. I glance at Canto, whose face is the very definition of expressionless. He motions calmly for Uzi to pry Maya's other wrist from her chest, plants his thumb on its pulse point, and continues his prayers. Maya tips her head back and moans, a loud, hoarse sound, like an animal's birthing cry, the call of terror and pain and desperation.

Canto doesn't even blink. Is this guy for real? Or is he just an automaton going through the motions of a healing session, oblivious to the client's response or needs, wholly focused on the American dollars he'll receive at the end?

Everything I stand for tells me to get up right now and walk out the door, taking Maya with me, but to hijack the effort-in-progress might be interpreted as a loud and resonant *fuck you* to my husband and his beliefs. Do I want to risk that? Then Maya makes that god-awful moaning sound again, and choking noises start coming from her throat, and I do a fast flip-flop from feeling ambivalent to feeling officially scared. And there is nothing that propels me into action faster than fear.

I stand abruptly, clutching Maya against my chest.

"That's it," I say. "Enough. We're done."

Canto drops Maya's wrist and looks up from the floor to Uzi.

"Can we just . . ." Uzi starts.

"I said, *we're done.*" He knows better than to push against this edge in my voice. I'm going to hear about my attitude later tonight, but I can't worry about that now. Right now, all my willpower is narrowed into a hard little knob of purpose: to remove my daughter from this house.

"We're going outside," I say.

Taking action is easier than I imagined. With Maya wrapped around me like a little monkey, I turn my back on the men. I face the door. I walk through it, and I don't look back.

On the grass, a single baby chick teeters past us, trying to catch up to the line of siblings following their mother hen. I try to interest Maya in the chick's plight—"Look, Maya! A baby chick! So cute! Look, Maya! Look!"—but she's stuck in an exhausted, hysterical loop, and nothing I can say can pull her out.

"That man!" she shrieks, kneeing me in the ribs. "That man tried! That man tried to take my cough!"

The children next door glide over to watch. One of the boys points at Maya and mumbles something to a younger child, who covers his mouth and laughs. What is it they know? I have the sudden, furious urge to smack their little cheeks and send them flying across the grass, to push over their barrel of fire with both hands and break into an uninhibited, maniacal dance as the field around us goes up in flames. I tighten my grip on Maya and hurry toward the van, sliding the door shut behind us with a yank so hard it feels like punctuation.

"That man tried to take my cough away and put it in the fire!" Maya cries as she pounds on the seat cushion, coughing and spitting. A thin line of saliva drips from her mouth to the bench.

I wipe her chin with the hem of my T-shirt. "How could he take your cough away? He's not a doctor."

"He did! He tried to take my cough away with his hand! And put it in the fire!"

"The fire?" I say. "No, no. The fire was all the way outside."

"I want to get out of here right now! Now! I want to go home now!"

"Shhh, shhh." I reach for her. "We'll go as soon as Daddy gets here. Shhh."

I have to come up with some kind of distraction, to get her to focus on something else, but my resources are sorely limited in the van. What am I supposed to give her, Dramamine? But then Dramamine makes me think of flying, and the thought of flying reminds me: I have gum in my bag. The bubble gum I bought at the airport. I pull out two pieces, stuff them in my mouth, and chew them fast.

"Look, Maya," I say. I blow a perfect round bubble. "You can pop it," I mumble around the fragile sphere. She usually loves doing this. "Go ahead," I urge when she doesn't move. "It's okay."

She jabs a straight index finger square into the bubble's center, popping it all over her finger and my chin, and the surprise of it eases her out of the hysteria.

She sniffles. "Again."

I blow another bubble. She pops it. I blow another bubble. She pops it. I blow a bubble inside of a bubble, on purpose, and she pops them both. In this manner, we pass the next twenty minutes until she puts her head down on my shoulder.

"Shh," I say, rocking her. I rock her until my arms ache, until her elbows drop loose and the dead weight of her tells me she's crossed the threshold into a feverish sleep.

When her breathing evens out, I lift my fist and slam it into the van window. It hurts, but not enough. I punch the glass again, hard enough this time for my knuckles to ache afterward.

I can't believe I just did that. What was I thinking? No, really. What was I *thinking*? That I could brazenly stride in here and get what I wanted, at my daughter's expense, just because I wanted it?

Through the windshield I see Uzi following Canto into the jungle. One second their backs are framed against the greenery and the next they've been fully enveloped by the trees. Victor sits on a tree stump about fifty yards away, absorbed in earnest conversation with a local man. And then I see, coming from all the way on my left, a woman holding the hand of a girl of perhaps five or six, a little girl in a frilly white dress, both of them stepping gingerly across the wet field to the cabin's open front door.

I smash my fist into the window again. This time, the pain sends a surge from my throat to my eyes, and I squeeze my eyes shut to hold in the tears. Then I remember no one's here to see me, and I let them slide.

"What am I doing here?" I whisper to no one in particular. One reason I'm always eager to plant myself in worlds so different from my own has been to achieve the traveler's sense of disorientation that, ultimately, reaffirms who I am. This is the aspect of travel I love most, the deep, sweet reassurance that comes from surrounding myself with languages, food, music, and architecture that bear no likeness to any piece of my history and nevertheless finding that my thought patterns and memories remain static. Even in the face of complete cultural disorientation—feverish and wandering in the rain in Luxembourg or surrounded by angry Bedouin cabdrivers in Sinai—the "Me" that makes up the "me" never changes. I could be walking on Roman stones worn smooth from two thousand years of foot traffic and suddenly remember how my favorite high school teacher, Mrs. Davis, taught us to use index cards to organize the material for European history exams, or I could be realizing I just boarded the wrong ferry in Sydney Harbor while simultaneously thinking about the time I saw a water snake devour a mouse whole on the shore of a Long Island lake when I was ten.

Wherever you go, there you are. It's either an expression of monotony and despair, or of reassurance and relief. To me, it's always been the latter. When all the familiar landmarks disappear, the only source left from which to draw information or inspiration is the self, and I've always trusted myself to get me out of a fix. But here in San Antonio, that whole concept has been turned inside out. The more unfamiliar the day gets, the more disoriented I've become. I still retain all the same experiences and memories of thirty-six years, yes, of course, but for the first time it feels as if the way I synthesize them, retrieve them, and describe them are only the cultural constructs of a middle-class, medium-aged white woman from New York. Here my life experiences have no relevance. Here I understand nothing. I am a child, a baby, a newborn, square one of beginner's mind, and because I cannot yet comprehend what just happened, I have no words to describe it. And without words I am doubly lost, because words are my currency, and without them I cannot make sense of anything.

It is both my instinct and my profession to elaborate, to explain, to decode. So here in this white van, I search for words from my worldview that might create a bridge toward understanding this one.

Tantrum. Prayer. Exorcism.

Exorcism. That's the word I can't push away. When the bush doctor touched Maya's wrist, her reaction was so violent it was impossible not to think of congregants writhing on the wood floor of a Pentecostal church, Linda Blair vomiting green pea soup, bodies convulsing at the sign of a cross. Who would have thought the Hollywood versions actually may have gotten it right?

The sun starts its slow descent, casting skinny shadows from the electric poles onto the dirt road. It must be at least four thirty by now. I wait for Uzi to return, and then I wait some more. When I get bored, I shuffle around inside my bag until I find the camera, and I hold it up to the window and snap a photo of the bush doctor's cabin. I pivot around a few times, but there's nothing else here I want to remember or record, so I put the camera back into my bag.

The chickens disappear around the back of the house. The dog finishes his nap and joins the children in their game, nipping at their ankles as they run circles around the burning drum. Victor still sits unperturbed on the tree stump talking to the man. They gesture with their hands, tilt their heads, and laugh. The mud puddles glisten, then deaden as the sun slips further toward the trees. I'm the only one here who seems anxious to move things along. I press the horn to get Victor's attention. Two short beeps. *Let's. Go.* He looks up, waves agreeably in my direction, and resumes his conversation.

There is plenty of time here in San Antonio, nothing but time. Well, that shouldn't be so surprising. The Maya themselves have been called the people of time. Their ancestors were the most accurate and obsessive timekeepers history has known. Without calculators, without even abacuses, they recorded cycles of time in an incredibly complex and sophisticated fashion. When they came up with the concepts of zero and place notation (three hundred years before the Hindus did) they suddenly had the capacity to count hundreds, thousands, even millions of years into the future and the past. Their Long Count calendar recorded the amount of time that had elapsed since the day they believed the Fifth World, the world of fire, began, which was— according to the most commonly accepted scholarly computation— August 11, 3114 B.C. They measured time in units that were multiples of 20, 18, and 360, and their notation resulted in some pretty funky-looking dates. My birthday on our calendar—June 17, 1964—comes out as 12.17.10.14.1 on the Maya Long Count calendar. Which, according to their form of math, is another way of saying I was born 1,854,281 days after the beginning of time.

I stroke Maya's hair and shift her to my other shoulder. Whenever my mind veers back into the cabin, I direct it across the yard to the children still chasing one another around on the grass. There don't seem to be any rules to their game, but then I notice the younger kids darting between the older ones in a kind of deliberate pattern. The burning oil drum functions as some kind of marker, though not quite as simple as a home base. I feel a small rush of adrenaline each time one of the smaller kids runs too close to the flames. There don't seem to be any adults looking out for them. Except for Victor and his friend. And me.

I check my watch. A half hour has passed since I first brought Maya to the van. What's taking Uzi so long? Thoughts of armed bandits and guerrillas . . . wait—no, that's Guatemala. What if this is the day that the tenuous border balance between Guatemala and Belize shifts? What if Uzi doesn't make it out of the jungle? My heart starts doing double time, and a cold current creeps down my neck and vibrates down my arms. Oh, God. I'm sorry, I'm sorry for every mean thing I ever thought about him. Just bring him back safely.

I take a couple of deep breaths and count to a hundred to calm myself down. Really, I have got to get a grip.

Just as suddenly as they slipped into the brush they step out of it, two dark-haired men, one short, one tall, materializing like apparitions out of the green. My relief is enormous. There's no other way to describe it. From his left hand, Uzi swings a white plastic grocery bag stuffed full of leaves. As he gets closer, I see his sandals are almost entirely caked in wet, orange mud.

When they reach the van, he and Canto shake hands. I manage a small smile and a brief wave through the window. Then Uzi climbs in next to me, Victor hoists himself onto the front seat and starts the engine, and we do a fast K-turn and start heading out the same way we came in.

Uzi turns to me. I'm looking straight ahead, wholly focused on the road that will lead us away from here.

"Is she okay?" he asks.

I nod and shrug at the same time.

"Are you?"

I shake my head no.

"Are you mad?"

I shake my head again. "I'm way past mad," I say. "Now I'm just freaked out." I watch the town float by in reverse order: clotheslines, Don Elijio's cement-block house, the yellow Coca-Cola shack. It all looks so different the second time around.

"I can't *believe* we just did that," I whisper. We bump along the dirt road. Uzi sighs and takes my hand.

"Did you pay him?" I ask.

"He only wanted money for the medicine. I gave him twenty for it and an extra twenty." He frowns tightly. "That's all I had with me. You think it was enough?"

Enough? I'm so far outside my normal frames of reference here, I don't have any sense of what might be enough. Forty American dollars has never felt like such an imprecise amount before. Forty dollars for a bush doctor's services could be a gross overpayment or an insult: I'd believe it either way. I think of the girl in the white dress clinging to her mother's hand as they stepped through the cabin door. Enough? How much would be enough?

Uzi is waiting for my answer. "I think it's fine," I say.

He holds up the grocery bag of freshly picked leaves. "We're supposed to boil this tonight and have her drink it. And also give her a bath in it. He wants to see her again tomorrow."

"Fat fucking chance."

Uzi strokes the top of Maya's head. "How is she?"

"All right now. But she screamed for almost fifteen minutes: *'That man tried to take my cough away and put it in the fire!'* She wasn't making any sense. And what happened in there. That was not okay."

Uzi exhales loudly and runs his hand through the front of his thick, dark hair. "How the hell did she know that?" he asks.

"What, about the cough? I have no idea."

"No, about the fire. Fire neutralizes negative energy. In Pranic Healing you push bad energy toward a fire, or you picture flames and send all the dark stuff there in your mind. Maybe they do something like that here."

A brief, powerful chill burrows straight up my spine. I clutch Maya to me tighter.

"I don't have any idea how she could have known that," I say.

I press my face into my daughter's warm neck, nuzzling around to find the spot where my lips always fit, no matter how much she grows. Maya smells like suntan lotion and little girl and Guatemala City hotel shampoo. I inhale deeply, as if I am a vacuum siphoning away all the noxious particles, as if I am a raging inferno sucking up all the bad air. I picture myself an oil drum full of flames. I am a mother on fire.

Bebé, bebé, I whisper. Send it all to me.

chapter seven
Cristo Rey, Belize
December 24–25, 2000

Jeronie, Victor's oldest son, plucks a heart-shaped leaf from the plastic grocery bag and twirls it by its stem. "This is *cordoncillo*," he says. "Also called Spanish elder."

We're standing in the Crystal Paradise kitchen. Behind us, a silver, twenty-gallon pot of water heats up on the industrial-size range as twilight advances on the lawns outside. After dark, you can walk across the grass with a flashlight pressed against your forehead and see hundreds of tiny green spider eyes sparkling among the blades. Night is when the rain forest comes to life: more than half of the animals here are nocturnal. Jaguars stalk the jungle floor, kinkajous glide across the canopy, and black howler monkeys wake the forest with their primeval grunts and moans. Nighttime is prime time, live time, getting-down-to-business time, so perhaps it's appropriate to be preparing Maya's leaf bath as the sun goes down.

Jeronie, a solid, handsome bear of a man with soft brown eyes and a neatly trimmed beard, holds up a different leaf for his mother, Teresa, to inspect. Teresa's father was a famous Cayo healer to whom, I imagine, the local medicinal leaves were as instantly recognizable as the over-the-counter-drug labels in my home medicine chest are to me. She looks at the specimen Jeronie holds, makes a murmuring sound, and shakes her head.

"I don't know," Jeronie says to us. "I think this one is poisonous."

"I'm sure it's not poisonous," Uzi says. "He wouldn't have given her a poisonous leaf to drink."

I don't think the leaf is poisonous, either, but how would I know? The sign on the bush doctor's wall claimed he was trained by Don Elijio Panti, but a handwritten résumé is hardly proof of competence.

"Do you know this bush doctor we saw, Ovencio Canto?" I ask Jeronie.

He shakes his head no. "I've heard of him. But I don't know him."

"We were hoping to see Rosita Arvigo," I tell him. "We had an appointment with her, but we missed it when we missed our flight from L.A. She didn't have another opening this week."

"Rosita's busy these days," he says. "A lot of people are coming to see her."

I imagine a line of cars snaking bumper to bumper through the rain forest to Dr. Arvigo's farm, the same way lines of people once formed on the road outside Don Elijio's house in San Antonio. It reminds me of the scene at the end of *Field of Dreams*, when the camera pans back to reveal a steady line of headlights blinking across the nighttime prairie on their way to the baseball diamond carved into an Iowa cornfield—*If you build it, they will come*—which then reminds me of the fields outside Iowa City, how they undulated gentle and green in the early autumn breeze when I would speed past them on my black mountain bike, trying to burn off the nervous energy that was blocking my ability to write. I feel that same nervous energy now, and then time and space do a weird pretzeling motion and I am both here and there simultaneously, both standing in this rain-forest kitchen and pedaling hard and fast alongside the high corn. I am driving on the muddy road to San Antonio and hurrying through the airport in San Salvador and sitting in a steamy bathroom holding Maya as she breathes ragged and croupy on my lap. It's the strangest, most disorienting feeling, to be standing here right now and yet also be everywhere at once, and if you were to tell me that I just left Iowa yesterday or that I can blink and be back in our Topanga kitchen in a moment's time, I'd believe it's somehow possible. I swear I would.

The pot gurgles and quakes on the burner in front of us. Teresa turns off the flame and places handfuls of leaves into the hot water to let them steep. Inside the pot, cell walls start to break down, membranes dissolve. I peer over the rim while Teresa stirs the leaves. The water has already turned a dark, inky green. The thought of drinking it brings up a fast gag reflex in me. Jeronie's use of the word "poisonous" comes right up with it.

I sidle over to Uzi. "There's no way we can let her drink that," I say, keeping my voice low. "A bath, okay, but she can't ingest it unless we know exactly what it is."

Maya is sitting in the dining hall on the other side of the curtained door, paging through the book about butterflies. It's a good thing she isn't here to look inside the pot. Forget about drinking it. If she saw that dark water, we'd have no hope of getting her within twenty feet of a bathtub full of it, either.

Uzi walks to the pot, takes a look over the rim, then returns to my side.

"Actually, I agree with you," he says.

He sounds surprised by how effortless it was to come up with an opinion identical to mine. Lately, our typical one-two sequence has been for me to make a decision and for Uzi to automatically resist, sometimes because he genuinely disagrees but other times, I suspect, because he doesn't want to cede control to me so easily. This time we started at different points yet independently arrived at the same conclusion, and the occasion is rare enough to leave us standing in this warm kitchen in Belize blinking at each other in the light of the discovery that such an event can unfold so naturally.

Teresa strains the leaves from the hot water and removes the pot from the stove. "Let it cool a while," she says.

Earlier, when we'd asked Teresa for help preparing the bath, she'd consented without even blinking, as if this were a perfectly reasonable after-dinner request for a pair of American tourists to make. Jeronie, too, has been acting as matter-of-fact about the whole enterprise as Victor did in the van when we first inquired about a bush doctor. I keep half expecting someone to snicker at our requests or to brush off traditional healing as a bunch of bunk and direct us to the hospital in Belize City instead, but that keeps not happening. I don't feel as if they're trying to humor us, either. Boiling leaves for a bath to cure a child appears to be as sensible a solution to the Tut family as taking that same child to a Wilshire Boulevard psychiatrist might be to a mother in Los Angeles. And though bathing a child in leaf water might sound like a primitive and ridiculous plan to that American mother, I've got the feeling that schlepping a child to weekly appointments with a psychiatrist or doling out behavioral medication would be considered equally absurd down here.

There's something undeniably seductive about the ease with which the Tut family assesses our situation and helps us take action. When I look into the silver pot, all I see is a pool of dark, impenetrable water, but seeing the Tuts, who are so knowledgeable about so many other local matters, treating it as an acceptable method of solving our problem makes me willing to try it, too.

Giving Maya a bath in our cabana is going to require some creativity, since the guest bathrooms have large, tiled stall showers but no tubs. Jeronie walks to the family's compound on the other side of the property and returns with a white plastic washbasin left over from Everald Junior's infancy. It's too small for Maya to sit in, but Uzi thinks maybe she can stand in it while we pour the green water over her body and head. Teresa gives me a large plastic cup for scooping the water. I'm not optimistic about this game plan, but I can't come up with a better one, so we head to the cabana to try.

In the bathroom, I push aside the plastic shower curtain and place the washtub on the shower floor. While I ease Maya's dress over her head and help her step out of her underwear, Uzi pours about four inches of bath-temperature water from the silver pot into the plastic tub.

Predictably, Maya doesn't want anything to do with it.

"Dodo doesn't want to," she says as soon as she sees the green water, jerking backward and whipping her head from side to side.

I glance at the water in the tub. The liquid is such a dark green it might as well be black, a tea of *cordoncillo* and God only knows what else. I wouldn't want to bathe in it, either. Except I'm the mother, and any revulsion I exhibit is going to be absorbed by Maya twofold.

"What if you just stand in it?" I ask. "Only with your feet. How does that sound?"

"I don't want to," she says, backing against the bathroom wall.

I swish my hand around in the water and lift it up to show her my skin hasn't turned green. "It's not really green water, see?" I say. I'm actually a little surprised to see this myself.

"I don't *want* to! No!"

Uzi wants to see this through to the end, and I think we should do it, too. So if we want Maya in the water, one of us is going to have to pick her up and put her there. I look over at Uzi, who's standing against the wall with his arms crossed. The move is mine, and the sooner I do it, the sooner it will be done.

I lift Maya under the armpits, raise her about six inches into the air, and try to set her into the tub, but just before her feet touch the water she kicks hard, catching the lip of the basin and sending a wave over the back rim and onto the shower floor. Uzi pours another inch from the pot into the basin to replace it.

"Maya," I say. I try to kiss the top of her head. My lips barely graze her hair. "Honey. For Mommy. Please."

"I don't want to."

"Can you try? Please?"

She stops kicking. That's a start. And she stops screaming, too. I lower her feet into the tub, where the water covers her ankles.

"Good girl, Maya," Uzi says. "You're doing great."

Except now she's standing naked in the water, sobbing, with her arms pressed against her sides and her head down in a position of complete submission. The combative, feisty Maya is hard enough to manage, but this new, defeated version, crying as if her spirit has been broken, is even worse. Every impulse I have tells me to lift her out of the tub and take her onto my lap. Yet I feel a conviction to see this ritual through to the end, partly out of curiosity and partly out of sheer determination. I'm getting impatient with the ambiguity here. This route we're taking either has validity or it doesn't, and I need to know which. Something happened at the bush doctor's cabin today, I know something happened, but then the story stops there. It's like Carmen with her egg. The results were real, I knew it, but not dramatic or conclusive enough for me to know what they meant.

With fast, fluid motions, I scoop up water with the plastic cup and start pouring it over Maya's legs. She tries to push it away with her hands. I pour the next cupful over her rounded stomach, still her three-year-old baby stomach, chubby and protruding and smooth.

"Mommy, no," she pleads.

I pour water over one shoulder, then the other, then dip down one last time and raise the cup high to pour the contents over her head, but before I have a chance to tip it sideways she flails out with her left arm and the cup goes flying. Water explodes in a spectacular array of drops that spray the sink, the mirror, the tiles. The cup ricochets off the tiled wall with a resounding crack, barely missing the doorframe, where Jeronie, I now see, is leaning with his arms crossed, watching us. I catch his eye, and we stare at each other silently. His face has no expression at all. Then he nods twice. That's all. Just nods.

In the morning, dozens of tiny winged bugs are stuck to the plastic bottles on my bathroom shelf, trapped there by the thin film of humidity that adheres to every surface in the room. Their wings are spread wide open, like miniature pinned butterflies. I peel one off with my fingernail and try to flick it into the air to give it a second chance, but it lands on the tile wall and stays there. It's a goner. Poor little guy.

My travel clock reads 6:49 A.M., which means 4:49 A.M. California time. I almost never wake this early at home, but I've just slept eight uninterrupted hours for the first time in months, and my body is rested and ready to go. Above my head, from somewhere in the bathroom's thatched roof, comes a loud, animated clicking noise. A bird? Dawn is prime birding time in Belize. Outside the cabana, the treetops already resonate with a symphony of chirps and whistles. At dinner last night Jeronie offered a 6 A.M. bird-watching tour of the property, and about two thirds of the guests immediately signed up. The rest of us looked at one another as if this was the most incomprehensible series of words ever strung together in a sentence. Six A.M.? Birds? Before *coffee*?

Uzi's side of our queen-size bed is empty. He must have gone for a walk, or maybe he's joined the birders? I don't think he's a bird person, but he's always interesting in learning something new. In the twin bed against the wall, Maya sleeps peacefully, sucking on the index and middle fingers of her right hand. I press my palm against her forehead. No fever. I close my eyes in a silent, private moment of gratitude. Whatever it was—the prayers, the green-water bath, the ointment from Canto, a good night's rest after two consecutive nights of broken sleep, or her immune system finally kicking in—I'm thankful.

One of the stubby bottles Canto gave us sits on the night table. It's made of cloudy white plastic, with a piece of Saran Wrap placed underneath the childproof cap. Half-inch dark segments of what look like leaves or bark float suspended inside the salve. I dip my index finger into the bottle and bring a dollop up to my nose. It smells faintly like Vicks VapoRub, but the consistency is thinner and more oily. Inside the plastic bottle it has a yellowish tint, but on my skin it's transparent and clear.

I pull back Maya's blanket and carefully lift the 101 Dalmatians nightgown I hastily bought for her in the San Salvador airport when I was certain our luggage was lost for good. I massage about a teaspoon of ointment into her chest. Last night after the bath, I tried to convince her to let me rub the salve on her skin or even to smear it on herself, like finger paint. When she crossed her arms against her chest and backed away, I let it go. God knew the kid had already had enough trauma for one day. We waited until she fell asleep for the night, then Uzi rubbed ointment on her chest. She made a face in her sleep as if she'd smelled something bad, then rolled over and slept uninterrupted through the night.

Tres veces, Canto had said. Three times. Three times a day for three days is how Uzi understood it. So nine times in all. As long as I wake up before her in the mornings and make sure she gets a good nap every day, I think I can sneak in all nine when she's asleep.

I wipe my fingers on a hand towel, and look for a book to read to pass the time. *Fodor's Belize & Guatemala* is lying on top of the desk, its pages starting to ripple in the humidity. From outside come the low murmurs and footsteps of guests as they head down to the dining hall. One thing you can say about the Tut family, they know how to run one tight ship of a resort. Breakfast starts at 7:30 A.M. sharp, even on Christmas Day, dinner is served at 6:00 P.M. on the dot, and they've got a whole transportation system running with daily airport shuttles and day trips to local points of interest. Carolyn wasn't kidding when she called it one of the best deals in Cayo.

I'd like to get a cup of coffee from the dining hall, but I don't want to leave Maya in the room alone, so I take *Sastun* out to the front porch and settle onto one of the hammocks to wait for Uzi. Getting into the hammock is like getting into a low-lying swing: you have to squat with your legs spread on either side and then sit down and lift your legs at the same time, whipping them around the sides of the hammock as you fall back. The end result wraps you tightly on three sides like a husk of corn, swinging just slightly above the floor.

I open *Sastun* to the first page of chapter seven, where we left off on the airplane. The author has just decided to stay over at the shaman Don Elijio's house three days per week to immerse herself in the training. The book has a different kind of density in my hands this morning than it had in Los Angeles last week or in the airplane hurtling over the Sea of Cortez just two days ago. Now that I've seen Don Elijio's house and stood in San Antonio, the story has a three-dimensional, almost real-time quality to it, as if we might drive back down the dirt road this afternoon and this time find Dr. Arvigo chopping herbs outside Don Elijio's hut while he sits inside at his wooden table feeling the pulse of a woman with an infant curled against her breast, even though the scenes in the book took place in the 1980s and Don Elijio died in 1996, at the age of 103.

Each chapter of *Sastun* begins with an italicized passage introducing a different Maya medicinal plant, or *xiv* (pronounced "shiv"). The *xiv* that leads off chapter seven is Spanish elder—also called buttonwood, *Piper amalgo*, and *cordoncillo*.

Huh. What were the chances of that?

"A common medicinal plant of many varieties, highly respected for its versatility as a traditional remedy in Maya healing," the paragraph reads. "The leaves and flowering tops are boiled as a tea and used to wash all manner of skin ailments, to aid insomnia, nervousness, headaches, swelling, pain, and coughs, and for the treatment of all children's disorders. The root is applied to the gums to relieve toothache. The raw exudate of the root heals cuts and prevents infection. The plant is one of the Nine Xiv used by Don Elijio for herbal baths."

That makes me feel better about finding *cordoncillo* in the bag of leaves last night. Much better.

The wooden door to my right whooshes open and gets pulled back shut with a soft slam.

"*Good* morning!" a voice sings out. Thus speaks our resident psychic, greeting the day.

"Morning, Shiva," I say, glancing up briefly from the book.

"Shakti," she corrects me.

"Right. Sorry. Shakti."

"Coming to breakfast?"

I shake my head. "Maya's still sleeping. I'm waiting for Uzi to get back."

"Where'd he go?"

"I don't know. He was already gone when I woke up."

"I can go look for him, if you want."

"That's okay," I say quickly. "He'll be back soon."

"Okay." She starts down the stairs, then changes her mind and turns around. "Can I get you a cup of tea?"

It's a kind request, even if I'm not a tea drinker, and it sounds genuine. I can't help it: I smile at her.

"Thanks," I say. "But I'm a coffee person."

"Eck," she says. "I used to drink coffee. Then I learned it's like pouring used motor oil down your throat."

I could have lived just fine, thank you, without that image in my head. I tell this to Shakti in exactly those words.

She laughs. "Yeah," she says. "It kind of flipped me out when I first heard it, too. You're sure you don't want me to find Uzi for you?"

"I'm sure." Oh yeah, I'm sure. "I'll see you later."

I watch Shakti head down the path to the dining hall, her tight, compact athlete's body moving like a single, synchronized unit instead of a collection of arms and legs. Shakti walks with substance, with a '30s gangster swagger, like someone packing heat. In the cartoon version of this morning, the ground would tremble slightly beneath each of her steps. Girls like her scared me in junior high. They still do.

I return to chapter seven, which opens on a chilly winter morning in San Antonio with insects buzzing and fan palms swaying in the distance, a morning—I notice as I briefly look up—strikingly similar to the one I'm sitting in the middle of right now. Don Elijio and Dr. Arvigo rise early to collect medicinal leaves and roots, entering the forest with their flour sacks and machetes. On this day, Don Elijio teaches his apprentice to say *ensalmos*, special prayers, as she picks plants for healing purposes. If one does not give thanks to the spirit of the plant before taking its leaves, he tells her, the spirit of the plant will remain in the plant and the picked leaves will not have healing power. "Many people say they gather what they see me gather, but it doesn't work for them," he explains. "That's because they haven't remembered to say the *ensalmo*."

I wonder if Canto said prayers of thanks when picking the leaves for Maya yesterday. He must have. I wonder if Uzi heard him, and I feel a small twinge of envy, although I'm not sure to whom it's directed: to Uzi, for possibly witnessing an ancient ritual of respect—making my anthropology minor itch with desire—or toward Canto, for believing so strongly in the spirit of a plant that he would acknowledge it out loud, without self-consciousness, before picking its leaves for use?

"And, Rosita," Don Elijio continues, "when you're gathering medicine, never say to yourself, 'I hope this works,' or 'Maybe this will work.' No, no, you must say with complete confidence in the plants and faith in God that these plants will heal. And they will, I promise you."

She tells him not to worry, that she is a person blessed with a great deal of faith.

"It is good to have faith. That is the most important lesson you will learn from me," he says. "With faith, everything is possible. Believe this, for it is true."

Faith. There's that word again. *It is good to have faith*. I don't doubt this is true. I just don't know what it would feel like. When someone instructs me to "have faith," I automatically think, *Surely, you must be kidding*. When you lose a parent young, you lose the illusion that a higher power is watching out for you. I long ago stopped believing that "things always work out for the best" or "everything happens for a reason." I don't have time for such platitudes. I'm too busy trying to ensure that whatever form of security I've managed to create for myself won't be taken away again. The kind of hypercompetence this fosters is what has saved me from despair, but it's also destroyed my capacity to have faith in anything other than myself. For people like me, a desire to "have faith" may still exist, but it lives far, far underneath the responsibilities of the everyday world and the omnipresent need to keep everything under control. To have faith, one has to loosen the grip on control, or at least on the illusion that one has control, and learn how to trust that someone else will provide. That's the step I just can't bring myself to take.

And yet. Sitting here in the deep green chair on the front porch of our cabana, underneath this roof thatched by hand, gazing out on a trellis of hot-pink bougainvillea while the gray horse munches on grass and the bees buzz and the mot-mot birds do their mysterious mot-mot things up in the canopy, a whole ecosystem waking up to a bright new day . . . well, I can't believe I'm going to say this. But when Don Elijio tells Rosita that with faith, anything is possible, the idea that other people can have such views without being completely delusional suckers . . . I can live with that right now.

A fast slapping noise comes heading toward me from the sidewalk, and then Uzi is bounding up the porch stairs, sweaty and breathless. His faded gray SO MANY BOOKS, SO LITTLE TIME T-shirt I picked up on a book tour years ago is drenched dark, front and back. Ah. He was out for a run.

"Hey, sweets," he says, leaning toward me for a kiss. Just in time I pull the sides of the hammock tight in front of my face.

"I love you, honey, but when you try to spread the sweat all over me? There's a limit to the sharing," I tell him.

He backs off with a grin and swipes at his forehead with the back of his wrist. "Am I that bad?" he asks.

"Not that bad. But a shower still comes highly recommended. Where'd you go?"

"Just along the road to town. It's not that muddy anymore."

"See anything interesting?"

"Dogs, chickens. Not that many people. It's still early, I guess."

"It's Christmas. Maybe everyone's sleeping in."

Uzi looks over toward the door. "Hi, Maya," he says.

I hadn't even heard the door open. I turn around to greet Maya, but there's just an empty doorway. Then I sense movement down near the floor, where she's wiggling across the tiles at the threshold.

"Guess what I am," she says.

This is a good sign. A very good sign.

"A snake?" Uzi asks.

Maya lifts her head and forcefully shakes it *no*.

"A fish?"

"No. A tah . . . tah . . ."

"Tarantula?"

"Dad! I'm not a tarantula!"

"What else starts with a *t*?"

"A tadpole," I say.

"Mom! You gave it away!"

Uzi squats and lightly bounces his index finger against the tip of Maya's nose. "How you feeling, tadpole?" he asks.

"Okay," she says and coughs loud and long. Well, maybe not so okay.

"Good," he says. He stands up, stretches his arms high above his head, raises his left shoulder in a stretch, then his right. "Well. If I'm not needed around here, I'll take a fast shower."

"You're always needed," I say.

"I mean right now."

"Okay. I'll bring Maya down for breakfast." I close my book and set it on the floor. "Are you hungry?" I ask Maya, hopefully.

"Do they have cereal?"

Relief inflates me like an elemental gas. The child is asking about food. She's better. She's better!

"I don't know, kiddo. We can ask Teresa. You'll have to get up off the floor, though."

She raises herself to sitting position. The front of her pink 101 Dalmatians nightshirt has a small smudge of dirt across Lucky the puppy's face. There is nothing extraordinary about this moment, which is what makes it, after this past week, so extraordinary.

I propel myself up and out of the hammock with a fierce, vibrant energy. If there's cereal anywhere on this property, I'll track it down. Cheerios, cornflakes, Raisin Bran: watch your backs. Here comes Mom.

"Ready?" I ask Maya.

She smiles up at me sweetly. "Dodo wants cereal for breakfast," she says. "I want cereal, too."

chapter eight
Cayo District, Belize
December 25, 2000

Everald Junior materializes at the bottom of our cabana steps after breakfast holding a pair of dice and a red alphabet toy in the shape of a flat plastic school bus. It's a two-year-old's unspoken request to play. Maya is out the door and on the lawn with him before I have the chance to introduce them. She's wearing jeans and hiking boots under her nightgown, with a long-sleeved denim shirt on top. Next to little Everald, in his Adidas T-shirt and knee-length navy shorts, she looks ready to climb K2. Whoever dressed Everald did it with knowledge of the afternoon heat in mind, whereas we'll be changing our clothes three or four times today, shedding and adding layers as the mercury rises and dips.

How can a child be so sick one day and so, well, *not sick* the very next? She's never bounced back from croup this fast before. Even Dr. Diane might be surprised by the speed of this recovery. It makes me doubt that Maya was really as ill as I thought she was, but no. The fever, the cough . . . it was real. I know it was real. And she's still not eating. Despite her request for cereal, she only sucked on a few cornflakes and sipped half a glass of water for breakfast. When she won't eat, my stomach knots up so badly that I can't eat either, so neither of us has been properly nourished this morning. But she has the interest and the stamina to play, so maybe I should let her? The alternative is to keep her barricaded in our room or to make her sit quietly on the porch with the adults, which seems more like punishment than prudence.

I check my watch: 8:58 A.M. I'll let her play with Everald for half an hour. That's my compromise.

At home in California, where we wake at six thirty, we'd already be past breakfast. We'd probably be standing on our upstairs deck, shading our eyes and pointing to the sky, to catch a fast glimpse of today's partial solar eclipse. Down here at tropical latitude we can't see it, but from the vantage point of our house in Topanga, the moon is passing between the earth and sun right now in just the right way to make it look as if a round bite has been taken from the sun's edge. The ancient Maya worshipped the sun as a god and viewed eclipses as such significant events that they created elaborate, complicated tables and charts to try to predict when future ones would happen. During a solar eclipse, they believed, a monster was devouring the sun. Depending on the specific Maya group, the monster was believed to be a snake, a lizard, a scorpion, or an ant. One can only imagine how they interpreted a rare total eclipse of the sun, when the sky goes completely dark during daytime and a shadow comes rushing across the land at 1,800 miles per hour. It must have made some of them have heart failure, literally, thinking the world was coming to an end.

Maya and Everald trek across the dewy grass holding hands. I settle into the green Adirondack chair with my black, leather-bound journal, the one I bought as a gift last year for Uzi, who later deeded it back to me. I can't help feeling envious of people who have the discipline to record pages of reflections and ideas in their journals every night. I'm more of a binge chronicler. I won't write anything for months, and then one day I'll sit for an hour and obsessively catalog every detail of a single event. My journal exists for the most utilitarian purposes possible: to record the funny things Maya says; to jot down ideas for future essays; or to describe dreams in which I come across my mother at a convalescent home and discover that her death has been a twenty-year cover-up. The way my mind works, it's the act of writing down the facts and seeing the words blossom across the page that commits them to memory. I hardly ever go back to read what I wrote. I keep a journal not so much as a tool for recalling things later but as a hedge against forgetting them now.

I want to get all of yesterday's details down before the small ones start slipping away, everything from the color of the pockmarked road to the milk crate of soiled women's shoes against the cabin wall. But when I open the journal to a blank cream page . . . I can't come up with a way to start. Regular words, my old reliables, suddenly feel too slippery, too insubstantial, too vague.

Virtually every person I know has had at least one nonordinary experience he knows to be real but lacks the language to describe. I'm talking about the unexpected check that arrives in the mail the same day the bank was set to foreclose, or the chance encounter at the base of a stupa in Kathmandu that altered the course of both New Yorkers' lives, or the 3 A.M. conversation with Aunt Gloria three months after she died. Maybe in German there's a consonant-laden, polysyllabic word for "relative who comes back to visit after her death," giving the experience cultural legitimacy, but English comes up short. Apparition? Visitation? Ghost? Without a widely accepted, recognizable vocabulary for these kind of events, we have to fall back on broad, familiar terms—*coincidence, vision, figment of imagination*—that barely begin to capture the experience and its impact on us. Or we become adjective factories, spitting out words such as *extraordinary. Amazing. Inexplicable. Weird.* I look over at Uzi, who's swinging gently in the woven hammock on Shakti's side of the porch. Does he have the same problem when writing in Hebrew? You'd think with all those mystical Old Testament events, biblical Hebrew would have had a precise, concise word for "voice that emanates from the heavens" or "child born to a woman long after her childbearing years should have ended."

"Uzi," I say, intending to ask him. He looks up from his book with a peaceful smile and raises his eyebrows slightly in a patient *yes?* My God, he is so calm and so handsome, this man. I should just let him be.

"Nothing," I say. "Just I love you."

He kisses the air, a pantomime of affection. "Love you too," he says.

I click the top of my black ballpoint pen once, twice, three times.

The ancient Mesoamerican scribes who lived on this land recorded their people's achievements and stories on elaborately carved towers of stone, painted them onto ceramic pottery, and inked them onto folded sheets of ficus bark coated with limestone powder. Most of their inscriptions began with dates, followed by a factual accounting of events. I think of my college newswriting professor Dick Hainey, a legendary, old-school Chicago newspaperman who retired from editing to teach college sophomores how to write news stories. "Keep it simple, people!" he would holler at us from the front of the room. "Who! What! Where! When! Why!"

Dates. Facts. It's a way to start.

> *December 25, 2000*
> Arrived in Belize yesterday, after a 2-night detour—1st in a Sheraton near LAX, then at the Princesa Reforma in Guatemala City, courtesy of TACA. Victor from Crystal Paradise picked us up at . . .

The pen stalls midsentence, without even a warning sputter. Out of ink. Inside the cabana, all I can find is a blue felt-tip. It'll have to do.

> . . . the airport. Maya is hardly eating or drinking—and her cough became markedly worse after two nights of severely compromised sleep. Yet she is in good spirits, and every decision feels like a tough parenting call. Yesterday after we arrived at Crystal Paradise, Victor took us a few miles down a bumpy dirt road the color of squashed mango pulp . . .

As if perfectly on cue, Victor rounds the side of the cabana and settles himself comfortably on the top step, elbow resting on his knee.

"How is the little one today?" he asks.

I gesture toward the lawn, where she and Everald junior are standing hand in hand about thirty feet from the gray horse. "Better," I say. "She took a few bites of cereal for breakfast."

"Good, good. I heard just now from the bush doctor. He sent a message he can see her again today."

"Can we get a ride over there?" Uzi asks.

"No, the cars are all being used this afternoon. He said he would come here. He'll borrow a bicycle."

The image of the bush doctor pedaling six miles on a borrowed bicycle along that pockmarked road to attend to Maya on Christmas Day gives me a weary, sad feeling in the cellar of my stomach. He may have helped her yesterday, I think it's actually possible, but there's no way I'm putting her through the trauma of being touched by him again.

"Victor," I say, "can you tell him we said thank you, thank you very, very much, but that Maya is doing better today so we don't think we need another appointment?"

"You sure?" Victor asks.

"Wait a minute," Uzi says. "I think we should consider it."

"I'm sure," I tell Victor. "I really think she's better today. And can you also tell him the ointment seems to be working?"

Victor shrugs. "Okay," he says, rising slowly. He takes off in the direction of the office. Watching him retreat, I wonder if I've just breached a form of local etiquette. If a bush doctor says he wants to see you, are you supposed to see him, no questions asked, because he's got the connections to know what you need better than you know yourself? If you refuse, are you snubbing him or insulting his culture? I hope not.

Maya and Everald run up the stairs and hurtle into our cabana, slamming the door behind them.

"I wish you wouldn't do that," Uzi says. He says it calmly, but the fact that he waited until Maya and Everald were out of earshot tells me he's annoyed.

"Wouldn't do what?" I ask. I feel my heartbeat speed up slightly, the way it always does when I realize, too late, that I shouldn't have done whatever it was I just did.

"Make decisions like that without me. I'm sitting right here. You can consult with me first."

He's right, I know he's right, but the truth is, he's been around so little lately to consult with, I've become accustomed to making snap decisions on my own. What he just saw wasn't a wife dismissing her husband's opinion but a wife who's been conditioned to make parenting decisions herself. But trying to explain that to him is only going to make him defensive, because he's right, he *is* sitting right here now. And if he becomes defensive, I'm going to argue my position even more fervently, and we're going to get into another argument about who does how much and when, which will stray too far from the point. Which is Maya. Which has to be Maya.

"The man's willing to ride all the way here on a bicycle," Uzi says. "He wants to help."

On the other side of the screen door, the dice skitter across the guest room tiles and plink against a stucco wall. "I'm winning!" Maya shouts. "I'm winning so hard!"

"What happened yesterday didn't look like 'help,'" I say. "I don't want to put her through that again." But even as I say the words, I'm not sure I fully believe them. It didn't *look* as if Canto was helping Maya in the cabin, yet today she's clearly better, and it happened freakishly fast. A part of me is ready to believe that the prayers and leaves, simple as they seemed, had a measurable effect, while at the same time my intellect is fighting to discredit that impulse. *You know what you're seeing is real, even if you don't fully understand it*, the first part says, until the other part comes slamming back. *Give me a break! Bodies heal on their own all the time. And what happened in that cabin was some weird shit. You can't let him do that again.*

It's the strangest feeling, to be caught up in this kind of argument with . . . myself. I still have no idea how it's possible to believe in the potential of something while simultaneously refuting its right to exist, but it is.

"She's better," Uzi presses on. "You said so yourself. That should be reason enough to see him again. This isn't like a regular doctor, where it's a one-shot deal."

"When did you go all Machiavellian on me?" I say. "The ends don't justify the means."

He shakes his head slowly, as if my response defies belief. He'll drop the argument for now, but he won't forget it, I know.

Victor comes round the corner again and resumes his prior position on the steps. I wait for another message from San Antonio, but when he doesn't speak I realize he just wants to sit. Everyone else is off on excursions; we're the only guests left on the premises today. The day stretches ahead of us, long, damp, and green.

Maya and Everald come frog-hopping out of the guest room, her in front, him following, and Victor laughs jovially.

"You want me to guess?" I say, and Maya nods. "You're frogs, right?"

"The tadpoles growed up," she says.

"You know how to say 'frog' in Spanish?" Victor asks her. "*Rana.* Almost like *reina.*"

"*Reina rana,*" I say. "The Frog Queen."

Maya gives us a crooked smile, as if she's not sure what to make of that. "Okay," she says and hops off with Everald to the lawn.

"You want to do something this afternoon?" Victor asks us. "You want to go somewhere? Maybe we can take you later."

"How about Tikal?" Uzi asks.

Tikal? The ancient Maya city? That's in northern Guatemala, at least a two-hour drive from here. Maya is better, but I don't think she's that much better.

"Tikal?" Victor asks. He makes it sound even less feasible than it sounded to me. "Tikal is a whole-day trip. There's a van going tomorrow. I think there's room. You want Tikal, you can go to Tikal tomorrow. Maybe today we can see the Mennonites. You need furniture? They make good furniture."

The Mennonite community came to Belize from Mexico in the

1950s and now produces most of the country's dairy and eggs. One of their settlements, Spanish Lookout, is about thirty minutes from here. I've heard their farms are pristine and orderly and worth seeing. But it's Christmas. I'm pretty sure everything in Spanish Lookout will be shut down for the day.

"Do we need furniture?" Uzi asks me.

"Not really. Plus, how would we get it home? It'd probably cost as much to ship it as it would to buy it. Anyway, it's Christmas. Everything's probably closed."

"Oh, right," Victor says. "Maybe tomorrow, then. I can call over there and see."

"The Mennonites have phones?"

"Oh, sure. Phones, cars, even computers! These Mennonites, they have everything."

"*Computers?*" I say. My house in Iowa wasn't far from an Amish community, but that was serious Old Order Amish, windmills and horses and buggies, the whole thing. I know Mennonites are more modern than the Amish, but I didn't realize they were quite that modern. "Do they have email?" I ask.

Victor gives a little laugh. I love the way Victor laughs. His shoulders go up and down just the tiniest bit and the sound comes out like an actual "hee-hee."

"I don't know," he says. "Probably!" He checks his watch. "What about canoeing? Maybe my son Everald can take you canoeing on the Macal."

"On Christmas Day?" I ask. I feel bad taking anyone away from their family on Christmas. On the other hand, the resort is open, it's a workday for the family, and we're still their clients. Maybe that makes it all right.

"Sure, sure," Victor says. "It's no problem. You can go down the river to San Ignacio for lunch. I know a very nice place there, Sri Lankan owners. You like Sri Lankan food?"

"I don't think I've ever had Sri Lankan food," I say. "But if it's like Indian food, we'll like it. They're open on Christmas?" I'm starting to sound like a one-note wonder, I know, but it's hard to believe such full service is available today. Movie theaters and Chinese restaurants: that's all you find open at home on Christmas Day.

"Sure. It's a big day. Lots of tourists are here now. They have to eat somewhere. So you want to go canoeing?"

I look at Uzi, who shrugs in an amiable *fine by me* gesture.

"Can Maya just sit in the canoe?" I ask Victor. "I don't want her to do anything too strenuous."

"Sure," he says. "The little one can just sit in the middle like a queen and look at the birds."

"And all four of us can fit in one canoe?" If we have to depend on my summer-camp paddling skills, we'll wind up in Honduras.

Victor closes his eyes and gives an amused little laugh. I'm asking a lot of picky questions, I know. "Four can fit," he says. "Everald and your husband can paddle. You and the little one just sit and enjoy the view."

The Macal River curves gently around Cristo Rey, cradling the village in a slightly open palm. Everald Senior guides the pale green Crystal Paradise canoe between the banks, his paddle slicing through the cool, clean water with steady, strong *plup . . . plup . . . plup*s. The river smells mulchy and fertile, like something freshly pulled from the earth. A coolness rises from it and winds its way into the back of my nostrils. I trail my hand in the water, causing a little ripple to form alongside the canoe.

"Watch out for turtles," Everald says from behind me, and I jerk my hand back so fast that droplets of water spray onto the thighs of my khaki pants.

The Macal is a lazy river on a late December morning, taking its canoeists for a leisurely stroll rather than a brisk jog. Walls of dark green foliage rise on both sides of the bank. Along some stretches, the branches bend forty-five degrees downriver as if held in place by a strong wind. It's residual damage from Hurricane Keith in October, when the Macal, which is prone to flash floods, rose twenty feet above its normal level.

It's hard to imagine such power churning through a river as placid as today's. We need only two paddlers to follow the mild current downstream and could probably make do with one. This renders me virtually useless from my perch in the middle of the canoe, so I hold Maya between my knees and point out the landmarks as Everald narrates them from behind us.

"Ceiba," he says, aiming his paddle at a tall tree whose light gray, branchless trunk rises ten feet above the surrounding tree canopy before bursting into a brilliant half sphere of green. "The national tree of Guatemala."

Yax Che, the Maya called the ceiba, or "First Tree." In the Maya story of Creation, the world began as a primordial sea in a field of unbroken darkness. Then First Father raised the World Tree, the *Wakah-Chan*, to separate Earth from sky and invite the sun's light in. According to legend, he positioned the tree's crown in the north sky, thus creating the central axis of the cosmos around which all the celestial constellations revolve. To the ancient Maya, the flowering, towering ceiba was the earthly representation of this mythical World Tree. Its upper reaches extend through the thirteen layers of the Upperworld, or heavens; its branches lie in the Middleworld, where the cycles of human activity and nature occur; and its roots extend down through the nine layers of the Underworld. Along its mystically charged central channel, heavenly deities could travel to Earth when summoned and human souls could travel down into the Underworld after death. Like the World Tree of Norse mythology; the Jewish Tree of Life, *Etz HaChayim*; the Bodhi tree of the Baghavad-Gita; and the Cosmic Tree of numerous shamanic cultures—as if a symbolic arboreal consciousness percolated up all over the globe at roughly the same time—the Maya World Tree offered its people a template for human cosmology. It placed humans and their behaviors within the context of an expansive universe and revealed humanity's connection to the divine.

But I don't know any of this yet as I sit here in this canoe, and if Everald knows it, he's not telling. He's pointing to a grove of bamboo growing on a riverbank to our left. Uzi tells him how popular bamboo floors have become in green-conscious Los Angeles, because bamboo replaces itself in the environment faster than hardwoods such as maple and oak.

"I heard somewhere that you have to cut bamboo at a certain time or it's not as durable," Uzi says. "Have you ever heard that?"

"Farmers here cut it after a full moon."

"Why after a full moon?"

"That way it doesn't have insects, and the wood lasts longer," Everald explains.

"Interesting."

"Crocodile," Everald says.

"What?"

"Over there." He aims his paddle at a shallow sand spit on the right, where a small brown crocodile, the size of a large monitor lizard, lounges by the water's edge. "Look, Maya!" Uzi and I shout. "A real live crocodile! Look!" I pull the camera from my bag and take three or four quick, successive shots. "Where?" Maya shouts. "Where?" She springs onto her knees for a better look, rocking the canoe dangerously. The crocodile takes a few leisurely steps into the river and disappears beneath its surface. Everald keeps dipping his paddle into the water with slow, circular strokes, unimpressed.

Ahead of us, a black bird with a long, thin beak perches on a wooden post in the water. With a loud cry, it stretches its black feathery wings and fans them gently, drying them in the sun.

"Cormorant," Everald says.

Everald is the pithiest tour guide I've ever encountered. I suppose once you've identified an object in the path, there really isn't anything critical to add unless your clients ask for elaboration, but still, most tour guides drone on and on even in the absence of questions just to give clients their money's worth. Everald seems more comfortable with silence. I heard somewhere, maybe from Carolyn the travel agent, that he has an encyclopedic knowledge of Maya archaeology and is considered an expert on the ruined city of Caracol, twenty-five miles south of here, but he doesn't wear the title for anyone to see. He seems equally as content paddling a family of Californians downriver as he might be picking his way through a crumbling palace in the jungle. Whatever store of knowledge he holds seems to be more an interesting fact about him than a defining characteristic.

I feel Everald shift his weight behind me, and the pace of his paddling picks up. "Rapids up there," he says.

"Where?" Uzi asks. I sit up straight. Victor didn't say anything about rapids.

"Just up there. Have you paddled rapids before?"

"Once or twice," Uzi says.

I have, several times, but that was thirteen years ago with river outfitters in eastern Tennessee, where I was wearing a hard helmet and paddling in an enormous, inflatable yellow raft with five other people, while a guide in the back yelled, "Left! Right! Left! Left!" A well-worn fiberglass canoe and a couple of baseball caps in western Belize? Not the same thing.

"Class one?" I ask Everald, trying to gauge what degree of rapids to expect. "Class two?"

"It's usually class one, but with so much extra water in the river, I don't know what it is today," he says. "Stay all the way to the left of the rocks up there," he instructs Uzi. "When the current starts moving fast, paddle hard."

Ahead of us, I can see the water riffling and spurting around a few table rocks in the middle of the river. There isn't anything for me to do except hold tight to Maya, so I hold tight to Maya.

"Ready," Everald says, steering us on a straight course for a narrow slip on the left. "Now!" He and Uzi start paddling furiously as we're sucked into the teeming passage. The water next to the canoe folds over itself again and then again and again, like a mechanical braid.

Just as quickly as we were pulled in, we're spit out the other side. The canoe practically stalls out on the tranquil water. That was the shortest rapid I've ever traveled. I have to turn around to verify we just came through what I think we came through. We did.

"Everyone okay?" Everald asks.

"That was the wimpiest rapid in history!" I say. "It was like class one half. It was a Jacuzzi!"

Everald laughs. "It's enough for some people," he says.

It was enough for me today, too, but I can't resist the temptation to make him crack a smile. Actually, I feel a little foolish to have gotten so worked up over nothing. I release Maya and lean forward to check how she's doing. She's sitting cross-legged on the bottom of the canoe, playing with the two little stuffed leopards from home I handed to her back in the cabana, thinking we didn't need to be fishing a Hursula out of the Macal. Her cheeks are pink, but from sunshine, not fever. It's the first time since we left Los Angeles that she's sitting quietly out of contentment rather than illness. Her serenity, so rare these past months, makes me want to capture the moment and hold on to its image.

I pull the Minolta back out of my bag, loop the strap around my neck, and aim it in her direction.

"Maya," I say, to get her attention. She turns around.

"Nyah!" she shouts when she sees the camera, so loudly it makes me jerk back on the seat and collide with Everald's kneecaps. She lashes at me with her right arm, and the leopard gripped tightly in her hand makes purchase with the camera. The blow sends it careening around over my right shoulder, pulling the thick black nylon strap taut against my throat as it passes.

"Jesus, Maya!" I say, pulling the camera strap from my skin. Everald gently hands the camera back over my shoulder. "What was that for?"

"Nyah!" she scowls again, her mouth twisted into an angry smear. She doesn't even resemble the same child she was before I lifted the camera to my face. Uzi turns around and shoots me a quiet look of concern over his shoulder.

"Iguana," Everald says.

"What?"

"Up there." He points to the high branches of a fig tree on the right bank.

Maya has been waiting for an iguana since the one she missed on the ride in from the airport. She whips her head around. "Where?" she asks.

"Right there." Everald points forty-five degrees skyward.

"I can't see it," I say.

"Right there, halfway up." The canoe glides alongside the tree. "You can't see it now. It's right above us."

Maya and I turn around as the canoe passes the tree, and from this angle, with the branches backlit by the sun, I see what looks like the silhouette of a grotesquely large, furry caterpillar lying flush along the top of a long branch. The iguana blends right into the tree bark, a nearly perfect camouflage. Only the jagged spines along its back comb give it away.

"Right there," Everald says, pointing at the spot, at the precise moment Maya shouts, "I see it!"

She leans back, satisfied, and plugs her second and third fingers into her mouth. Crisis averted, for now.

Uzi rests his paddle on his lap and watches the trees pass. Everald is silent behind me.

We float downstream. There's no sense of urgency to get where we're going. Time hangs suspended between the banks. Only the river moves.

We float.

We float.

Six years from now, a writer friend of mine will read an early draft of this story and tell me the characters spend too much time getting from one place to another. "You're always on an airplane or in a car or a canoe," she will say. I will have nothing to say in my defense. We *have* spent a lot of time in transit these past few days. But is that so unusual? All of us, all the time, are in perpetual states of motion, like sharks, which have to swim constantly to keep oxygen coursing through their gills, like rodents in winter intent on keeping their body temperatures high enough to survive. Nearly all our waking hours are spent in transit: stumbling from the bedroom to the bathroom, racing from the subway to the office, gliding from the supermarket parking lot to the produce section to the toothpaste aisle to the checkout line. I cross the room to pick up the telephone; head down the driveway to the mailbox, then turn around and head back up; roll my office chair between my desk and the file cabinet and the bookshelf thirteen times a day. We are all, always, in the process of trying to get somewhere else.

When I was in graduate school, one of my writing professors invited our class to her home, a renovated one-room schoolhouse in the middle of Amish country. That winter evening, as we sat around the woodstove, we were encouraged to read excerpts from works in progress. One of my classmates was writing about her relationship with a young professor at the university, a man in the process of scrambling up the ladder of a brilliant academic career. "When you fall in love with a person on their way from one place to another, you fall in love with someone who doesn't exist," she read out loud. I was twenty-six, coming out of a relationship with an aspiring novelist, and thought I'd never heard a truer statement.

I left Iowa a little more than a year later, on my way to New York City, where I would finish writing my first book. Soon after its publication, my father landed in the hospital with heart trouble. My father landed in the hospital with heart trouble, it turned out, because he was in catastrophic financial trouble. He was in catastrophic financial trouble because . . . well, I won't go into the details, but trust me: they were bad. Homelessness was not out of the question. I had to hire a private investigator to parse years of facts from fiction. I was the oldest child in the family and the only one living in New York at the time, so it was up to me to figure out what to do.

For the next few weeks, I juggled magazine and radio interviews for my book with visits to the hospital and endless appointments with lawyers and accountants, who all had different ideas about how to fix the mess. It was an extremely crappy couple of weeks. There were moments, many of them, when I felt I was in too far over my head, with too much at stake for my father, but I refused to let myself fall apart in front of people I had to rely on for help. The only time during the day when I would let down my guard was in the small pockets of time between appointments. So I became the kind of person I had always scoffed at before: a public crier. I cried in the back of cabs, on subway platforms, and while rushing down Park Avenue in wobbly high heels. As soon as I exited one meeting and started heading to another, a switch would be flipped and the sobbing would begin. When the cab pulled up in front of a designated building or when I stepped into a lobby, I could turn off the tears like a faucet. It was compartmentalization of the highest order.

This was New York, where nearly all transportation is public, which meant all this was happening in front of an audience. Normally this would have mortified me, but I didn't have the time or the presence of mind to care. And something remarkable happened as a result. Total strangers were kinder to me than they had ever been in New York before. A Sri Lankan cabbie promised he would pray for me and my family when he got home that night, and I believe he meant it. An enormous African-American woman at Grand Central Station put her arms around me and tried to give me her well-worn Bible. It was as if the sight of a woman crying alone called forth an essential humanity in New Yorkers that they otherwise chose to suppress. The man in the brown leather jacket sitting across from me on the F train didn't say a word, but he reached down into his paper bag of groceries, carefully removed the plastic from a new roll of paper towels, and handed me the first sheet. I could barely stand all this kindness. I kept thanking everyone, profusely, for every small act of compassion, like an urban gratitude machine. During those two weeks, I fell in love with my fellow New Yorkers. I don't mean that I blithely loved them, I mean I *loved* them, with a radiance and purity and sense of oneness I don't recall ever having experienced before.

I had never felt more lost or more frightened or more overwhelmed than I did during those two weeks, yet at the same time, I had also never felt more liberated, more connected to others, or more real.

When I let down the barricades I normally kept erected between me and the rest of the world, I was no longer a first-time author or the girlfriend of a writer who lived on Fifty-first Street or a lecturer who stood in front of a hundred paying attendees on Thursday nights talking about early mother loss. I was just a girl on a train who was scared for her father and wished her mother were still here to help her. I was a human being with human emotions, the same as every other human being in the world. And it was then that I realized my classmate in graduate school had been wrong. A person on the way from one place to another is not someone in a state of suspension, a self in the process of becoming. A person in the act of traveling from one place to another is a person stripped down to her very essence, perhaps the truest self that can exist.

Here in this canoe on the Macal River between Cristo Rey Village and San Ignacio Town, I am a woman in transit. A person, floating. Waiting. Watching. Trying. Impatient. Imperfect. Hopeful.

Myself. Nothing more.

chapter nine
San Ignacio Town/Cristo Rey, Belize
December 25, 2000

The Hawkesworth suspension bridge stretches across the Macal River, linking San Ignacio with its smaller sister town of Santa Elena. Constructed in 1949, the Hawkesworth looks a like a scaled-down, red-steel version of the Brooklyn Bridge. Everald and Uzi paddle us between the two towering cement piers and over to a small sand spit on the river's left bank. Ahead of us, a single car glides across a second, simpler wooden bridge that almost grazes the water. At its base, a small group of people has waded in, fully clothed, up to their thighs. The children splash and shout in high-pitched tinny cries and send glistening arcs of water catapulting through the air.

Everald steps out into the shallow water and drags the canoe up onto the bank, where he'll wait for Victor to come retrieve it with the van. He points us toward a gentle rise leading into town. Uzi lifts Maya onto his hip, and we follow two tire tracks etched in the grass to a deserted side street lined with mostly vacant, boxy cinder-block buildings. Around a corner we bump into the edge of the town's square, where a red-and-orange gazebo sits smack in the middle of a concrete sea.

We've just arrived at the capital of the Cayo District, where the Macal and Mopan rivers meet, forming what was once a natural hub for the timber and chicle industries. A hundred years ago, the region was flush with lumberjacks and *chicleros*, who scaled sapodilla trees to extract the natural latex for chewing gum. Today in San Ignacio Town, the third largest population center in Belize, you're far more likely to find district administrators and ecotourists walking on the streets. The town's population is mainly mestizo—a mix of European and native ancestry—and Maya, with smaller groups of Creoles who've migrated from the north and east, Mennonite farmers from nearby Spanish Lookout, Lebanese whose grandfathers and great-grandfathers came as chicle traders in the early 1900s, and Chinese immigrants who came from Guangzhou in the mid–twentieth century and now operate many of Cayo's grocery stores and bakeries. For its size, San Ignacio is a town of remarkable diversity, even for a country as remarkably diverse as Belize.

With 13,000 residents, San Ignacio is normally a bustling, honking urban hive, but at 1 P.M. on Christmas it's just a slim notch above deserted. Here and there we see a random person on the sidewalk, but only a few lonely cars cruise the narrow streets. The black-and-white license plates all sport the tagline BELIZE, C.A., and the first eight times I see this I automatically read, "Belize, California," a subconscious pull toward home. Next to the town square, a two-room, yellow wooden bus station isn't seeing much action today. A clerk sits behind a swinging wooden window, idly watching a black-and-white television, while two taxi drivers lean cross-armed against their cars, staring at the empty street.

"Check this out," Uzi says, tipping his head toward the opposite wall, where the weekly bus schedule is hand-painted onto the yellow wooden planks. You can board a bus here and go to the Guatemalan border, to Belmopan, even all the way to Belize City, for U.S. $3.50 or less.

The air is as still as an abandoned movie set. The taxi drivers nod at us silently as we walk by. We listen to our footsteps slapping against the pavement as we walk uphill.

"It's so *quiet* here," I say to Uzi. Even in a whisper, my voice sounds like an interruption. He nods.

One block off the town square we find Burns Avenue, a paved road lined with dilapidated wooden buildings sitting shoulder to shoulder in alternating shades of yellow, green, and blue. The ground floors house restaurants, tour operators, or variety stores; the second floors all sport narrow balconies and guest rooms for rent. Electrical wires crisscross overhead in haphazard combinations. Except for the omnipresent Sprite, Pepsi, and Belikin beer advertisements, all the signage here is hand-painted, giving the town a makeshift, frontierlike feel. If you plucked a street out of the Old West, stuck it in the middle of the tropics, and painted the buildings every color of the rainbow, that would pretty well describe the scene. Everything about it shouts, "Laid-back, low-cost option!" and it makes me feel a small tug of nostalgia for the years when I could show up in a strange town with a backpack and a guidebook, tired and dirty and happy, and trek from door to door, inquiring about a cheap place to sleep. The sign jutting out from the balcony above Eva's Restaurant reads, "Backpackers Budget Hotel, Reasonable Rates, Friendly Atmosphere" and I swear: peel away ten years, a family, and a mortgage, and I'd sleep like a baby in one of those upstairs rooms, drifting off to the melody of a traveler's beat-up acoustic guitar and beer bottles clinking softly downstairs.

The Sri Lankan restaurant sits up and across the street from Eva's. On the sign nailed to its yellow outer wall, someone has painted small outlines of Belize and Sri Lanka side by side. This unlikely pairing occurred when the restaurant's owner came to Belize to work for the British Navy, Army and Air Force Institutes and stayed. He named his business Serendib, from the old Arabic name for Sri Lanka. In 1754, the English writer Horace Walpole used this name to create a new word, *serendipity*, to describe a lucky accident. He got the idea from the Persian fairy tale *The Three Princes of Serendip*, whose traveling heroes, he wrote, "were always making discoveries, by accident and sagacity, of things they were not in quest of."

Inside the restaurant, a cool breeze runs from the front door straight through to the crowded patio in back. Victor was right: tourists always need a place to eat on Christmas, and most of us seem to be doing it here. The main room is simple and clean, with a fully stocked bar on the right; walls paneled in blond faux wood like a 1970s basement rec room; red and green tablecloths trapped under square glass table-tops; and a string of Christmas lights winding around a center pole. The dull scent of curry hovers in the room like a faint perfume. In the back corner, two women sitting underneath a black-and-white portrait of Princess Diana are engaged in earnest conversation. The one with the brown ponytail wears a yellow Los Angeles Lakers baseball cap.

We sit down in straight-backed wooden chairs at the only empty table, in the middle of the room. Maya scrambles onto her knees and starts bouncing up and down. She's excited to be here. Her preschool teacher is Sri Lankan, and to a three-year-old that means she's in the know.

"Look, Maya," Uzi says, pointing to a poster hanging in another corner of the room. It's a large Asian elephant and two smaller elephants standing in a clearing, with the words "Sri Lanka" printed across the bottom.

"A mommy, a baby, and a baby," Maya observes, pointing at each one in turn.

A waiter materializes at my left elbow and takes a few swipes at the glass tabletop, cleaning an already spotless surface.

"Merry Christmas," he greets us, placing two menus on the table.

"Merry Christmas," Uzi and I chime back.

"Christmas?" Maya asks. She pulls her face into a tight, puzzled frown, and I can almost see the little gears clicking and turning inside her head. Christmas? Where's Santa . . . the music . . . the tree? She was so sick before we left California that we didn't take her to any public displays, not to the street in the San Fernando Valley where every house goes all out with lights, not even to see Santa at the Santa Monica mall. Tonight is also the fifth night of Hanukkah, and except for lighting candles in our dining room at home on the first night and giving Maya a few gifts, we haven't been celebrating that, either. It's a little confusing for me too, actually.

"Christmas is different here than at home," I say. It's a weak explanation but seems to satisfy her. She looks up and smiles shyly at the waiter.

"Do you know Prema?" she asks.

"Excuse me?" he says, politely.

"She's talking about her teacher," I explain. "Who comes from Sri Lanka. I don't think he knows her, honey," I tell Maya. "Prema lives all the way in California." It occurs to me that Maya has no concept whatsoever of how far we are from home. Notions of time and distance and geography exist at only the most simplistic level in her mind. In April when we were in Israel, she started crying in the car one afternoon, demanding that we keep driving until we reached our house. A two-hour drive to the next county, a three-day flight around the world, a week on a camel in the Gobi, to a three-year-old the result is always the same: not home.

"Do you know Helen?" Maya asks the waiter, hopefully.

The waiter tilts his head patiently.

"That's Prema's sister," I tell him. I turn to Maya and shake my head no. "Sri Lanka is a very big country. Maybe a long time ago his parents knew their parents, but even then, I doubt it."

A family in the back of the room starts waving for the waiter's attention. "We have to order now," I tell Maya, who has slumped down a little in disappointment.

"Well, do you know the *elephants*?" she asks. Her tone says that at least he should know the *elephants*. She's talking about the ones in the poster, but the waiter has no way of knowing that.

"Ah, yes," he says. "There are many elephants in Sri Lanka."

Maya nods and gives him a dazzling smile of accomplishment. I take the opportunity to move things along. "Can you tell us what on the menu would be good for a child?"

He points to the section titled "Snacks." It lists six kinds of hamburgers, a fish burger, and a ham-and-cheese sandwich. "Children also like the rice . . ."

"I don't want rice," Maya says. I give her the one-minute sign to let the waiter continue.

". . . and we can make a very mild curry with vegetables and chicken."

"I don't want vegetables!" Maya shouts, banging her fist on the table. "Dodo says no vegetables!" The waiter looks startled by the abrupt outburst. The woman in the Lakers cap glances in our direction and immediately looks down.

I glance at Uzi, whose expression says, *Let's emphasize the positive, please*. Maya's fever has broken, and I think she might finally eat something today. Okay, those are two indisputable positives.

"*No* vegetables!" Maya shouts again, clutching the table's rim. The man in the back who's been frantically waving for the waiter yanks his hand back down. Everyone's looking at us now.

"I'll take her outside," Uzi says, leaping into action. "We'll go wash our hands. You can order for me." He hoists Maya into the air before she has a chance to object and quickly shuttles her out the back door.

"I'm sorry," I say to the waiter, who offers a sympathetic nod.

I ask for two orders of yellow rice with chicken curry and an omelet with fries for Maya. I hope she'll eat it. I hand my menu to the waiter and glance out at the patio, where a single long table of diners is accumulating bottles of Belikin beer.

"And one bottle of Belikin," I add.

A small painted portrait of Jesus hangs directly above the restaurant's back door, on top of the exit sign. I wonder, has it been strategically placed there like a Tibetan prayer flag, to bless all who pass beneath it? In the portrait, Jesus faces the restaurant wrapped in a long white robe, a golden halo of light hovering around his head and rays of red and white light emanating from his chest. He looks so . . . *peaceful*. I've always thought of Jesus as the original divine leader. Blessed are the meek; turn the other cheek: he handed us all the key insights we need for living in equality and peace. It makes you look around the world and wonder, *what if?* What if more people lived by the purity of his teachings, instead of by the dogma that grew out of them?

The waiter returns with a cold bottle of Belikin. I pick it up and automatically start to peel off the paper label, an old habit from college, except there is no paper label. The Belikin logo is printed right onto the dark glass, a black-and-white illustration of a Maya temple, framed by green and red squares. I scratch one of the white corners with my fingernail, but the paint is stuck fast to the side of the cold glass.

The table on the back patio breaks out in a spontaneous, raucous cheer, and I jump a little in my seat. Uzi and Maya are still outside in the bathroom. But washing hands for this long? I feel my chest tighten just a notch, bracing myself in case something else is about to go wrong. This is how it feels most of the time: as if I'm driving down the road, steady and smooth, yet ready for a brick wall to come shooting up in front of me at any time. I shared this metaphor with Sarah just before we left for Belize. She said it sounded as if I were spending too much time in the car.

"Excuse me," someone says.

I look up. It's the woman with the ponytail and the Lakers hat, stopping at our table on her way to the front door.

"I heard you mention California," she says. "By any chance are you from L.A.?"

"We're from Topanga Canyon. Near Malibu."

"Was that your daughter?"

I nod.

"How old is she? About four?"

Oh, no. Did Maya's shouting bother her? I hope not, because I am not in the mood for an earful about my child's behavior right now.

"She just turned three," I say. "Why?"

The woman makes an apologetic little *oh* sound. "Sorry. I should have introduced myself first. I'm Robin Goldstein." She extends her hand for me to shake. Then she reaches into the black fanny pack at her waist and starts fumbling around. She pulls out a business card and hands it to me.

Advantage Casting. Oh my God. Uzi is never going to believe this.

"I run a casting agency in L.A. that represents kids, and I was noticing your daughter. I know a cute kid when I see one, and I'm telling you, that is one cute kid."

It is truly a glorious world when humor shines through at moments like this. I can't help it. I laugh out loud.

"Thanks," I say, "but"—how to phrase this?—"I don't think she's quite ready for prime time."

"That's okay," Robin says, zipping up her fanny pack. "She's still young. Hang on to the card, and give me a call when she's ready. But don't wait too long. Sometimes little kids are very cute, and then all of a sudden they're not so cute anymore."

"Believe me," I say. "I know all about not so cute." I hold up her card and use it to give her a little wave good-bye. "Have a good rest of your trip," I call out as she leaves.

"Merry Christmas," she calls back.

"Merry Christmas!" I say. And there you have it: two Jews from Los Angeles wishing each other Merry Christmas in a Sri Lankan restaurant in Belize. You can't not love this place.

The food arrives at the table on round white plates, with Maya and Uzi following close behind. "Sorry," Uzi says. "I couldn't get her to wash her hands." Maya takes a bite of a French fry and immediately spits it back onto the plate. Too hot. She leans over the rest of them and blows out a loud, "Foo! Foo!" like Uzi has taught her to do. The older couple at the next table look over. This time they smile.

"Here," Uzi says, picking up a fry. He exhales two loud "Foo!"s and hands it to Maya. "Ultimate Foo!" he announces. She looks at him uncertainly but takes a small bite, chews, and swallows.

"What's that?" Uzi points at the business card on the center of the table.

"A card from a casting agent in L.A. She was one of the women sitting over there in the corner. She saw Maya from across the room and wants us to give her a call. She said she's 'one cute kid.'"

Uzi's mouth is full of food, so the laugh exits through his nose. "You're kidding me, right?" he says.

"Honey, I can't make up stuff this good. I'd be writing fiction if I could."

I cut a small piece of omelet for Maya and hold it out to her on the fork. She obediently opens her mouth, chews, and spits it out on the plate.

"Yuck! Dodo hates it!" she says.

"All right, all right. Then just eat the French fries," I say. They're potatoes, and potatoes are food: I'll settle for that. I watch her eat one, then another, and a third. I take a few bites of salad and rice. She eats another fry. I mix some curry sauce into my rice. It tastes good. Better than good. I'm hungrier than I thought. Maya eats a sixth fry.

Six French fries! Who would have thought that watching a child eat six fries could make me this ecstatic?

Maya reaches out and drinks half the glass of water. This *is* a glorious day. Forty-five degrees above us, Jesus gazes down beatifically from the exit sign, streams of red and white light emanating from his chest. With the long hair and the carpentry skills, he'd be a quintessential Topangan. The string of lights around the restaurant's central pole blinks off and on. It's Christmas Day, December 25, 2000. On the Jewish calendar, it's the twenty-eighth day of Kislev in the year 5761, the fifth night of the Festival of Lights. On the ancient Maya Long Count calendar, it's 12.9.7.15.1, exactly 1,867,621 days since the Fifth World began. And on the Maya Tzolk'in calendar, the sacred 260-day count still in use, today is 6 Imix. Imix is the day of the alligator, the first day of the sacred year, a propitious time for starting something new.

Before the East Indians, before the Mennonites, even before the Lebanese arrived, African slaves were brought to Central America by the shipload to provide labor for sugar plantations and logging companies. In Belize, the descendants of these slaves mixed with Europeans to form the Creole culture that gives Belize much of its vibrancy today. The Africans couldn't carry much with them overseas, but they brought the rhythms of their homeland and the memory of their instruments. It's believed that the West African balaphon, a series of tuned wooden keys played with two padded mallets, blended with a pre-Columbian Maya instrument to create what's now known as the Central American marimba. Four hundred years later, the marimba is the national instrument of Guatemala and a favored instrument of mestizo culture in Costa Rica, Honduras, and Belize. You can hear its vibrational melodies all over the region, at festivals and on the street, as common in these parts as the Andean pan flute is in Peru. Which is a long way of explaining how the featured entertainment tonight at the Crystal Paradise Christmas party came to be a three-man marimba band.

The evening's performers begin setting up their instrument and microphones at the far side of the dining hall as the sun goes down. They wear large white cotton embroidered shirts with colorful patterns looped around the deep V-neck collars. Their marimba resembles an enormous rosewood xylophone. It's so big it takes all three of them to carry it down the steps, and they stand shoulder to shoulder behind the keyboard to play it.

"Hey, *niña*, want to try?" one of the marimba players asks Maya, handing her a padded mallet. She gets up on her toes for a better view and tentatively bounces the mallet against one of the wooden keys. A rich note reverberates throughout the dining hall. She smiles and hits the next one much harder. This time the effect is more like a loud, hollow gong.

"Whoa, whoa, whoa!" the musician laughs, taking the mallet back.

The party is scheduled for seven thirty, but by eight o'clock there's still no sign of an imminent show. The musicians are sitting around the tables drinking beers with the guests while Shakti tries out her Spanish on them. They all tip their heads back and smack their thighs with loud laughter when she makes a mistake. Quite a few of the guests seem to be locals, friends or family of the Tuts, and I'm happy to see they finally have a chance to celebrate the holiday. Everyone's pulling Belikins and sodas from the self-service bar. Just before eight thirty, the musicians amble over to the marimba, pick up their mallets, give one another a fast nod, and—just like that—the dining hall bursts into a series of loud, harmonious plunks.

I look over at Maya to see how she's handling the noise. She's so tired she's struggling to keep her head from dropping onto the table. Uzi is deeply engaged in conversation with a man with spiky blond hair and round John Lennon glasses, a fortyish biomedical engineer from Houston who designs prosthetic limbs. His name is Brian, and he's traveling alone. We sat with him at dinner, where he entertained us with stories about a caving trip he'd taken earlier in the day that involved swimming in his clothes, climbing over wet boulders, and seeing ancient Maya skeletons embedded in the mud. He strikes me as exceptionally intelligent and more than a little nervous about safety, the kind of guy who probably kept both hands flush against the cave wall the entire time. As I would have no doubt done myself.

I yawn widely to clear that thought from my head. Then I touch Uzi's shoulder. "I need to take Maya up to bed. Do you want to stay here?"

"I'll come up in a little while and switch with you," he offers.

In the cabana, I help Maya brush her teeth and get into her pajamas, then tuck the Hursulas under the covers by her side. She sticks her middle and ring finger into her mouth. She's asleep less than a minute after closing her eyes. I rub Canto's ointment on her chest and then try to read on my bed by the light of our single flashlight. We're leaving for the town of Placencia, on the Caribbean coast, in two days, and I want to read up on what to expect when we get there, but after only about ten minutes the flashlight batteries start to go dim. I slip my Tevas back on and try the hammock outside, but the marimba music is too loud for me to concentrate. I read the same paragraph about Placencia's history four times without absorbing any of it, while all manner and size of flying bugs whop and sizzle against the exposed bulb of the porch light.

The party careens along below me, the marimba keys sounding at a furious pace, the shouts and laughter of the guests leaking out between the notes. I give up on reading and walk out onto the lawn. If I step a few paces deeper into the grass, I can strategically turn one way and see our front porch, another way and see the back end of the dining hall. The musicians are bent over their instrument, elbows pumping wildly as they bang the mallets up and down the strip of wooden keys. Over their shoulders, I see a couple dancing across the floor in a quick lock-step fashion, the woman's long black hair twirling in her wake like a dark veil. It makes me wish, for a moment, that I were down there with the crowd. If I were, Uzi and I might step onto the dance floor, too, bumping hip bones and stepping on each other's toes, laughing so hard there'd be nothing left to do but stop pretending we know any real moves and start making up silly ones of our own. I do a fast little two-step on the lawn, the cool grass tickling the sides of my feet, but then I feel ridiculous dancing out here on the lawn alone.

The dancers part for a moment, and between the couples I catch a fast glimpse of Uzi sitting at a table, laughing. Next to him is Shakti, leaning her head toward his. She's laughing, too. My heart does a little fish flop in my chest. In the five years since Uzi and I met, I can't recall feeling jealous or even suspicious of another woman's interest in him, not even once. Until now.

I turn my back on the party and look out at the dark expanse of lawn and trees. I take three deep, cleansing breaths. That's better. It's a new moon tonight, cloudless and clear. Overhead, the stars spread across the sky like five hundred sparks of light glittering through random pinpricks in a black tent. I know how to pick out only the most familiar patterns in the night sky, the ones that anyone can find: Orion, the two dippers, and Venus. Our deck at home sits under the flight path between LAX and San Francisco, and when you stand out there you have to stare at each light for a few seconds to determine if it's moving or stationary. Here, all the stars are fixed. Or, rather, they migrate so slowly and in such total sync that you can't discern movement happening until it's already occurred.

We don't rely on stars for much anymore, not with clocks and calendars to record the passage of time. But standing here underneath such celestial splendor, to be unable to read the sky feels like a form of illiteracy. To the people who lived here thousands of years ago, the heavens were a world as rich and animated as the one they inhabited on earth. They believed the patterns of stars and planets were the means by which gods, ancestors, and spirits communicated with the Middle-world of people and pyramids and trees, and to ignore their divine messages was not only a sign of disrespect but a sure recipe for cosmic disaster.

The ancient Maya were expert naked-eye astronomers, spending countless nights atop their pyramids tracking the progress of stars and planets across the sky. They relied on celestial cycles to tell them when to plant crops and when to harvest, when to wage war, and how to calibrate the most elaborate calendar in the pre-Columbian world. The astronomical charts the Maya created to track Venus and pre-dict eclipses were so elaborate and so precise it's nearly impossible to comprehend they were made with only the most rudimentary forms of instrumentation. Forget about not having telescopes or calibration devices: these people didn't even have *metal*. It's believed they used pairs of crossed sticks to pinpoint places on the horizon where celestial objects rose and set, planted the sticks in the ground to mark the spots, and recorded how long it took for the star or planet to return to the same place. Some may have done similar sightings using their own crossed legs as measurement sticks. It took them decades, in some cases centuries, to achieve their degree of exactitude. I've always believed that a culture is only as smart as its current systems of technology allow it to be, but then along came the Maya, who mapped out astonishingly accurate astronomical charts with only a couple of sticks, their bare legs, and enough time to get it right. Talk about making the most of what you have.

Over there on the right, a single point outshines all the others in the sky. That must be Venus. Right now it's the Evening Star, rising at sunset in the west. In a while it'll disappear for eight days before rising in the east before dawn as the brilliant Morning Star. Venus was, hands down, the most important celestial body in the ancient Maya sky, so important that kings timed wars, coronations, and human sacrifices according to its position. The Maya believed Venus to be the heavenly equivalent of their feathered serpent god, Kukulkan (known as Quetzalcoatl to the Aztecs), their celestial messenger who once lived on Earth as a man.

Soft footsteps pad up the patio stairs behind me, and I whip my head around to see who's there. Oh. It's just Shakti, going into her cabana. By herself. Good. I turn back to the sky.

I don't see the Big Dipper anywhere tonight, but up there, directly overhead, are the three stars in the belt of Orion. The one on the left, Alnitak, joins with two others, Saiph and Rigel, to form a perfect equilateral triangle. To the Maya this is the First-Three-Stone-Place, the sky spot where humanity was born. According to the Maya creation myth, the Maize gods who were assigned the task of creating life paddled to the center of the universe in a cosmic canoe. They lay down three hearthstones, creating the First-Three-Stone-Place to contain the Fire of Creation that would give rise to humanity. Five hundred and forty-two days later, they squared the cosmos with four corners and four sides, to give it shape and order. Then First Father lifted the World Tree—represented by the Milky Way in the heavens and on paper as a cross—to separate heaven from Earth, placing its roots on the southern horizon and its crest pointing north. The gods used the motions of a weaver to spin the constellations around the tree's northernmost axis, thereby giving humans a method for measuring time.

The gods set up the Three-Stone-Place on the zero day of the Maya Long Count calendar, considered the day of creation or—in our calendar system—August 11, 3114 B.C. On every August 11 in the tropics to this day, the constellations rise and set in a celestial pageant that allows the story of creation to play out visually overhead. The stars that form the cosmic canoe move across the sky before dipping down as the rotation of the Milky Way brings the First-Three-Stone-Place directly overhead. Five hundred and forty-two days later, on every February 5, First Father raises the World Tree as the Milky Way lifts from the horizon to arc from north to south across the sky.

I hear a quiet rustling sound behind me in the grass and turn to see Shakti approaching, gripping a bottle of Belikin by its long brown stem. She's wearing a little headlamp attached to her forehead with two blue nylon straps, like a stylish miner.

"Coming back down?" she asks.

"Maya's sleeping. I'm waiting here until Uzi can switch with me."

"I can wait up here with her if you want, so you can go to the party."

"That's okay. I'm not so in the mood for a party right now," I say.

She nods, and the light on her forehead casts a bobbling shadow onto the grass. "Okay, then," she says. "I guess I'll go back down to Uzi."

I feel compelled to point out the following: Shakti doesn't say she'll go back down to her son or back down to the dining hall or back down to the party. She says she'll go back down to Uzi, *my husband.*

On the outside, I might look like a medium-aged mother with a messy ponytail and clothing that looks like pajamas, but inside, I'm a middleweight prizefighter dancing around on my toes, gloves at face level, ready to take a jab.

I plant my hands on my hips and turn to face her.

"Listen, *Shakti,*" I say, taking extra care to get the name right. "You need to back off my husband. Right now. Do you understand?"

In the light from her headlamp, I watch the smile on her face melt into neutral and then keep going. Just when I expect her eyes to harden for a fight, they do something else entirely.

"But I didn't mean . . . I wasn't . . ." she sputters.

When I was writing my first book, I traveled around the country interviewing more than a hundred women who'd lost mothers during childhood or adolescence. I sat with them, one at a time, in living rooms, in cafés, on backyard picnic blankets, even once on a houseboat docked in Puget Sound. They shared some of the saddest stories of loss and neglect you could imagine and a couple of uplifting ones, too. Most of the time, I didn't need to say much. The women had been waiting in some cases for thirty or forty years for someone who wanted to listen. I needed only to ask a question here or there for clarification. This freed me to watch each woman's face closely as she talked, and it wasn't long before I noticed that about forty-five minutes into each story, a woman's countenance would start to soften, to become more vulnerable and less guarded. The years would lift from her face until I swear I could see the outline of her younger self emerge. I could see the shape of her eight-year-old eyes behind the crow's-feet; I could picture how she must have looked in braids. Then both women—the girl and the adult—would finish telling the story together. This was how I came to understand that the eight-year-old does not precede the thirty-year-old any more than the fifty-year-old negates the twelve-year-old. One does not replace the other. In the most beautiful way imaginable, they coexist.

This is what I see when Shakti's tough-chick mask melts away: the ten-year-old who looks as if she's just been smacked and had no idea it could hurt so bad. Her haughty self-assurance dissolves into a childlike pain, and my anger disintegrates with it.

"I'm so sorry," Shakti says. "I was just trying to be friendly to you guys. I didn't mean to cause any problems." Even her voice has changed. It's higher, thinner, and stripped of the false bravado we've heard in it since we arrived.

"It's all right," I say, and mean it. "I'm the one who's sorry. I didn't mean to hurt you." The memory of my petty jealousy makes me cringe. Did I really just say, *Do you understand?* "I'm not usually like this," I add. "I've been in a real state for a while. I've got a lot going on right now."

Shakti nods slowly. "I can see that."

"You can?"

"It's hard not to."

"I guess it's pretty obvious," I say. "Anyway, I'm sorry. I didn't mean to jump on you. It's just . . . you've been showing a lot of interest in my husband. Sometimes right in front of me. I had to say something."

"He's a nice guy," she says. "I like the way he thinks."

"It's a little unusual sometimes. But I like it, too. It definitely keeps things interesting."

Shakti nods. It's a slow nod, a quiet nod, devoid of anger or judgment, just a gentle, pure form of agreement. It says, *I hear what you're saying*, and against all odds, it makes me want to tell her more.

I hug my arms against my chest and stare out at the whole mess of stars smeared across the sky. The Maya saw the stars as much more than timekeeping devices and oracles. They believed the cosmos was our essence, our source, and that we humans are so closely connected to the heavens that what happens light-years above us is mirrored in our behavior here on Earth.

"You know," I tell Shakti, "back home I was trying to convince myself, oh, this thing with Maya isn't such a big deal. Maybe you're just making it up because you need to have conflict or drama in your life or whatever. Because whenever I insisted there was a problem with Maya, people would start looking at me like *I* was the one with the problem, and I started thinking maybe I was. Then I'd be even more determined to figure out what was going on with her and fix it, just to prove everyone wrong. But down here, the problem is real. No one even considers it might be in my head. It's like stepping into an alternate reality. So you'd think I'd like that, but it's actually freaking me out a little. I'm not used to being taken seriously on this."

The words pour out of me, as if they've been pent up behind a locked gate. Now I know how the women who sat down for interviews with me must have felt: unrestrained and grateful and relieved.

"Down here, the verdict seems to be clear: my kid has a spiritual problem that needs to be cured," I continue. "I don't know if I totally believe that, but it's tempting for me to get swept up in that kind of jungle logic. I want to have that kind of certainty. I think everyone does. But then, before you know it, you're pouring plant water on top of your kid's head because that's what you're supposed to do here, and you don't even recognize the person who's doing it any more. You look at your hands pouring the water, and you think, *These used to be my hands. Who do they belong to now?* How crazy is that?"

"It doesn't sound that crazy to me," Shakti says.

"Well, it *feels* crazy. Not while I'm doing it, but definitely after."

"This trip is going to change your life, you know," Shakti says. "I think you and Uzi are really brave to be doing it."

"Brave? I don't know. Sometimes I think 'brave' would be to wait it out and see if Maya gets better on her own, like everyone at home says she will. Sometimes I think that pushing for a resolution instead of admitting I don't have control is the cowardly act, not the brave one."

"No, I think what you and Uzi are doing takes courage. And faith. And you know, just exposing your daughter to this way of thinking is going to expand her consciousness. She's lucky."

"Shakti? I have to tell you. When you say things like that, they just go right over my head."

She laughs. "Yeah, I hear that a lot. Don't worry. It'll make sense to you one day."

"One day tomorrow, or one day ten years from now?"

She shoves her hands down deep in the front pockets of her trail shorts and rocks from one foot to the other. "One day whenever," she says. "I don't know."

"And you call yourself a psychic?"

She laughs again, and the light on her forehead bobs up and down a little. "I'll let you in on a secret," she says. "The future unfolds on its own, whether I can see it or not."

"So, free will and determinism? It's just a bunch of bunk?"

"Not exactly. You can change the course of events in your life, more or less. But why would you want to? It's much more exciting to discover the plan."

"That's what I'm talking about," I say. I make the *whoosh*ing motion with my hand over the crown of my head. "Right over the top."

"Ask Uzi," she says. "He knows what I mean."

"Hey," I say, in a voice of mock toughness. "You leave my husband out of it." I give her the little ha-ha elbow jab in the upper arm, but she's shorter than me so it gets her in the shoulder. She returns it with an elbow into my waist.

"Want some?" She extends her Belikin bottle to me.

"No, thanks. I'll go down and get my own later."

We stand on the lawn just a little longer looking at the sky, as the marimba music amps up in the dining hall behind us. I can't see the musicians, but from the sound of it they must be a flurry of shoulders and arms, hitting key after key in a nearly manic frenzy to keep the tempo going this fast for so long.

I point to the bright star to the west, riding just a little higher in the sky now than it was before.

"That's Venus," I say.

"Cool." Shakti points directly overhead and just slightly to the left. "There's Orion," she says.

Inside the First-Three-Stone-Place, a smudge of stars glows diffusely, like a cosmic thumbprint in the sky. The Orion Nebula. You can see it through a telescope but not so easily with the naked eye. The Maya identified this spot as the Fire of Creation, the place where human life began. Modern-day astronomers describe it as a stellar nursery, a place where new stars are born. How the Maya could have known that two thousand years ago with only their sticks, legs, and eyes for detection is anybody's guess.

The music behind us comes to an abrupt halt, as if all three musicians decided in unison to abandon the song on the same note. The silence feels unfamiliar and deep. Then muffled applause from the guests filters up to us on the grass. Uzi comes bounding out of the dining hall and up the stairs to the lawn to switch with me when he realizes the party is coming close to an end.

Beneath my feet, tiny spiders sit tucked between the grass blades, their eyes gleaming like emerald sparks in the dark. High above in the nebula, elemental gases combine and explode to create dazzling new sources of light. Here in the middle layer, two women stand together on a vast lawn, gazing up at a narrative suspended in the sky.

Shakti pivots toward the dining hall, the beam of her headlamp casting a wide, lit-up wedge across the lawn for me to follow. Then she turns to make sure I'm behind her.

"Ready?" she says.

chapter ten
Tikal National Park, Guatemala
December 26, 2000

The entrance to Parque Nacional Tikal is shaped like a corbeled arch, a modern-day replica of the structural vaults built here two millennia ago. It looks like a tall, narrow hallway with walls that rise straight up then start slowly slanting inward until they're joined by a capstone at the top. Stick a triangle on top of a rectangle, and you've got the basic idea.

Our blue van pulls up at the entrance, next to a wooden sign that reads MA'LO' TALEL TI TIK'AL in Itza Mayan. WELCOME TO THE PLACE OF THE SPIRIT VOICES. The name "Tikal" was given to the site by nineteenth-century explorers who swore they heard voices carried by the winds. In ancient times, the city's name was Mutul, and its written glyph was a tied-bundle symbol closely resembling the hair knot worn by males of the ruling elite. So essentially, we're visiting what's left of a city named after a two-thousand-year-old hairdo. It promises to be an interesting day.

On the other side of the arch, an entry guard uses a hand pulley to lift a weighted metal pole, giving us passage into the park. We've just traveled ninety minutes from the border of Belize with five other Crystal Paradise guests. Our companions for the day are Brian the engineer and a family of four from Montreal with two twentysomething daughters. Marie, the mother in the family, keeps doting over Maya and sharing stories with me about her daughters' early illnesses. She doesn't seem the least bit fazed that we're taking Maya to Guatemala, and earlier this morning Teresa Tut assessed her as healthy enough to make the trip, but I'm still not convinced it's the right choice. Maya has been fever-free for more than twenty-four hours now, which is my benchmark for sending her back to school, but taking her into Guatemala?

"It's an easy drive," Victor said.

All that walking around in the ruins?

"I'll carry her," Uzi promised. We lugged the child backpack all the way from Los Angeles for a purpose, he said. Besides, we leave Cayo for the Caribbean coast tomorrow, and what's the point of sitting around the cabana all afternoon on our last day in the rain forest? These arguments made me feel like an insufferable killjoy. So when the Crystal Paradise van was ready to leave for the border, we joined the group headed for Tikal. A half hour later, Victor walked us through the departure hall on the Belize side of the border and passed us off to Hugo, a young Guatemalan driver in baggy khaki pants and a Jimi Hendrix T-shirt waiting for us on the other side.

The sticker on Hugo's back window reads TURISMO in jaunty, sky-blue script. This either protects us from bandits or advertises us as targets, I'm not sure which. As soon as we're settled in the van, Hugo, who speaks minimal English, starts talking to us in a fast and steady stream of Spanish, which, fortunately, Marie's older daughter, Karen, can understand.

"The ride will be about an hour and a half," she translates from the backseat. "If anyone needs the bathroom, just tell Hugo. Or I guess you should tell me, and I'll tell Hugo for you."

Karen wears a Greenpeace T-shirt, cargo shorts, and Teva sandals. Her wavy chestnut hair is cut in a no-nonsense, chin-length style. When we first met this morning, she looked back and forth between

Uzi and me and said, "You're American?" though the way she asked it was more of a statement than a question.

"Don't even talk to me about our election," I said. "I'm still recovering."

"That answers my question," she said, breaking into a smile, and we all got along fine from that point on.

The drive to Tikal cuts straight through the heart of the department of El Petén, the least populated area of the country. The Petén is the fat chimney of Guatemala, the squared-off, northernmost chunk that juts up toward Mexico. It's the poorest and largest region, occupying about one third of the country's area but containing only 3 percent of the total population. About half of the residents here are Kekchi, Mopan, and Itza Maya, pushed north into the Petén first by a program promising acreage to landless, poor Indians and later by Guatemala's thirty-six-year civil war.

The contrast between Benque Viejo del Carmen, the border town on the Belize side, and this region of Guatemala isn't quite as stark as, say, the difference between San Diego and Tijuana, but it's obvious nonetheless. In Belize you see cars everywhere. In the Petén, not as many. We share the road here with townspeople riding horses or donkeys and lots of people on foot. Unlike in Belize, where every house is made from concrete or wood, about a third of the structures we pass are built in the traditional Maya round-house style that's been used for thousands of years, with walls made of tall sticks bound together and roofs thatched with dried palm leaves. Full wash lines hang in every yard or swing between front-porch poles, where barefoot women in cotton dresses swipe at the ground with straw brooms as tight clusters of children peer from the doorways behind them.

"Why do you think everyone here does wash on the same day?" I ask Uzi.

"I think if you don't have much clothing, you do wash all the time," he says.

In the backseat, Marie and her husband close their eyes and tip their heads together to create a nap tepee. Uzi opens the past-lives book and starts a new chapter. I place my forearms on the seat in front of me, leaning forward to let Maya rest against my back, and open up my well-worn copy of *Sastun*. I'm up to chapter twenty, almost at the end of the book. Two parents have just shown up at Dr. Rosita's office with their eight-year-old daughter, who's paralyzed from the waist down after a bout with the flu. The hospital in Belmopan hasn't been able to help them, and they don't have money to take her to doctors in Guatemala or the United States. My God. Rosita diagnoses her with a pocket of infection in her spinal column, left over from the flu. Through a series of naprapathic treatments, steam baths with three local herbs, and a tincture made from local plants to combat the virus, the family and Rosita together get the child walking after six weeks, and 95 percent recovered in three months' time. Whoa.

I wonder what our trip would have been like if we hadn't missed our appointment with her, if Maya would have gotten better faster or slower, completely or not at all. The disappointment I neglected to feel when Carolyn the travel agent said she couldn't reschedule our appointment with Rosita comes to me now. If we'd been able to better describe Maya's predicament and had been able to communicate better during the treatment at Canto's cabin, perhaps we would have had a different outcome. Uzi would say everything happens for a reason, but I say it's a pity events unfolded the way they did.

I place the book in my lap and watch the Petén landscape rush by. On this side of the border, the wood-plank houses are bisected by color like national flags, the top half painted one hue and the bottom another. On the most weather-beaten homes, only the front doors are painted, a splurge of optimism against an otherwise dreary palette of gray wood. Shiny, colorful cellophane banners loop over door frames and across porches as residual Christmas cheer. CRISTO VIENE read the hand-painted wood signs nailed to houses and trees. CHRIST IS COMING.

Several times Hugo slows down to let a string of chickens or a cow safely cross the road. A light rain begins to fall. One-room stores painted turquoise or purple appear here and there with bags of chips and plastic water bottles displayed inside dark windows. Nylon hammocks scoop across nearly every front porch. CRISTO SALVA, the signs read. *CHRIST SAVES*.

Along one lonely stretch of road, a boy no more than six or seven rides a burro against traffic. His striped cotton saddlebags bulge with produce. I try to imagine Maya, three years from now, riding a horse along Topanga Canyon Boulevard alone. That is so not happening. A little farther up, a smashed van lies tipped into a ditch off the right side of the road. As we pass, I catch a glimpse of a *TURISMO* sign lying askew on the dashboard.

"*Accidente?*" I lean forward further to ask Hugo. "*Qué pasó?*"

Hugo answers over his shoulder in fast Spanish. I catch the phrase *no hay muertos*.

"Nobody died," I tell Uzi, settling back into my seat.

"*Bandidos?*" Uzi asks.

Hugo laughs out loud. "*No. Es un accidente,*" he says. "*Los bandidos no molestan a los turistas en este camino. Solo se preocupan por las drogas.*"

"Molested?" Brian the engineer's head snaps up from his guidebook. "Did he say tourists were molested?"

"*Molesta* means 'bother,'" Karen says from behind us. "He said the *bandidos* don't bother tourists here. They only care about drugs."

"Oh, *that* makes me feel better," Brian says.

"*Qué dice?*" Hugo asks.

"*Dice . . . qué le hace sentir mejor,*" Karen says.

Hugo throws his chin up and laughs. "*Bien,*" he says. "*Todos los turistas dicen lo mismo. No se preocupan. Mientras estén en la camioneta conmigo y el guía en el parque estarán seguros.*"

"What did he say?" Brian asks me. I look back at Karen, who's gazing peacefully out of the side window. She's been translating almost nonstop since we left Crystal Paradise. I don't want to bother her again.

All I caught was *No se preocupan* and *parque*. No words to worry about, such as *muertos* or *molestan*. "He said don't worry and something about the park," I say. I shift my position a little to stretch my back. Maya has been leaning against me in the same position for nearly an hour. "Beyond that, I've got no clue."

We drive out from beneath the shadow of a dark cloud, and the rain tapers off. The sky ahead of us is cloudy but bright. FARMACIA LUCKY, the sign by the side of the road reads, with an arrow pointing to the right, as we speed by.

A network of Maya city-states once stretched from Mexico's Yucatán Peninsula all the way through Belize and Guatemala down into Honduras and as far west as Chiapas, incorporating a population of millions. Slicing and dicing the territory into dozens of competing factions wasn't a terribly efficient system of government, but it managed to last for more than two thousand years. The main seats of power developed in the lowlands of southern Yucatán and northern Petén, where the great cities of Calakmul, El Mirador, Uaxactun, and Tikal flourished.

Today Tikal National Park is a UNESCO World Heritage Site sprawling across 222 square miles of Guatemalan jungle. On 23 of them sit the ruins of the ancient Maya city-state. The first Maya in the region are believed to have settled at Tikal around 2,500 years ago, creating a culture that thrived into the ninth century A.D., at which point the entire population just up and left its homes, dispersing and restructuring into small-town life. Tikal wasn't the only city where this happened; virtually every Maya city-state had emptied out by the year 900. Historians and anthropologists have long been debating why such large-scale urban abandonment might have occurred: warfare, drought, soil depletion, disease, and social revolution have been the main contenders, but no single explanation has sufficed. The palaces and temples and plazas left behind at Tikal were slowly overrun by the jungle and lay dormant for nine hundred years, existing only as legend until 1848, when a local chicle tapper chanced upon the towering temples of the lost city and ran back to tell the governor of El Petén. A century of expeditions, excavations, and restorations followed, including a thirteen-year project run by the University of Pennsylvania to map and uncover many of the four thousand known structures in the park.

Tikal is the largest excavated archaeological site in the Americas, and escorting more than 100,000 visitors per year through the ruins is a tightly run operation. Hugo pulls our van into a parking lot alongside a dozen other tourist vans and we tumble out the side door into the late-morning sun. Uzi swings the steel-frame child carrier onto his back while I reach for Maya to help her jump from the van's side door.

"Dodo goes first," she insists.

I sigh deeply and pretend to lift an invisible child from the van onto the ground. Then Maya puts her arms around my neck and I swing her onto the pavement.

"*Su muñeca*," Hugo says, handing us Hursula One from the van.

"Whew," I say, taking her. "*Gracias*. Good catch."

A stout, middle-aged man across the parking lot peels away from a cluster of other men when he sees us and heads directly for our group. "*Este es el guía*," Hugo informs us, stepping back in a perfectly choreo-graphed exchange as the man approaches.

The other guides on the curb wear cargo shorts and knit polo shirts, but our guy is dressed for a day at the office in a short-sleeved, button-down maroon shirt, formal slacks, and rubber-soled black shoes. The front of his dark hair dips up and back like an Elvis wave. It's only 10 A.M., but the temperature must already be in the eighties. A thin layer of perspiration clings to his forehead.

"*Buenos días*," the guide greets us.

"*Buenos días*," we echo.

"This morning your ride was . . ."

"Long," Brian says.

"Fine, thanks," Karen says.

"Permit for me to introduce myself. My name is Rigoberto Sanchez, I am your tour guide for this day. In this park, I have been guiding seven years. I will do my best to make this an enjoyable day, interesting day full of history for everyone. Four hours approximately we will be in the park, then on the premises we will eat lunch, after when I will return you to Hugo." His English is an interesting mix of sophisticated vocabulary and creative syntax. "Everyone now is ready to begin, yes?"

We head past a patch of grass, where three oscillated turkeys peck

at the ground, oblivious to our presence. Their feathers shine iridescent in the sunlight. Maya runs directly into their midst, flapping her
arms to provoke a response, just as she does every Friday afternoon
with the flock of pigeons that likes to caucus outside the Pacific Palisades post office. The turkeys scatter in three directions.

"Maya!" Uzi scolds her. "That's not nice to the birds!"

"Do you want to get in the backpack?" I call after her as she runs
ahead to catch up with the rest of the group. Uzi chases after her, the
empty backpack bouncing against his hips.

"Guess not," I say out loud to myself.

The walk to the ruins takes us down a wide dirt causeway littered
with small rocks and dried leaves that crackle under our hiking shoes.
The air is heavy and pungent with the scent of wet soil and rotting
leaves. Virgin jungle presses up against the path on both sides,
branches joining hands over our heads to nearly obliterate our view of
the sky. We're walking through a tube of green. This is the habitat of
spider monkeys and toucans, of jaguars and coatis. A gentle chorus
of clicking and squawking filters down to us from the canopy above.
Brian wears his binoculars around his neck but holds them in his hands
as he walks, ready to train them up toward the high branches as soon as
Rigoberto gives the sign. A birder always travels prepared.

Uzi points down to the ground, where a steady, two-lane highway
of leaf-cutter ants has blazed a four-inch-wide, bare swath through the
carpet of dead matter. I crouch down low and point it out to Maya.

"Ants," she observes with a brief glance, and keeps on walking. Her
attitude might just as well be saying, "They've got 535 kinds of butterflies here, more than a hundred species of mammals, and fifty kinds of
snakes, and the best you can come up with is *ants*?" I shrug, stand up,
and walk on.

The path is wide and clear enough for other groups to pass ours
easily. Without pressure from behind, our progress is slow. Rigoberto
stops about every hundred feet to reward us with a small packet of narration jammed with numbers and dates and facts.

"Here in the jungle, you see many trees and leaves, but this vegetation no was here in the time of the ancient Maya, why? At the largest Tikal was city of we think more than fifty thousand inhabitants, being even larger than London or Paris at those times, and land was to have been cleared for farms and houses to support so many people. But all Mayas left this city approximately 900 A.D. and then trees and vegetation grew in to cover the structures."

Maya tugs at my hand. "The man said my name," she says.

"Yes," I tell her. "The people who used to live here were called the Maya Indians. The same name as yours."

"I don't want them to have my name," she says.

"Well, that's kind of hard," I tell her, "because that's what the people who lived here called themselves. But they haven't lived here for a long time. I bet that today you're the only one here with the name Maya." She looks at me dubiously, but lets the matter drop.

". . . and more than two hundred species of bird are here at Tikal, plus many animals, jaguar too, if you are so lucky to see one," Rigoberto continues.

Brian raises his hand to shoulder level. He has an earnest, almost nerdy, desire for continuous learning. I find it kind of endearing. Every time I've seen him, he has a tour book or birding guide in his hand. I hope I'll be as willing to absorb new information in another ten years.

"I thought jaguars were nocturnal," Brian says.

"Yes," Rigoberto says. "Sometimes in the early morning they can be seen, but very rare. Next time you come, you may choose to stay at one of the lodges in the park, why? So you can walk here for more than one day. Today, we see only a little of this magnificent place, but enough for you to understand what important center it was to the Maya who lived here and around here."

"Did we consider staying for a night?" Uzi asks me as the group starts walking again.

"We could have done a night down the road in Flores, but we wanted to keep it simple," I remind him. "You don't remember?"

"Next time," he says. There won't be a next time, and we both know it—this is the kind of place remote and unique enough to visit just once in a lifetime—but saying "next time" creates an open-ended vista, an absence of closure, that we both prefer. Uzi tosses his arm around my shoulder and the empty backpack bumps against the side of my head. Maya races ahead to catch up with the group, then stops in the middle of the trail to cough. It's not as loud or as deep as a few days ago, but it's still phlegmy and turns some heads in a group of tourists heading the other way.

"Can we put her in the backpack soon?" I ask Uzi. "I'm getting a little worried about all this running around."

"She's fine," he says.

I watch my husband loping through the forest, with the air of calm serenity and quiet interest in his surroundings that he carries everywhere he goes. In his version of these past two days, we had a child with a problem, we took her to a bush doctor, and now she's fine. Problem, solution, positive outcome: that's the standard, predictable sequence in Uzi's world. He is nothing if not consistent, like a box you open every holiday to find precisely the same present inside. Open me up, on the other hand, and the gift you get depends on the holiday, the season, the temperature in the room, the day of my menstrual cycle, and the amount of time since my last cup of coffee. I'm not so easily convinced that Maya is fine. Better, granted. But not fine.

Maya marches ahead of us in her little flowered pants, long-sleeved denim shirt, and pink-and-white sneakers. Her pace is starting to lag a little. I'm the only one who can detect the subtle slowdown, the slight slump of her shoulders, the way the right toe of her sneaker drags behind her every eighth or ninth step.

Rigoberto stops at the foot of an enormous pale gray tree trunk with buttresses so large they look like a giant webbed foot.

"Here we have the ceiba tree, also known as the kapok, sacred tree of the Maya," he tells us.

"He said my name again!" Maya cries at my thigh. "I want him to stop saying my name!"

"Shh," I tell her, ruffling her curls with my hand. "He's talking about the tree, not you."

"When it is young the trunk has many thorns so animals no can attack the bark, but this ceiba is mature, thirty meters in height. One hundred feet almost."

We tip our heads back in unison. The trunk juts straight up like a perfect cylinder for at least fifty feet without interruption. And what's going on with the branches up there? Each one looks as if it's wearing a furry brown sleeve.

"Up there, you see air plants on the branches," Rigoberto says, anticipating the question before anyone can ask it. "They grow on the tree like a parasite, without soil, just needing light and water up so high. Many times they are growing on a ceiba. Any questions, okay?"

There are no questions. We keep walking.

"I didn't know plants could grow without soil and still be plants," I say to Rigoberto as we fall into step in the middle of the group.

"These are special kinds of plant," he says. "Also known as epiphytes."

"You're a botanist?"

He shakes his head. "No, no. In university, I studied anthropology. The plants I know just from being here. But I like to talk about them so you can learn more than just the history."

"Do you live near the park?"

"No, in Cobán, about four hours' driving."

"That's some commute," I say.

"There is much to do here every day. So here I am during the week and with my family just on the weekend."

For about four months last year Uzi flew to New York every Tuesday morning and came home late every Friday night. The kind of separation Rigoberto is describing can't be easy on any family.

"How many children do you have?" I'm genuinely interested, but I know that sometimes my curiosity is misinterpreted as an interrogation. *No more questions*, I tell myself.

"Four, but not little like yours. My smallest one almost is fourteen. You have just the one?"

"So far," I say.

"Children are a blessing. You must to have more so you will be even more blessed. Ah, here we are." He stops in front of a small, scrappy tree by the side of the trail and pulls off a few leaves. He crushes them between his fingers and extends his arm to us. "Who knows this smell?" he asks, as we obediently line up for a sniff. He brings his hand down low so Maya can bring her nose close, too.

"Cookies?" she says.

She's right: the scent is reminiscent of gingerbread. There's something strikingly familiar about it, but I can't put my finger on exactly what it is. Not cinnamon. Not nutmeg. Almost like an aromatic dark tea.

"Some kind of spice," Brian says.

"Cloves?" Marie guesses.

"Very close," Rigoberto says. "Allspice. People think 'allspice' is meaning many spices but only it is one. Here the leaves of allspice are used for many things, often in tea to help with the stomach. Also some people chew them for toothaches. Very useful leaves."

Brian raises his hand. "Can I take some?" he asks.

"Some few," Rigoberto says. He watches while Brian pulls a few leaves from a branch and stuffs them into his fanny pack.

A short distance up the trail, the path widens and splits, allowing the sky to reappear overhead. We stop in front of a pole structure with a corrugated tin roof, shielding an illustrated map the size of a trucker's windshield. The time it takes to walk each trail is indicated on each yellow path. While we wait for the tour group standing in front of the map to move on, Rigoberto revs up the narration. There is to be no wasted time today.

"Before we go in the park, I will give you short history of the Maya who lived here, so you know a little of background. First Mayas settled here around 600 B.C. and began to build structures that are under what plazas and pyramids we see today. From 600 B.C. to approximately

250 A.D. is what we call Preclassic Period, followed by from 250 A.D. to 900 A.D. is what we call Classic Period. In all these times, Mayas built more than four thousand structures, and six pyramids tall like sky-scrapers, four you will see today. Later part of Classic Period is known as Late Classic, also what we call *Golden Age of Tikal*." He says this slowly and with great emphasis. "Most of what you will see at Tikal today is from Golden Age, which was lasting for one hundred thirty-five years and for six kings of Tikal until the city got abandoned. Then from 900 A.D. until the coming of Spanish conquerors in 1500s is what we call Postclassic Period, with no one left living here at Tikal."

The guide ahead of us finishes and herds his group down the path to the left. Rigoberto steps up to the map and points to a spot roughly in the middle.

"This is where we are here," he says, pointing to a painted hut marked GARITA DE CONTROL. He slides his finger along a thin, yellow path marked "10 MIN" through the painted trees until it comes to rest at two small white triangles in a row. "Here we start with Complex Q. Only one pyramid here have been uncovered, which you can climb up it. Then Complex R. Complex R not have been uncovered. And next up here, North Zone, where you will see pyramid with temple on top, a little older, built around 700 A.D., *Golden Age of Tikal*. There you will get idea of what kind of a structure they used for ceremonies at Tikal. And then." He runs his finger down and to the left, along a trail marked "20 MIN" that ends behind a white pyramid labeled in red type TEMPLO II. "And here just to the south probably will be one of the highlights of your day. This is Main Plaza of Tikal, what is this? Main Plaza is most important political and religious plaza Mayas introduced around whole city. Built also in *Golden Age of Tikal*. Remember, Tikal was not mostly for residential purposes, but was *ceremonial center* of the region, where religious events and calendar ceremonies were held for all the people. And here on east side of Main Plaza we have located Temple One, which is most popular building from Tikal, Temple of the Great Jaguar, at height one hundred and forty-five feet. Right across we have Temple Two, smaller a little. They are facing one each other, they are only temples totally uncovered in Tikal, but Temple One is no allowed for hiking, why? The staircase of that building is original, the steps they are not in a good condition, some time some people fell down, so that's why they don't let us hike Temple One. But you can do Temple Two."

Maya is crouched down on her haunches drawing in the dirt with a stick. I notice she's holding three small rocks she's collected in her left hand.

"This looks like an awful lot of walking," I whisper to Uzi.

"Don't worry, I'll carry her."

". . . and then we hike around here to Temple Four. This is tallest temple in all of Tikal, how tall? Two hundred and twelve feet. From the top you will find most beautiful photo of jungle with pyramids coming up from the trees, making you see why Tikal has got the nickname, 'Manhattan of the Maya.'"

"How much of this are you getting?" I whisper to Uzi.

"People who built pyramids lived here a long time ago," he whispers back. "They don't live here anymore."

"Exactly."

". . . lunch on the premises, after which your driver will take you home," Rigoberto concludes. "Any questions, okay?"

There are no questions. Rigoberto nods and smiles. "Then moving now along!" he announces. He makes an "after you, please" gesture with both hands to guide us toward the path to the right.

"Maya, are you ready for the backpack?" I ask. She nods and raises her arms to Uzi, who crouches down so I can lift her into the pack on his back. Her legs pop through the designated holes and she shifts around a little to find a comfortable position. Uzi pushes off the ground and stands up in one motion. That would kill my thighs, but he makes it look easy.

"Do you want me to hold your rocks?" I ask Maya as we follow the group.

She clutches them tighter in her hand and presses her fist against her chest. "They're Dodo's," she says.

I step off the trail to the right to let a pickup truck pass. The path to Complex Q is narrower than the causeway that led into the park and winds up a slight hill. In here, it's more like a rugged day hike through the jungle.

"I can hold them for Dodo. You'll be more comfortable there with your hands free," I say.

She whips her head from side to side. "Dodo says no. He doesn't like you."

Uzi shoots me a little *uh-oh* look to indicate he heard, but I'm stuck on that last sentence. Dodo doesn't *like* me? I feel a small, irrational twinge of injustice upon hearing it. What did I ever do to Dodo? Well, besides trying to get rid of him. Okay: I just answered my own question.

"What about Dad? Does he like Dad?" I ask Maya. I'm wondering if Uzi is being held in the same low esteem.

"Hey," Uzi says. "Don't drag me into this. I didn't do anything."

"Dodo doesn't care about Daddy," Maya says. "He doesn't like you."

"That figures," I say. "*Everyone* blames the mother."

Maya scrunches up her nose in confusion. "What?" she asks.

"Oh, stop it," Uzi says. "No one's blaming you."

"Dodo's blaming me."

"Dodo's not real!" he says, exasperated.

"Dodo is too real!" Maya shouts, whacking Uzi in the back of the head with her free hand.

"Ow!" he yells.

"Oh, my God!" I say. "Enough! I'm going up there to walk with the normal people!"

I double-time it to the head of the group and fall into step beside Rigoberto, who's walking with Marie and her husband, George. "The kings were building them for celebration after every twenty years," Rigoberto says.

"What are we talking about?" I whisper to Marie.

"Twin pyramids," she whispers back. "Like the ones we're going to see. They're unique to Tikal."

"They built them every twenty years?" George asks. "Then there should be a lot of them here."

"Only seven that have been found," Rigoberto says, "but some pyramids got built on top of parts of old pyramids. We call it 'onion construction system' with buildings superimposed on top of each other. So underneath a pyramid we see can be more."

The day is warming up fast, even through the clouds. I wiggle out of my denim shirt and tie it around my waist. I glance back quickly at Uzi and Maya, who look fine. Uzi is wearing a windbreaker underneath the child backpack. He must be getting hot.

Ahead of us the path bends to the left, exposing a large grassy hill on our right. We walk along its side, and then *whoa*, that's not what I was expecting at all.

The hill isn't really a hill, it's a pyramid in disguise. Five platforms are stacked in layer-cake style, each ascending one slightly smaller than the one underneath. If you stand at just the right spot on the side of the hill, it's like looking at a split screen. To the left: ancient stone pyramid. To the right: overgrown hill. Pyramid, hill; pyramid, hill. It's an architectural wonder emerging from a hill, or flip the switch and it's a hill encroaching on a pyramid with a predatory determination. How a team of archaeologists could extract all this from a pile of so much nothing looks like a feat no less remarkable than building the thing in the first place.

Only the front of the pyramid has been excavated, revealing a steep rise of thirty-nine wide stone steps that lead straight up the center. In front of the steps a line of five-foot-tall stone markers stand in a row like oversized tombstones, eight in a row. The ninth stands in front like a dance teacher who wants the students behind her to follow her moves. Corresponding circles of stone lie in front of each tombstone, shaped like enormous wheels of cheese. All the stone surfaces are cracked and blackened, as if a wildfire passed through the jungle years ago. That's because the Maya here built with limestone, Rigoberto tells us, and over time limestone weathers to a dark gray.

"What was the original color?" Brian asks.

"Light," Rigoberto says. "Which then it had white stucco on top and on top again red paint." It occurs to me that I haven't seen a red house anywhere in Guatemala or Belize. Maybe red is reserved for holy sites?

We cluster tightly in front of one of the gravestones, which aren't gravestones at all, Rigoberto explains. Nothing here is what it seems: we're so far outside our cultural frames of reference that our guesses are all wrong. These vertical slabs are called stelae, on which dates and historical events were often carved. Walking into the park, we'd listened to Rigoberto talk about the ruins out of mild curiosity and politeness, but now, faced with the genuine article, our collective interest level has been cracked open wide. Even Maya, clinging to Uzi's back like a symbiotic creature, leans forward intently as Rigoberto speaks.

"This pyramid here dates from the rule of King Chitam, a great king during Golden Age of Tikal, who dedicated this pyramid in the year 771, why? It was to celebrate the end of a twenty-year cycle called *katun*. When twenty years ended, the king would build pyramids like this to make a celebration, and to say 'Hey, I am the king who has the success to lead you into this new time!' This is a radial pyramid having four stairs, one to each side, but only one of the stairs have been excavated, the one we are seeing. Over there is another pyramid like this one, under that mountain of dirt. Maya built these pyramids to face each other from east and west, they built them also with buildings on north and south of plaza to honor all four directions. Over there, on north side, was direction of sky and also of kings and there we see Building of the Heavens." We swing our heads to the right. All that's left of the original building is what looks like a high stone fence with a corbeled entry arch.

"Inside this north building you will find Stela Twenty-two, with picture carving of Chitam, this is how we know he is the one who built these pyramids," Rigoberto continues. "Stela Twenty-two is a copy, the original is in the Tikal Museum near the entrance which maybe you will see on your way out. In front of Stela Twenty-two is an altar, always the stela and altar come together like two. And there in the south"—he makes a sweeping gesture back toward a low, wide, crumbled structure on the other side of the entry road—"is South Building, the Palace of Nine Doorways, very common to Maya—"

Maya whops Uzi on the ear again. "The man said my name!" she shouts. Rigoberto pauses and the whole group turns to look at us.

"She's having a problem with hearing her name so much," I say. "It's okay. Go on." I grab hold of Maya's wrist and squeeze it lightly. "Stop it, Maya," I whisper loudly.

"If you look closely, you count nine doorways, Ma—people who lived here," Rigoberto corrects himself, with a glance in Maya's direction, "believed in nine lords of underworld so there are nine doorways, one for each one. Now. The open way of this plaza here suggests its use was for public function, to celebrate ending of the *katun*. At this time, people would come from far away for dancing and ceremony but only king and priests could go to top of pyramid, not all the people. Most of Ma—the life here was happening outside, this is why all the rooms are dark and small as you will later see. But now you will know what it is like to go up the pyramid like a king and look at people down under." He pauses and exhales heavily, as if winded by his own narration. "Before the exploring, you have questions, okay?"

"How were the pyramids built?" asks Brian the engineer.

"This is good question," Rigoberto says, "and tells how many people once must have lived at Tikal, because the bigger pyramids like especially Temple Four would take many, many people to build and maybe even years. And remember, the people of Tikal were to build these pyramids not with wheels or beasts of burden or tools of metal, but only with limestone and tools of flint and the power of man using many blocks of stone, and then also it would take many people to keep the pyramids clean and painted and not to let the jungle grow back on top of them."

"There must have been a whole working class just for this," Karen says.

"Yes, many common people who must have lived in small houses around the city, some of which have been excavated," Rigoberto says.

"Now. It is fine to climb up this pyramid here so you can pretend to be king for this day. Later when you climb Temple Four, whoa you will be high, and you can feel it even more. Please when climbing stay only on the steps and the top for safety and to preserve the stones. Also it is good to go and look at the north and south buildings, but please not to climb on the pyramid not uncovered so as not to disturb what is underneath."

The group starts moving toward the east pyramid in unison. Uzi crouches down so I can pull Maya out of the carrier. The sun presses down on our heads, heavy and hot. I set Maya down on the ground next to me and extract a small baseball hat for her from the backpack's outer pocket. "Do you want to take her up?" Uzi asks.

I look up at the top of the pyramid. It's probably seventy feet above the plaza floor. The steps have no railing and no obvious places to stop and rest. I was once so afraid of heights that looking over a second-floor atrium railing in a shopping mall made me so queasy I had to sit down immediately. I've gotten better in the past few years, mostly out of sheer determination, but I don't think I should push my luck.

"I'll sit this one out," I say, fixing the hat on top of Maya's head. She pulls it off. I take it from her hand and put it back on. "You want to take her?"

"Okay," he says, extending his hand to Maya. I watch them start the ascent, and when I see that Uzi is holding her hand tight, I wander over to investigate the ruin on the north side of the plaza. Inside the ring of crumbled wall a single, vertical stela with a round altar at its base stands sheltered underneath a triangular thatched-roof structure. A crude, square fence of sticks around it keeps people from getting too close to the stone. Most of the carving on this stela has eroded away, but I can make out what looks like an elaborate headdress in the upper right portion, a man's profile underneath it, and to the left of the profile, a vertical rectangle filled with carved designs.

"You can't see here, but Chitam, he was a big fat guy," says Rigoberto, from my right elbow. He must have followed me over. "Very unusual for the Maya, who were a small people." He holds a flat hand up to about my collarbone to demonstrate the average height. "You see he is looking at the west? That is direction of the underworld, all rulers look that way on stelae, maybe to see where they will one day go." He leans over and rests his forearms on the stick railing. "And right there, to left of the face, this is the writing. You can see?"

I lean over for a better angle. The carved rectangle is divided into columns of squares, six squares high and two squares wide. I can make out some bars and dots, but the rest looks like elaborately carved pebbles. I can't imagine how long it must have taken to craft a single word.

"Do you know what it says?" I ask.

"It tells about Chitam becoming king on 25 December 768 . . ."

"That was yesterday," I say.

Rigoberto briefly looks upward, as if consulting a sky calendar, and nods. "So it is," he says. "One can think then it was a day like this one. Also the writing I think says, 'We had completed twenty more years here together with me now as your king.' Carving like this was how they kept the history."

"They didn't have books to write in?" I ask. "That would have been a lot easier."

"They had many we think, but the Spanish when they came burned all the books because to them the Maya religion was from the Devil. And others came apart from water and air . . . disintegrate, I believe you say. So there are four books only existing now, of all the books once that were."

Images of books tossed into bonfires come to me from World War II–era film reels. We stare at the stela silently.

"I'm a writer," I say, "and this looks like the most difficult form of writing I've ever seen."

"Some is symbols, some is words, and some is pieces of words, very complicated a system of writing, very hard to read."

"Very hard to *write*." Compare this to typing on a computer keyboard, and man, do I have it easy.

"The scribes also were the artists, and they were held in very high reputation, doing a sacred art."

"Not in Los Angeles," I say. "In Los Angeles, writers are the low men on the totem pole."

"Ha! That is very funny to say, but not here at Tikal. Writers were very up high, doing a sacred act, maybe even they were part of the royal families, too. Did you see here, on the altar?" He points at the round slab of stone lying on the ground. "It is hard to find, but on it there is carved pictures of war captureds with hands tied."

I can see only the barest outlines of figures on its sides. "Is this where they cut the victims' hearts out?"

Rigoberto shakes his head in a tight little motion. "That was Aztecs," he says. He seems a little ruffled, as if I've offended him with the question. "But the Mayas did sacrifice, too, to offer blood to the gods. Only I tell about it when people ask, because sometimes it makes families sad to know."

"I guess it's not the most civilized chapter of their history."

"We think 'civilized' because we think we are here," he lifts his hand just above his head. "But the way I see things, a culture, it changes and grows over many years. Once there was sacrifice of people, then it was sacrifice of animals, now the Maya are modern like you and me and some of the young ones choose against eating animals. I have the most interest in parts that survive. The pyramids here, they are pyramids built for kings, but also for purpose to watch the stars and the sun and to bring people close to Heaven, to be connected to the spirit. The rest is like waves in the ocean, come and go, come and go. But all this here that you see, this is coming from the ocean itself."

Back on the plaza, Uzi and Maya are making their way slowly down the pyramid's steep stairs behind the rest of our group. Each step is so shallow Uzi has to take them sideways, and I see him trying to encourage Maya to do the same. I notice he's holding her hat. Rigoberto and I stroll back to the middle of the cleared plaza to wait for them to descend.

Maya urban planners modeled their plazas on the sacred quincunx, the four-corners-and-a-center design shaped like five points on dice. First they squared the space to honor the four cardinal directions, then they planted a ceiba tree in the middle to represent the central axis of the universe. In this way, they created heavenly, sacred space on earth for fifteen hundred years, but they didn't bargain for impermanence. By the late ninth century, they had left all their plazas, and if a ceiba tree was ever planted and cared for here at Complex Q, no sign of it remains.

Uzi and Maya reach the bottom of the stairs, and Maya makes a beeline across the grass to hug my thighs. Uzi jogs up behind her and hands me her hat.

"Mommy! We went up *high*."

"What did you see?"

"Nothing."

"What did it look like?" I ask Uzi.

"It was pretty. Mostly the tops of trees. There was just grass and dirt at the top. Maya wanted to run around, but I didn't want to risk it, so we just took a fast look and came back down."

"I forgot to give you the camera," I say.

"That's okay. I had my hands full."

Rigoberto claps twice and makes a reverse herding motion with both arms. "All right, our group!" he says. "Moving now along!"

The path between Complex Q and Tikal's North Zone is a terrarium of biodiversity, a tangled mass of trees and vines with a tunnel bored straight through. Treading on the moist earth, the air resplendent with the rich aromas of bark and wet leaves, it's not hard to see why this area was granted official protection ten years ago when the Maya Biosphere Reserve was formed.

Rigoberto keeps stopping to scan the branches overhead. Brian grips his binoculars to be ready for whatever he finds. The third time we pause, Rigoberto points at a spot directly overhead. "Up there," he says. "See them? Spider monkeys."

Brian tips back his head so far his khaki explorer hat goes tumbling down his back. I pick it up from the ground and hand it back to him.

"Where?" Uzi asks. Rigoberto steps between us and points again.

Up there? Way up high among the sun-dappled leaves, I see two dark figures, one slightly larger than the other, clinging to thin branches.

"There are three," Rigoberto says. "One of them has a baby. A monkey family."

"Where's a baby?" Maya asks from the backpack.

Brian hands his binoculars to Uzi, who takes a fast look through them and then adjusts them smaller for Maya. She holds them against her eyes and pivots her head wildly from left to right.

"Where? Where?" she asks.

"Way up," I say, gently guiding her head back with my hand.

I aim my camera at the high branches and turn it forty-five degrees to square both monkeys in the frame. It looks like a good picture through the viewfinder, but when my film is developed in two weeks' time, I will see how the sunlight played tricks with me that day, how the backlit monkeys looked dark against the leaves when I was standing on the path, but on film the picture comes out looking like an accidental shot of tree-tops where, if you look hard enough, you can barely make out two amorphous, shadowy areas that don't look like living things at all.

I slip the camera back into the zippered compartment on the backpack as Uzi starts walking away and accidentally get my fingers caught in the pouch, causing him to jerk backward and almost lose his balance.

"I'm sorry," I say. "My fault." He looked so vulnerable just then when he almost fell, my heart instinctively leapt in his direction. I plant a kiss on the shoulder of his jacket as we fall into step behind Rigoberto.

"You doing okay?" I ask.

"I'm fine. How's Maya back there?"

Maya is making Hursulas Zero and One talk to each other on either side of Uzi's head, alternating between speakers by wiggling the one that's talking.

"She's fine," I say, "but she's going to need food soon."

"I've got some granola bars in the backpack we can take out when we stop next."

"Okay. Maybe I can find some place in the park selling fruit."

"Good idea." Then he puts his arm around my shoulder and adds, just so I don't miss it, "See how agreeable I am? How did you ever find someone so agreeable?"

"As I remember it, you were standing on a street corner in New York, waiting for someone who needed an agreeable partner, and because you're so agreeable, when I came along and said, 'That one, please!' you said okay."

"I agree!" he says and kisses the side of my head. Light and witty: this is how we used to be when we first met. It feels good to slip back into the pattern again.

"How come you're being so nice to me on this trip?" he asks.

"What do you mean?" I say. "I'm always nice to you."

"Not always."

Part of me automatically resists the criticism, but a larger part wants to consider what he's saying. Despite the stresses of this trip, I haven't felt the constant, low-level resentment that eats at me at home when I'm alone with Maya and he's always at the office or away on business. Here we're on a level playing field, facing decisions and solving problems in real time together. I could live without the problems part, but if I have to face some, I'd rather face them in the same time zone as my husband.

"You've spent four solid days with us," I tell him. "We haven't seen this much of you in months. And you're engaged with what we're doing. It makes a difference."

"I'm engaged because you're being nice to me. It's not that complicated."

"And I'm being nice to you because you're acting engaged."

"Woof!" Uzi says. "The chicken or the egg?"

The path heads up a steep hill. Rigoberto guides us into a dirt clearing, and it happens again. Without any warning, a pyramid.

"Ladies and gentlemen," Rigoberto announces. "I introduce you to Tikal structure 3D-43."

This one looks nothing like the one Uzi and Maya just climbed.

Whereas the pyramid in Complex Q was square and steep, 3D-43 is rectangular and rises slowly from the plaza floor. And whereas the top of Compex Q was flat and empty, 3D-43 has the remains of a one-story temple on top. A large chunk of masonry in front of the structure has collapsed, but the rest of the building appears intact. A wide, open doorway in the center gives the impression of a gaping mouth or the entrance to a darkened cave.

The area to the right of the stairs is still buried under a slope of dirt, but the left side has been excavated to reveal five layered platforms of crudely cut limestone blocks, ranging down in size from filing cabinet to cantaloupe. The mortar between them has turned black over the ages, and a green, mossy skin climbs up the front of everything. It's a field archaeologist's work in progress, this structure 3D-43, cleared just enough for visitors to appreciate the grand gist of it.

"So here we have North Zone pyramid with temple on top," Rigoberto explains. "We think built around 700 A.D., maybe older, by who? We do not know. This is smaller pyramid temple than the great pyramids still to see, why? Also we do not know, maybe this one was used only for special ceremony or for short times. Inside the temple you will find three rooms, these are the biggest rooms found in all of Tikal, they are a little smaller than each the other as you walk back. Up there is where the king did prayers and asked for the help of gods and ancestors and to show respect."

"The king said the prayers, not the priests?" Karen asks.

"The king, he was a priest too, and also a shaman in Ma—in ancient time," Rigoberto explains. "He was busy guy. Also the ancient people believed their king had bloodline to the gods, like they were human but had some god parts, and they only were the ones who could communicate with the gods and the ancestors. The king would go up there to the temple, at the top he would do incense and he would dance and give his blood and eat no food, then in a few days he would see the gods and talk with them and get answers and make protection for the people. To the Maya"—I check to see if Maya caught the slip, but she doesn't seem to have noticed—"the temple was a . . . how do you say? A special place opening where the king could go up to Heaven and the Heaven could come down?"

"A portal?" Uzi guesses.

"Yes. This is what they were believing. Now in the three rooms up top, if you look at the walls there you can see drawings by ancient people, maybe from the shaman kings even, maybe when they were in special mind state, so look closely to see. Okay. Any questions?"

There are no questions. Everyone just wants to climb. Uzi sits on a tree stump so I can lift Maya from the backpack carrier. "Do you want to do this one?" he asks. I can tell from the slight hesitation in his voice that he's hoping I'll take Maya, so he can explore the top alone this time.

I shield my eyes from the sun and peer at the pyramid steps. They're wider than the ones at Complex Q and not terribly steep, and the temple door is only about forty feet above the plaza. The rooms at the top look dark and slightly ominous, but the graffiti in them might be worth the effort.

"Maybe," I say. "You can leave Maya down here with me, if you want."

"I want to go up," she says.

"Maybe in a little while," I say. "Let's go look at those big rocks over there."

Across the plaza, a group of broken stelae lie rakishly in the dirt like stone driftwood washed up on a landlocked beach. We circle the limestone fragments, but there isn't anything more to see there, so we walk back into the plaza. At the top of the temple stairs, Uzi, Brian, Marie, George, Karen, and Karen's sister are posing in a row while Rigoberto stands in the plaza and snaps a photo of them with Marie's camera. "One more!" I shout, pulling our camera from my bag. I snap a fast shot before they wave and disappear one by one into the temple's dark interior.

"Bye, Daddy!" Maya shouts.

"She doesn't want to go up?" Rigoberto asks. He stands in front of a grove of young trees with his arms crossed, slowly rocking back and forth on his feet. No matter how much history this place contains, it's got to be tedious to steer groups of foreigners from ruin to ruin every day, reciting the same dates and facts.

"She does. It's me who's not so sure."

"Ah, you can go! This one is like a trainer. You go up this one for training to climb Temple Four."

"Not me. I won't be climbing Temple Four." I don't know exactly what climbing Temple Four involves, but he's already told us it's the tallest temple at Tikal and that's as much information as I need.

"Everyone wants to climb Temple Four," Rigoberto says. "It is the Manhattan of the Maya!"

I whip my head around to make sure Maya didn't hear him say her name again, just in time to see her taking off toward the pyramid, her little elbows pumping with determination. How did she just get from here to there so fast?

"Where are you going?" I shout, chasing after her.

"Up!" she calls over her shoulder. What chutzpah this child packs, in such a small frame.

"Not by yourself!" I look to the top of the pyramid for Uzi, but he's still inside the temple. Maya starts heading up the wide stone stairs, carefully picking her way up one by one.

Okay. I guess I'm going up. At the base of the stairs I cast a quick glance back at Rigoberto, who raises a hand in acknowledgment.

I step onto the first rough, black step. It's nowhere near deep enough for my size-ten shoe, so I angle my body to the right and slowly sidestep my way up. My hands instinctively reach out to both sides in search of something to grasp. A few steps above me, Maya climbs straight up, steady and sure, her little pink-and-white sneakers a perfect fit on the shallow stairs. I drop my butt a few inches and creep up another two steps, then pause. I don't trust my sense of balance at all. I must look like a lunatic from down below with my surfer's stance. I steal a fast glance at Rigoberto, who gives me an encouraging wave.

That wasn't such a good idea, to look down. I concentrate on my feet beneath me. Left foot up, right foot follows. Left foot up, right foot follows.

"Maya?" I call out after about eight of these slow steps, just to hear her voice.

"Maya?" I call a little louder, when she doesn't respond.

I stop and look up, doing a little tightrope wobble with my arms to stay stable, as both Hursulas go bouncing past me down the limestone steps, tumbling heads over toes. About six or seven steps above me, Maya has both hands pressed against her eyes as if she's playing peek-a-boo with someone higher up, but why would she be doing that here? and just as I realize there's absolutely no reason why she'd be doing that here, the bloodcurdling scream from the bush doctor's cabin fills the space just below structure 3D-43.

Oh, sweet Jesus. Not again.

"Maya? What is it?" I shout, trying to make my way up to her faster. In my haste, the arch of my right shoe nicks the side of a step and I hurtle forward, landing hard on my left elbow and left hip. For a substance that can be cut by flint, limestone is shockingly hard. I bump gracelessly down two steps, my hands trying to make purchase against the rough, mossy stone. From the corner of my eye, I see Rigoberto's maroon shirt heading off to the right. He's leaving us? *Now?*

I crawl back up the stairs to Maya and grab her around the knees. She twists away from me, her mouth an ugly grimace.

"What is it? What happened?" I ask.

"No!" she shrieks, pointing toward the top of the pyramid. *"No, no, no!"*

I look toward the temple, but all I see is the gaping black entry door. "There's nothing there," I tell her. "It's just a door. Look!" She twists the upper half of her body from left to right in a full-body "no" with such force I'm afraid she's going to topple over.

Damn it. Damn it, damn it, damn it. Of all the places she's ever melted down, this has got to be the most inexplicable and least manageable. Why do I keep finding myself in these situations alone? Why is nobody—not Uzi, not my parents or family or friends—ever here to help when I need it most? If I were the kind of person who believed in "the universe," maybe I'd say it's because I alone have something to learn, but even if I were that kind of person, damn it again, you'd think I would have learned whatever it is I'm supposed to learn by now. Why can't my lesson be one of collaboration, rather than continual self-reliance?

There's no way I can carry Maya down all these steps myself. I have to get her to calm down first. "Come to Mommy," I say, extending my hand to her, but she smacks it away. "No!" she howls again and again, "No! No! No!" like a broken siren.

I scoot across the steps on my butt and reach for her again. This must be what it feels like to be physically disabled when mobility becomes an imperative: panicked, helpless, stuck. Marie steps out of the temple door, sees me struggling with Maya, turns around and walks back in.

"No!" Maya shouts. *"No, no!"*

Rigoberto comes bounding up the steps on a sharp diagonal, taking them two at a time. So that's where he was heading. He's breathing heavily when he reaches us. His front hair wave dangles rakishly over his right eye.

"What happens?" he asks.

"No!" Maya shouts, clamping both hands over her ears. *"No!"*

"I don't know. She won't stop screaming," I tell him. "I can't get her down."

"Maybe she lets me." He reaches his hand out to Maya, who does three quick little side steps in the opposite direction and screams again.

"What's going on?" Uzi calls from the top of the stairs, Marie right behind him.

"I don't know!" I yell back. "She won't go up, and I can't get her down!"

He hurries sideways down the steps. "What the hell, Maya?" he says. Maya takes a swing at him when he reaches for her, but he's faster. He tosses her over his shoulder like a sack of flour and descends steadily, one step at a time, oblivious to her fists pounding against his back.

"I want everyone to stop saying my name!" she wails as he whisks her away. "I want them to stop saying my name!"

Brian, Marie, and the others make their way down to me. "What happened?" Brian asks.

"I don't know. We were climbing up, and then she started screaming." I press my hands against my chest to slow down my heart. "I just need a minute," I say.

Marie pats my shoulder while the rest of the group waits. When I'm ready to stand, Rigoberto offers his arm and I cling to it for balance as we pick our way down the stairs. My left hip aches hard where it collided with the stone. On the plaza, Uzi is crouching in front of Maya, who has stopped crying and is now wiping her nose with the back of her hand.

"She looks okay now," Karen says.

"She does?" I can't look down. Right foot, left foot. Right foot, left foot. Stay focused and upright.

"She will be fine," Rigoberto says, as he swoops down to pick up Hursula Zero from the final stair. We take the last step onto the plaza, where I release his arm with a thank-you, and bend down to retrieve Hursula One from the grass. "I have seen it, sometimes, children who get scared here," he says.

"What causes it?"

He raises both shoulders. "Who can know?"

Uzi waves at us as we approach. "It's okay," he says, trying to sound upbeat. "She's fine. She was fine as soon as she got off the stairs." He tilts his head in her direction with a wry smile. "Maya ruins Guatemala," he says, giving me a little elbow jab to extract a laugh. But I'm not in the mood for humor right now, and he can tell.

I may not understand what I just witnessed on those stairs or be able to adequately convey Maya's terror to a father who didn't see it, but I do know this: despite all we've tried to do for her so far, our child is not "fine." Tomorrow morning we will leave Cayo, and five days later we will leave Belize, and when we get back to California, nothing will be different, and nothing will be fine. Nothing.

"Uzi," I say. "Honey. She is not fine."

My husband stares at me for a long moment. The skin between his eyebrows pinches and rises just slightly, the hurt, confused look of a child who's been misunderstood. That's when, for the first time, I see past his facade of steady certainty to a hidden, vulnerable core of doubt. He knows Maya isn't fine. He knows. And now we both know that his calmness isn't unchecked optimism or willful self-delusion but an attempt to protect us from what we both know. Mostly to protect me.

"All right," Rigoberto says, with less enthusiasm than usual. "Moving now along!"

I look from left to right. "Where's Maya?" I ask.

Uzi points to the center of the plaza, where Maya is standing with her arms extended outward, her face lifted to the sky. She does one slow, full revolution, then another, graceful and controlled. The rest of the group stops to look at her, too. She is the flowering World Tree, the mighty ceiba that anchors the quincunx. The center of the cosmos. Our child. She is the point around which all the stars revolve.

For weeks after my mother died in the summer of 1981, my father couldn't bring himself to clear out her dresser or her closet. The first snow had fallen before he was able to pack up the items she'd left on her side of the bed. For a man who rarely showed his devotion or even simple affection in front of others, his grief seemed to have no bounds. Even for a teenager, it was heartbreaking to watch. Yet it also made me uncomfortable and impatient. One year, two years, three years after her death, he couldn't get back into a predictable family groove. Ten years later, he still couldn't talk about her death without crying. And his drinking, which had been daily but moderate when she was alive, became heavier each year after she died.

At thirty-six, I can understand his devastation in a way I never could have at seventeen. Physical demonstrativeness, as I've learned, is only one gauge of devotion, and often a misleading one at that. Yes, I may complain about my husband's behavior, I may roll my eyes at his beliefs, I may even entertain random fantasies of leaving him to live more simply as a single mother. Nonetheless. If he were to leave me, I would find a way to survive, but if he were to die? I don't think I would ever recover. I'm not sure I could do more than barely exist. I'm often careless about showing it, but such is the depth of my love.

Perhaps the last half hour with Maya has left me feeling raw and exposed, primed for thinking this way, or maybe it's just the sheer, awe-inspiring immensity of the Plaza and the love story of its two high temple pyramids that bring on this state of poignant melancholy. When Rigoberto walks our group into the Plaza, the first things we see are Temples One and Two facing each other in an east-west axis across a large expanse of grass. Directly to the north sits the North Acropolis, a series of rising platforms where sixteen smaller temples once stood. At the southeast edge of the plaza lies a collection of ruined palaces that once housed noble families and administrative offices. The scale of the place is nearly unimaginable. We are just tiny ants crawling around a ruined metropolis. In nine months, when I see photos of minuscule rescue workers scaling the monolithic piles of debris that once formed the World Trade Center, I will remember this scene.

Rigoberto assembles us at the corner of Temple Two to tell us the story of King Hasaw, also known as Ah Cacau, or Lord Chocolate. He was the grandfather of King Chitam and the ruler who pulled Tikal out of a century of depressed domination by a neighboring city-state to restore it to its earlier splendor. When he married Lady Twelve Macaw, a noblewoman from a neighboring city, their union cemented a political alliance and merged two powerful family lines.

Even for Maya nobility, Lord Chocolate led a life of extreme privilege. He stood nearly a foot taller than his subjects, which meant he'd had more and better food to eat than others and that his children had a higher likelihood of surviving to adulthood. Unlike the majority of Tikalites, most of whom lived in small houses made of sticks or stones, his residence was a duplex stone palace. He wore robes fashioned from jaguar pelts and necklaces heavy with jade. And he adored his beautiful wife, his "precious flower," who bore him a son in the year 691, on the night of a new moon. When she died young in the year 703, Lord Chocolate commissioned a 122-foot pyramid in her honor, taller than any structure attempted before at Tikal. In an unconventional urban planning move, he placed her pyramid on the western edge of the Plaza instead of on the North Acropolis, which had always been the traditional resting place for the nobility.

Today, Lady Twelve Macaw's pyramid is prosaically known as Temple Two, or the Temple of the Masks, after the extravagantly carved masks on its facade. Its three fat platforms support a three-room temple on top. On a massive limestone roofcomb, a wall of stone that extends up from the back half of the temple roof, Lord Chocolate had artists carve a likeness of his departed queen facing east, the direction of the rising sun. (This was the Maya version of a portrait over the mantle, only eighty times as labor-intensive and one hundred times as large.)

Lord Chocolate lived for at least another thirty years, ruling for fifty-two years in total—an eternity in Maya history. When he died, he was buried in a tomb on the east side of the Grand Plaza, directly across the plaza from Temple Two. On top of his burial site a second towering pyramid was built, probably erected by his son Yik'in. This one—known as Temple One, or the Temple of the Giant Jaguar—is the iconic image of Tikal found on every postcard, its nine steep terraces built to represent the nine layers of the underworld. Carved into its imposing roofcomb on top is a portrait of Lord Chocolate holding his sun shield and his royal scepter, facing west toward the setting sun. And so the images of Lady Twelve Macaw and Lord Chocolate were literally set in stone on opposite sides of the Grand Plaza, to gaze at each other into eternity as testimony to the enduring power of their love.

"Would you build one of those for me if I died?" I whisper to Uzi.

"Absolutely. Even bigger."

"Make sure my hair looks good in the carving. Blow-dried straight, the way I like it."

He laughs. "Okay," he says. "I promise."

I reach up to the backpack and stroke Maya's hair, feeding her crackers and bottled water as Rigoberto sets us free for the next twenty minutes to explore the Grand Plaza on our own. We can climb Temple

Two but not Temple One, he reminds us. "People have died from falling down from the stairs there," he tells us again.

Uzi and I don't need the deterrent, since neither of us has the inclination to climb anything after our last escapade. We release Maya to run across the grass, and she takes off clutching Hursulas Zero and One under her arms. The plaza is about the size of a football field, maybe a little smaller. "Don't go too far!" I call after her.

A Guatemalan family walks past us in a tight three-abreast formation, the older man and teenage boy in Western clothing flanking an older woman whose hair falls down her back in a long black braid. She wears a traditional Maya *huipil*, an embroidered square-cut blouse, woven in shades of red, green, and blue. When she sees me looking at her, she smiles and shyly looks down. Her face is deeply creased, the countenance of an elder, and I'm reminded of how little time I spend in the company of older women. If my mother were alive, she'd have turned sixty-two this year. That's a piece of data I can't seem to properly digest, no matter how many times I try. I get stuck chewing on how implausible it seems.

I watch Maya burn off energy by running figure eights between two rows of stelae lined up on the plaza's north side. Some of them are shielded from the elements by small thatched roofs held up by pole frames. Behind them, another wide, stone staircase leads up to the North Acropolis, which supports a series of crumbled temples connected by platforms and stairs that rise, fall, and turn like something out of an Escher drawing. It's a light day for visitors, too close to Christmas to draw much of a crowd. About forty people stroll across the grass and wander up and down the sequential levels of stairs. Tourists in baseball caps and sneakers with backpacks slung over their shoulders dot the stone staircases. Everywhere I look, someone is posing for a photograph or standing atop a ruined temple with arms raised in a victorious Y, Rocky Balboa–style. Two women crouch in front of a low, rectangular thatched-roof structure on the middle platform and stick their cameras through the gaps between its supporting sticks to get a shot of something inside.

The plaza today contains probably about a twentieth of the activity that would have taken place here during the Golden Age. The Grand Plaza was the nexus of Tikal, and to a visitor from a smaller town or to overland traders stopping here on their way from the Caribbean to the Pacific, the sheer majesty of the city's layout must have been a phenomenal sight. The plaza beneath our feet would have been plastered white instead of covered with grass and dirt, and the air would have been filled with the loud hum of priests, city officials, and townspeople going about their daily business rather than the low drones of tour guides. The temples, instead of displaying aged and crumbling stone, would have been plastered smooth and painted red. At ritual ceremonies, thousands of royal subjects would have crowded into the plaza to watch their king ascend the temple stairs in an elaborate headdress and a heavy costume of shells and jade, accompanied by the din of drums and bells, before disappearing into his temple aerie to call upon the gods and his ancestors for sun, good harvest, or rain.

Brian comes jogging across the grass toward us at a fast clip. "You're staying down here, right?" he asks. "Can you do me a favor? Stand here until I get up to the top. I read the acoustics here were designed so that a king speaking in a normal voice at the top of a pyramid could be heard by the people in the plaza, and I want to test it out."

"Sure, why not?" Uzi says.

Brian runs back in the direction of Temple Two. From where I stand on the Grand Plaza, Temple Two looks like a squatter, fatter version of Temple One. A wide, steep staircase angles directly up the front to the top platform, where another, smaller flight of stairs leads up to the temple's single door. A large block of stone sits right in front of the opening. That's where the kings once stood to address their people below. I try to make out the outline of Lady Twelve Macaw on what remains of the roofcomb, but the slab up there is too broken and eroded. At best, I think I see the barest hint of a head and shoulders.

I turn to check on Maya, who's now running circles around a pit of ashes in the center of the plaza behind me. A vague campfire smell hangs in the air, mixed with the faint scent of some kind of incense or dried herb, duller and smokier than sage but not as musky as frankincense.

To climb Temple Two, Brian has to take the wooden staircase built on the south side to accommodate tourists. It's a little like having to use the servants' entrance, only with a better view. Uzi and I wait for him to appear in front of the temple.

"What do you think he'll say when he gets there?" I ask.

"'Testing, testing.' I'll bet you ten bucks that's what he says."

"You want to bet me? Why? If you give me ten dollars, I'll just use it for our groceries."

"Exactly," he says.

We see Brian's khaki explorer hat moving across the front of the temple. He takes a big step up onto the stone speaking block and waves his arms overhead wildly to get our attention. Even lifted on the regal perch he's tiny up there, only about a centimeter high if I frame him between my forefinger and thumb. A king looking down at his subjects from that vantage point would have seen a colorful tapestry of people spread out beneath him, but the people looking up would have seen only a lone, little figure dwarfed by a structure of his own creation.

I wave back and give Brian the double thumbs-up sign.

"Do you hear anything?" I ask Uzi after a moment. We're too far away from him to see if Brian's mouth is moving.

"*Nada.*"

I lift my elbows high and give Brian the double thumbs-down sign in a big, exaggerated fashion. "Try again!" I shout, even though I know he can't hear me.

Rigoberto slides up alongside me on the left. "What happens?" he asks.

"We're trying to see if it's true that if you speak up there in a normal voice, people down here can hear you."

"You can hear from the tops of one to another temple, but not from the tops to the bottoms," he explains.

I don't know how to convey this information to Brian, who's still standing in front of the temple up there, futilely speaking into the void.

I try a windshield wiper motion back and forth with both hands to indicate "Don't go any further," and when he doesn't respond, I try a finger-across-the-neck gesture to mean "Cut it off." In response, Brian waves his arms overhead again and points at me.

I point at my own chest. *Me?* It's like playing long-distance charades.

He waves even more wildly and points again, jumping up and down. If we were actually playing charades, he'd be miming, *Yes! You got it!*

"Do you know what he's saying?" I ask Rigoberto and Uzi. Brian points again, this time with an arcing motion that sends his line of sight back over the top of my head. The three of us turn around to see Maya climbing up the narrow stone staircase of Temple One, the one forbidden to tourists.

"This is not allowed!" Rigoberto shouts.

We take off across the grass in a group sprint, darting around the fire pit. Temple One's stairs are so narrow only one person can climb at a time, and we create a messy bottleneck at their base when we realize there's room for only one of us. Uzi breaks free and bounds up the stairs in two huge leaps, grabbing Maya from behind.

"*Maya,*" I say, when Uzi brings her back down. "Rigoberto *told* us not to climb that temple." She hides her face in Uzi's shoulder. But even as I scold her, the admonishment feels weak and wrongly aimed, an attempt for me to save face in front of Rigoberto. I shouldn't have taken my eyes off her, not even for a moment. Or I should have let Uzi come here with the group and stayed back at Crystal Paradise with Maya when my early-morning instincts told me this was no place for a child. Because this is definitely shaping up to be no place for a child.

Rigoberto pinches the space between his eyebrows with his thumb and forefinger. "There is more to see there, up the stairs," he says, gesturing behind him toward the raised platforms of the North Acropolis. "Main religious center of Tikal, each new pyramid built one atop the other. Also there is big mask to see, but you have to look down into the fence where it is. You can go now." He sounds tired and weary of us, and I can't blame him. Maya could have just cost him his job. He shoos us away with his hand. "Back here we will meet again in ten minutes of time."

So there was Lord Chocolate the grandfather, Chitam the grandson, and between them in the family line was Yik'in Chan K'awil. It's getting hard to keep track of all these guys. "It is not for worrying about the names," Rigoberto reassures us as we leave the Grand Plaza and step back into the forest. He has rebounded to his prior upbeat, informative self. "I am telling you only for your interest."

Yik'in, the father of Chitam, was the twenty-eighth ruler of Tikal. His name means "Darkness of the Night Sky," probably because this was the first thing his father saw upon leaving the birthing room. He ascended the throne in 734 at the age of forty-three, after Lord Chocolate died. Once established as king, Yik'in assumed and expanded his father's role as grand architect of Tikal. Over the next three decades, he oversaw some of the greatest public works ever constructed in the city, including the mighty Temple Four, which is the next destination on Rigoberto's jungle walking tour.

Our first glimpse of Temple Four is from a distance, when its stout roofcomb appears through a triangular clearing in the trees. In perfect Pavlovian fashion, we all reach for our cameras at the same time and tilt them forty-five degrees toward the sky. The same photograph must be sitting in thousands of family vacation albums around the world: the gray stone temple and the roofcomb rise out of the lush greenery as if resting on the distant treetops, the tiny specks of people milling in front of the temple's single entry door, the tree branches framing the image that were trimmed back for the purpose of giving us this photogenic view. Uzi slips the camera back into its pouch, hands it to me to put in the pocket of the backpack, and we all move on.

There's been a noticeable decline in group energy since we left the Grand Plaza. By this point, we're tired and hungry and our legs are starting to ache, but it also feels like a collective letdown to have left the splendor of the Grand Plaza just to enter the woods again. As we walk west, I can feel the presence of Temples One and Two and the North Acropolis looming behind us, pulling us back in imagination and desire. All those staircases we didn't have enough time to climb, all those abandoned pyramids we didn't get the chance to explore. The palaces we didn't see! Hiking to another pyramid-temple feels like a ho-hum, been-there enterprise, although Rigoberto keeps assuring us that this final trek is worth the time. And I'm hoping he's right, because if I've got the spatial orientation correct here, we're walking away from the park entrance instead of toward it, meaning we'll have to double back later to get to lunch and Hugo's van.

Rigoberto stops and slaps his hand against a tree, then points to where a series of Xs crisscross all the way up the rough bark. "This here is the chicle tree," he says. "Also known as the zapote or the sapodilla. This is from where the sap for chewing gum comes. But now chewing gum is made from synthetic, so where once this forest was full of *chicleros* who climbed to take sap from the trees, there are none anymore."

I slip behind Brian to check on Maya, who's riding in the pack on Uzi's back again. She's sleeping with her cheek resting on his shoulder. I look at my watch: 1:09 P.M. It's early for her naptime, but all the walking has tired her out. I'm feeling as if I could use a nap myself, but we're still a good hour away from finishing the tour.

"Also this tree has the very, very hard wood what Ma"—Rigoberto checks to make sure Maya's sleeping, then continues—"Maya builders liked to use, why? Because it was so hard, and also because the insects could not eat it. They used sapodilla to make the beams that go on top of the door in palaces and temples. Any questions, okay?"

There are no questions. We trudge on silently until the path empties into a dirt clearing and—*voilà*—the trail ends at the foot of Temple Four.

Temple Four is so massive—212 feet—that from its unexcavated base you can barely tell the hill alongside you has a temple on top, only that something very, very large is obliterating the sky. (For comparison's sake, the very first steel-framed skyscraper, built in Chicago in 1885, was only 138 feet high.) To build Temple Four took 250,000 cubic yards of stone, an estimated two years, and so much manpower, some anthropologists have hypothesized, that diverting that many people from the fields to the quarries might have created a citywide shortage of food.

Unearthing the entire pyramid today would be an undertaking of nearly equivalent scale, so only the temple and broad roofcomb at the top have been cleared of jungle debris. Two narrow wooden staircases snake up one of the sides at rakish angles, bypassing mature trees and thick roots jutting out of the base's unexcavated mound of dirt.

Brian, Marie, George, and their daughters head for the staircase and gamely start climbing. I spy a small refreshment stand off to the left and wander over to see what's for sale. There's the obligatory lineup of bottled water and soft drinks on display, along with several kinds of chips and a few pieces of fruit. I buy an orange Fanta and three bananas and sit down with Uzi and Rigoberto on a wooden bench.

"Guess what?" Uzi says as I sit down. "He's a shaman."

"Who's a shaman?"

"Rigoberto."

"You are?" I ask Rigoberto. I hand him a banana. "You don't look like a shaman."

"What is it a shaman looks like?"

I flip through a fast slide show of Arthur my Mesquakie friend, Burt the drug counselor in Iowa, Canto in his straw hat and rubber boots. "I don't know what a shaman looks like," I say. "But you look way too normal to me."

Rigoberto laughs, exposing two rows of gleaming white teeth. It's the first time we've seen him laugh today. "I am just still learning," he says. "I meet with my teacher when I am at home."

I peel the second banana, break it in half, and hand the top part to Uzi. "We brought Maya to see a shaman in Belize two days ago," I tell Rigoberto.

"Your husband was telling me," he says. "She has the imagined friend."

"Right."

"And what did the shaman do?"

"He didn't get a chance to do much. When he touched her wrist and said prayers, she started screaming and kicking and spitting. It was such a violent reaction I rushed her back outside. The ointment he gave us to put on her chest seems to have worked, though. She's better now, you can see."

"This is what really happened?" Rigoberto asks. He looks visibly disturbed.

"Yeah," I say. "That's what happened."

"Then you will need to go back," Rigoberto says.

"Go back? Why?"

"Because the way it sounds, it did not get finished."

Uzi shoots me a fast *I told you so* look, and I have an image of Canto pedaling hard and fast down a muddy road in his worn workshirt and rubber boots, just before I have a sinking feeling that he knew exactly what he was doing in the cabin and that his calmness came not from disinterest but from a place of deep knowledge and a corresponding lack of alarm.

"Can you help us if it needs finishing?" Uzi asks him.

Rigoberto shakes his head. "Today I am a guide, and I cannot mix the both."

"Maybe we can come back," Uzi says, although we both know how impossible that would be. Tomorrow morning we're leaving the Cayo District for six days on the Caribbean coast. Plus, I don't think it's a good idea to grab just any shaman off the street, although for God's sake, there do seem to be a fair number of them milling around down here. "Or maybe you can come to us tomorrow?" Uzi adds.

Rigoberto shakes his head again. "Tomorrow I work," he says. "I am sorry."

We sit quietly and watch a steady stream of foreigners and locals carefully make their way up and down the steep flights of wooden stairs, holding on to the handrails for support. What Rigoberto just said has lodged in my upper chest like a tight fist. Not only did I screw up the process by rushing Maya out of Canto's cabin, it seems, but I made matters worse by refusing to take her back. Whereas only a few days ago I was questioning my motives for taking my child to a shaman, I'm now questioning my decision to keep her away from one. Forget about not being able to keep up with all the new information coming at me; I can't even keep up with the competing messages inside of me.

"Rigoberto," I say. "What do you think is really going on when kids get scared here? Not as a tour guide, but as a shaman. Or as a normal guy, if you can't mix the two."

Rigoberto stares at me for a moment, as if trying to size up what I'll do with the answer. "Okay," he says. "This is what I think only, not the position of Tikal Park. I think maybe they are small enough still to see things or hear things that we cannot anymore."

"That's what I was thinking," I tell him. "Thanks."

A small brown animal with a long, ringed tail emerges from some low brush, steps daintily over an exposed tree root, then starts burrowing around in a pile of dead leaves. It looks like a cross between a small monkey and a raccoon. Six or seven park visitors surround the animal, pointing and snapping photos. "Coati, coati!" a child shouts, hopping around in a circle and pointing.

"Want to take a photo for Maya?" Uzi asks. I take the camera from the zippered pocket behind Maya's legs and snap a shot.

I check my watch. Fifteen minutes have passed since the rest of our group started the climb.

"You want to go up?" Rigoberto asks us. "There is still a little time."

"I don't want to wake Maya," Uzi says. "But you should go," he urges me. "Go. Maya and I are fine."

I massage my calves and consider it. The stairs look steep but not treacherous, and there are handrails all the way up. The question is how I'm going to feel once I get to the top.

"What's up there?" I ask.

"You have seen *Star Wars*?" Rigoberto says.

"A long time ago. When I was twelve."

"At the end, one of the planets is the view from top of Temple Four. It does look like a place on another world."

"Is there someplace to sit down? And something to hold on to?"

"You can sit on the temple stairs with everyone. It is very safe, you will see."

The people streaming down the left staircase don't look traumatized or overexerted. Then again, neither do most people exiting amusement-park rides, which reduce me to a nauseous crawl. Still, to have come all this way and spent the whole time at ground level, to miss out on what's meant to be the crowning moment of the day: it does seem like a bit of a waste. I peer around the backpack to check on Maya. Still sleeping.

I stand and brush some stray banana strings from the front of my pants. "Okay," I say. "I'll give it a try." I hand the third banana to Uzi for Maya to eat when she wakes up and kiss him on the top of his hair.

The stairs are even more rudimentary than they looked from the bench. A small brown sign posted at the bottom reads *RECOMENDAMOS SUBIR CON PRECAUCIÓN*. Climb with precaution. Close up, they're just a series of two-by-ten planks, angled like a forty-five-degree version of a cartoon bridge that swings over a ravine. But the banisters are sturdy and the staircase is narrow enough for me to easily hold on with both hands as I climb.

No one's coming up behind me, so I take the ascent steady and slow. By the halfway point, I'm breathing hard and sweating, with a dull pain in my upper chest. I stop on a small platform and lean back against the railing to catch my breath. Trees wrap around me on four sides, surrounding me with the soft twitters of concealed insects and birds. I look around to make sure no one is watching, then lift the hem of my black T-shirt to wipe my face. A small explosion of leaves flapping on my right signals a bird taking off from a branch. I make the mistake of looking back toward the ground, and my stomach and head swirl in opposite directions like fitted gears.

Three sixtyish Central American women in flip-flops, sundresses, and matching powder blue baseball hats pass me on their way down. I must look as unsteady as I feel. "Okay?" one of them asks me.

I smile back. "Okay. *Gracias.*"

When I feel ready to climb again, I take the second half of the stairs without stopping. They end at the side of the top platform, where a stone path wraps along the limestone wall. I press my back against the blocks and sidestep until I clear the front corner, where I see Brian and the others perched on the temple's shallow stone stairs, gazing to the east.

"Hey!" Karen says as I offer a feeble wave. "Look who's here!"

I can't believe how high up we are. I catch a glimpse of the treetops and reach out for the steps, slithering onto the nearest one. I keep my eyes on Karen and Brian for a moment before risking a half turn to the east.

Rigoberto was right. The view from up here is so otherworldly, it's easy to imagine why George Lucas chose it for the landscape of an alien planet. An expanse of bumpy green treetops, like the crown of a bunch of broccoli, extends far out to the north, south, and east, interrupted only by three gray temple roofcombs poking through the jungle canopy. Straight ahead, the back of Temple Two rises above the trees and, just beyond it, the front of Temple One. Over there to the right is the tall, narrow roofcomb of Temple Three, and somewhere beyond it lie Temples Five and Six. Way, way out there in the distance, seventy-five miles away and barely outlined in a blue-green haze, are the Maya Mountains of Belize, Crystal Paradise, the village of San Antonio, and the cabin where Canto lives.

"We're going to check out the inside of the temple," Karen says, rising to her feet. "Want to come?"

I glance up the ten additional steps to the temple's door. They're taller than they are deep, with no handholds. Maybe I could crawl up them on my hands and knees—but then how would I get down? Sliding on my butt, in front of everyone? Plus, from where I'm sitting I can see partway into the temple's narrow first chamber, which looks dark and damp. There could be bats.

"No, thanks," I say. "I'm fine right here for now."

A woman with short brown curly hair to my left is meditating in a modified lotus position on the stairs, with the backs of her hands resting against her knees and her thumbs and forefingers touching. Only a few other people are up here before lunch. It's low tide at Temple Four. Peak time is just before dawn, when tourists sit elbow to elbow on the stairs to watch the sun rise over the park. The moment must be magnificent, when the sun breaks free of the horizon to illuminate an ocean of fog suspended above the trees, the howler monkeys letting loose with their primordial calls, as the jungle wakes to another day.

Sitting here, I can understand why Maya royalty chose to lift themselves high above ground to communicate with their dead. Looking down on this unbroken expanse of life must have felt as close as one could get to visiting the Upperworld of their mythology. At night, Yik'in must have thought he was on a par with the surrounding stars, confirming his divine origins. Perhaps this proximity to the heavens convinced him that his ancestors could hear his prayers, that the boundary between his mortal world and their supernatural one could be traversed more easily from up high.

Once, only once, after years of fruitless attempts, did I feel my mother's presence after she died, and I was also perched above ground level at the time. It was just a few days after my father's heart trouble began, and that morning he'd lent me his car so I could travel between my apartment in Greenwich Village and his suburban hospital room. I drove the car back into the city in the late afternoon, parked it on the street in front of my building, and went upstairs to make some phone calls. When I came down an hour later, the car was gone. I double-checked the signs: it had been a legal parking spot. Towed? No, according to the tow pound when I called. Stolen? That's how it looked.

I didn't see how the week could possibly get worse. The doctors, the lawyers, the accountants, the confused and frustrated family members, a private investigator, and now a stolen car? My boyfriend, worried about leaving me alone for the night, insisted I sleep at his apartment. Not that I could sleep much. Around midnight, I wandered into his living room. I felt I needed to have a big, noisy cry—but where? I didn't want to wake him, which meant my choices were either the fire escape outside the living room or the hallway out near the elevator. It was early July, a balmy night, so I climbed through the living room window five floors above East Fifty-first Street in my T-shirt and bare legs. I sat on the iron stairs between two ficus plants and wrapped my arms around my knees.

As soon as I sat down it was as if a dam burst, and I started crying hard and fast and loud. The noise from the street, even after midnight, was enough to drown me out, so I let it go as loud as it needed to. I cried for my father's sudden brush with death; for his trouble with the IRS; for the illusion of family security that had just been shattered; and for my own bank account, which was too small to fix the problems. And then, in the midst of all that crying, words began to form, purely on their own.

"Mom," I cried, "I'm not strong enough to do this alone. If you can hear me, wherever you are, and you can help me, please try. I need you to send me some help. Please help me be strong enough to get through this. And Grandma," I pleaded, "if you can hear me, please, please, help me too."

As if a hand were passing in front of my face, a sensation of complete calm and well-being washed over me. I let go of a few more sobs, and then the crying just . . . stopped. I found myself sitting on a fire escape in an oversized T-shirt between two ficus plants with no good reason for being there anymore. So I climbed back through the window and into bed next to my boyfriend, where I slept deeply for the next seven hours.

In the morning, I left to catch a subway back to my apartment, only to realize I'd left my house keys back on my boyfriend's kitchen counter. So I doubled back to his apartment, where he met me at the door with the cordless telephone pressed to his ear.

"It's your editor," he said with a look of pure amazement. He handed me the phone. "Your book just made the *New York Times* bestseller list."

It was a Tuesday, which made no sense. The list was printed in the Sunday papers. I didn't even know enough to know it was sent to publishers in advance. I took the phone to the sound of my editor's joyous screams. "You did it!" she shouted. "The *New York Times*, baby!"

I nearly sailed the forty-four blocks home. Somehow, I had to believe, this was a sign. Somehow, I hoped, this news would parlay itself into some kind of income I could use to help my father.

When I got back to my apartment, I went to call my father's auto insurance company to report his car stolen . . . but I hung up before I finished dialing the number. Before I started all the paperwork, I figured, it was worth calling the tow pound one more time.

"The car was brought in at 6:10 A.M.," the clerk there informed me. "No damage. You can come pick it up now."

"*No damage?*"

"That's what I said."

If you know anything at all about car theft in Manhattan, you'll know what truly exceptional news this was. To have a stolen car returned with all of its tires and windows intact, with all four hubcaps still affixed, with all of its CDs still in their nesting places and more than a half tank of gas—more than the car had when it was stolen—is an exceedingly rare event. And it was then I felt that somehow, the barriers between wherever my mother was and where I am had been penetrated, and for that one morning she'd passed through to help me in whatever way she could.

From far below Temple Four's limestone stairs comes the distant crunching of tires against gravel. A tinny voice shouts "Wait up!" somewhere down between the trees. The three other people on the limestone stairs head back to the wooden staircase, leaving me at the top of Temple Four alone. I look up toward the temple door, but Karen and the others are still inside. High above the temple, the roofcomb rises, wide and imposing.

The K'awil family dynasty that ruled Tikal put twenty-seven consecutive kings on their limestone thrones. Family lineage meant everything here. Yik'in climbed these stairs to communicate with his dead ancestors, offering them incense, prayers, and blood in exchange for their insights and protection. This temple behind me is where Yik'in would have fasted and pierced his skin with obsidian shards and stingray spines to let his blood pour into offering bowls. He would have chanted and prayed, probably alone, inhaling the gray plumes of incense smoke that rose into the sky, dancing himself into a dreamlike state of exhaustion until he heard the voice of an ancestor perforate the night, and then another, and another. Did he feel he'd earned his place in the community of his forefathers when he heard them call out his name? Did it reaffirm his self-perception as a deity among men? The first time he heard a dead person speaking to him, was he scared? In some indigenous cultures, the schizophrenics are the shamans, the prophets, the seers, revered for hearing the voices that others cannot detect. How different might our family's path have been if Dr. Diane had told us we were raising a pint-size medium or if my sister had gotten down on her knees in supplication in our kitchen, eager for Dodo's next words?

I look up at the dark, bumpy roofcomb behind me. You can't see it any more, but a portrait of Yik'in was carved into it the year the temple was built, 741 A.D. He would have turned fifty that year. He was only twelve when his mother, Lady Twelve Macaw, died—two years younger than my sister was when we lost our mother and three years older than my brother. Thirty-eight years later, when Yik'in built the largest pyramid-temple in the Americas, he was a husband and a father, but the roofcomb he commissioned reveals that even as a middle-aged man, he never stopped being a son. More than twelve hundred years ago, when he stood on these steps, he wouldn't have been looking at the treetops I see today. Back then, his city was a thriving metropolis. The land would have been cleared down to the dirt, white causeways would have run between the temples, and the outskirts of the city would have been organized with housing clusters and orderly orchards and gardens. From the top of Temple Four, Yik'in would have had a direct sight line to the back of his mother's temple and the front of his father's, facing each other across the Grand Plaza. Of all the possible views in Tikal, this was the one he claimed for the site of his own monumental public work.

Maybe I'm reading too much into the orientation here, assuming close family relationships where there may have been none. After all, Temple Four is also positioned so that someone standing at its top would see the winter solstice sun rise over the top of Temple Three on December 21 every year. But I can't imagine that the emotional trial of losing a mother at age twelve was fundamentally different twelve hundred years ago than what it feels like today. Yik'in may have been a ruthless warrior, overconfident about natural resources, and delusional about the divinity he possessed. But he would never have stopped being a boy who lost his mother at twelve. You can feel it here on his temple stairs, his sadness, his longing, the childlike sweetness of his impulse to build a structure so tall, taller than anything ever attempted before. Tall enough that his own likeness could gaze down for eternity at the carvings of his parents gazing at each other. Watching over them. A family threesome set in stone.

chapter eleven
Cayo District, Belize
December 27, 2000

Our last breakfast at Crystal Paradise is both reunion and diaspora. Shakti and her son rejoin the Tikal group at one of the wooden tables, where we share bowls of scrambled eggs with green beans, plates of tortillas, and dishes of diced watermelon. And coffee—good, strong Guatemalan coffee. Behind us, three families who arrived last night eat at separate tables. They'll introduce themselves in the back of a van this afternoon or over Belikins from the self-service bar tonight. By tomorrow they'll be sitting together at breakfast like us, quickly becoming characters in one another's vacation stories.

Marie and Uzi review the high points from our Tikal trip for Shakti and her son, who spent yesterday horseback riding to a nearby waterfall and natural pools. When Marie gets to the part where we climbed Temple Four and looked down on that vast shaggy green rug, Shakti's cheeks twitch in a small wince of regret.

"We should have gone with you," she says. "I'm feeling like we really missed out on all that."

"This way you're leaving something for next time," Uzi tells her.

Shakti's son looks up from his breakfast burrito. "Dude, there's no good surf here," he says. "Next time we're doing Costa Rica."

We've taken our last sips of coffee and tea, the breakfast dishes have been cleared away, and still we linger. Nobody wants to leave just yet, but the vans will be idling in the parking area soon. Victor strolls over with a steaming mug of fresh coffee to review the day's plans. Within the half hour, our group will be dispersing in every direction, like arrows on a compass. Marie and her family are heading to the airport for their flight back to Canada; Brian will go down the road to Francis Ford Coppola's Blancaneaux Lodge for three days of birding; Shakti and her son will share Marie's van to Belize City, where they'll take a water taxi farther east to the island of Ambergris Caye for four days of snorkeling and, as Shakti puts it, "serious beach chill time." And Jeronie will be driving Uzi, Maya, and me four hours southeast to the town of Placencia on the central Caribbean coast for the second half of our trip.

Everald Junior peeks around the kitchen door, looking for Maya. "Can I play?" she asks me.

"It's fine," I tell her, "but make sure you stay on the lawn where we can see you."

She runs off, then runs back just a minute or two later. "Hursulas," she explains, grabbing them both from the table before she takes off again.

When Victor leaves to prepare the vans, it's our cue to settle our bills and finish the last-minute packing. "I'm soglad we hadthis tiiime togethuh," Brian sings in an intentionally corny Carol Burnett imitation as we head off to our cabanas one last time. Yesterday on the ride back from Tikal, Brian and I talked for nearly an hour about the logistics of building a bionic man, a subject I wouldn't have thought I could sustain for ten minutes, but with an engaged audience Brian suddenly developed the speaking skills of a charismatic college professor. I'm going to miss his thirst for learning. Over breakfast he and Uzi exchanged business cards with a promise to swap photos from Tikal, but later, back at home, we'll find we misplaced his card somewhere between Crystal Paradise and L.A., and he may have done the same between Belize and Houston, because we won't hear from him again.

I check on Maya and Everald on the lawn and head into the cabana to finish our packing. A few items of clothing still hang in the open closet, and I tuck them into tight rolls and stack them neatly inside our respective bags. From the closet shelf I take the box of unused Hanukkah candles I brought from home and stuff them into an empty corner of my backpack. They've been useless without the menorah I forgot to pack. While I work, a four-inch lizard scuttles straight up the wall and disappears into the roof with a loud rustling noise.

On the closet floor I find the empty plastic bag that held Canto's leaves, which I can use to wrap up our half-used bottles of shampoo and conditioner. When I go to retrieve them from the shower, a tiny, tan, nearly transparent frog with beady black eyes stares up at me from a tile next to the drain. Four days ago I would have called Uzi in to escort this guy back outdoors, but now I scoop him up in a plastic cup and set him free outside the door. I swear, after this trip Topanga Canyon's wildlife is going to seem like an underfunded petting zoo.

I start piling our bags and backpacks at the foot of the bed for Uzi to carry to the van. "Knock-knock," Shakti says through our open screen door. "Coming to say good-bye."

She's wearing the same black tank top she had on the day we met her, with a colorfully woven Guatemalan headband stretched wide across the top of her head. Over her shoulder, I see Maya and Everald playing follow-the-leader in front of the purple bougainvillea tree. Maya's the leader.

"When are you kicking out of here?" Shakti asks.

"In about fifteen minutes. Jeronie's going to take us to the butterfly farm on the way. We can't check in at Placencia until after three o'clock, so we've got some time to kill."

"I thought it's two o'clock," Uzi says from the hammock.

"Three," I say, stepping out onto the porch. I'm certain it's three.

"Jeronie's a good driver," Shakti says, and I nod. Most of the road to Placencia is unpaved. I figure that's what she means.

She reaches out to hug me good-bye, and we hold each other in a tight grip. "It's been a real experience meeting you," I tell her. "I mean that in the best way possible. I hope you have a beautiful time at the beach."

"You're a good egg," she says. She gives me an extrahard squeeze and whispers in my ear. "Everything's going to be all right, you know."

"Thanks," I tell her. "And if I ever want a reading in Santa Cruz, I know who to call."

"Damn," she says. "I should have done one for you here. Why didn't I think of that?"

"How about a twenty-second good-bye version right now?"

"Meaning . . . ?"

"I don't know. Whatever you can see."

"Okay," she says, shrugging gamely. "Ask me a question."

One question? In the third grade, I had to write an essay about what I'd ask for if a magic genie lamp could grant me a single wish. I thought about it hard, and then I wrote that I'd ask for three more wishes. "Good idea!!!" the teacher penned in the margin, but I don't think this is what Shakti has in mind. Just one question? There's so much I want to ask. What's really going on with Dodo? Will I ever write another book? Will Uzi and I still be together in ten years? I need a question broad enough to be meaningful yet specific enough to offer real guidance. Or maybe I'm overthinking this. Shakti's waiting, and so is the van.

"What should we do for Maya?" I blurt out.

Shakti closes her eyes, takes a deep breath in and a slow breath out. Then she does it again. I wait. Her son comes up behind her and waits, too. Finally she opens her eyes.

"I see plants," she says.

"Shakti, we're in the tropics." I gesture out toward the lawn, where bougainvillea and orchids and about eleven other kinds of flowers grow in abundance. "I see plants everywhere, too."

"Good!" she says, laughing. She and Uzi exchange a fast hug, and then he grips her son's hand and shakes it firmly.

"Hope you find some good surf, dude," Uzi tells him.

"Me, too," the kid says glumly.

The van horn beeps twice. Shakti and her son sling their duffel bags over their shoulders and hurry down the steps. "See you!" I call after them, and the kid flashes me a peace sign and a grin as they turn the corner behind the cabana. And then, just like that, they're gone.

"So," Uzi says. There doesn't seem to be anything to add.

Each time our group diminishes in size, I feel a small yet palpable feeling of loss. We were ten at the breakfast table, then five at the cabana, and now we're down to three again. Four if you include Everald Junior, but he lives here. In only four days—have we really been here only four days?—we've created bonds with the other guests, not just out of circumstance but out of curiosity and genuine interest in one another's lives. Maybe one day Uzi and I will come back to these cabana steps and visit with the Tuts, but we'll never again be here in the same group of ten people, and this knowledge has me feeling nostalgic for the place even before we've left.

Jeronie comes to take our bags to the car, and Uzi calls Maya over from the lawn. Everald trails behind her, and I crouch down into a squat to say good-bye to him at eye level. He's such an adorable child, all barefoot smiles and holding hands, following Maya around the property like an adoring younger brother although they're only a few months apart in age.

"Thank you for playing with Maya," I tell him. "I hope we'll see you again sometime."

He smiles shyly and darts away in the direction of the family's house. "Bye, Everald!" Maya shouts after him. Her voice is loud and strong now, the congestion in her chest nearly gone. Last night would have been the ninth time I rubbed the ointment on her chest if I'd been doing it three times a day, but I managed to get it on her only seven times total. Still, it seems to have done some good.

Uzi does a final check of our room to make sure we've left nothing behind. This is his little ritual at the end of all our trips, opening and closing all the nightstand drawers, getting down on his knees to peer under the beds, peeling back the curtain in the shower. I'm chronically careless about these details, so neither of us is surprised when he comes out of the cabana carrying the shampoo and conditioner, a hairbrush, three crayons, and one of Maya's spotted leopards that had gotten wound up in her bedsheets.

"Good catch, Jim," I say, in my *Mission: Impossible* voice.

I stuff the items into my carry-on bag and stand on the porch for just another moment. Not a single molecule in my body is signaling me to leave.

"I want to stay here forever," I tell Uzi.

"We can come back sometime," he says.

"It's not the same."

I've traveled enough to know that this feeling of being rooted to a place where I've stayed only a few days is carefully cultivated, and when a resort gets it right, few guests will want to leave. Yet I don't feel that the Tuts have been manipulating the experience that way. They're just good people living in a beautiful place, sharing it with the travelers who book their rooms. What I'm feeling now is more than good marketing. A strong pull of intuition is telling me we're not done with this place. It's not time to go.

Is it Rigoberto's warning, that our visit with Canto did not get finished, that's making me feel this way? No, I don't think so. It's something else, something I can feel but can't shape into words.

I've always admired people who can make an abrupt about-face in their plans, who cancel a flight to spend their whole vacation at the first place on their itinerary instead of going on to the three other stops, or who quit a job they hate without another one lined up, and even those who cancel a wedding a week before the ceremony because they wake up and realize the marriage is destined to fail. One of my friends went to London for a ten-day visit and wound up staying six years. I can't imagine making such an impulsive choice. That kind of act requires the ability to know what you want, the courage to act, and a healthy degree of self-interest. That last point is where I keep getting stuck. When I think of unilaterally announcing that I'm not going to leave today, I immediately think of how that's going to screw up Jeronie's plan for the afternoon and how the guesthouse in Placencia will never fill our room at the last minute and probably won't refund our money and how Crystal Paradise may not even have room for us for another five days. The degree of complexity my decision would set into motion, and the hardships it might create for others, are enough to convince me to stick with the original plan.

But here's the problem with this: I get almost no pleasure from original plans. They're rote. They're boring. They have no spontaneity. Back home in Topanga, my days are predictable and routine, most of them spent alone or in the company of just Carmen and Maya in a house at the top of a canyon, waiting for Uzi to come home. The thought takes shape until it forms a perfect sentence: *I'm lonely at home.* I'm not lonely here. Here I've been surrounded by happy people and I've been laughing for the first time in months. Here I've been part of a community, as ephemeral as it is. Leaving it feels like the wrong choice to be making. Yet with everyone else disbanding, there's no real reason to stay. In the strangest of ways, I feel jealous of Maya for having Dodo, a friend who goes everywhere with her and never leaves her alone.

In six days, we'll head back to a place where the mind-set insists that imaginary friends are purely a child's mental invention, and when those friends become aggressive or troublesome it's the child's mind and not the culture's mind-set that needs to be fixed. In our brief time here, I've entered a culture that doesn't think of me as a crazy mother for wondering if Dodo could be more than a child's elaborate idea. If in the end it's a mental disturbance we're facing, I'd rather face it here, where the hope exists of fixing it from the outside in, instead of being pressured to change my child from the inside out.

I step down the cabana stairs and look at the bushes bursting with color, the orchids growing delicate and tall in the crotches of mature trees, the red-and-yellow cabana with the blue-and-white hammocks slung across the front porch, and I think, *Help me find a way to feel it's all right to be leaving. Help me find a way to feel that having gotten this far is enough.* Bringing Maya down here was an act of courage, Shakti said. I want to believe she was right. Maybe breaking the home routine for even a week is worth something, a small act of faith itself.

The car is waiting. It's time to go.

In the parking lot, Jeronie and Victor wait for us next to a four-wheel-drive Isuzu Trooper with our bags already packed into the back. They're talking quietly among themselves and Victor looks serious, but his face lifts into a smile when he sees us walking his way.

"So the little *reina* is leaving us already," he says, running his hair through the curls on the crest of Maya's head. "So soon?"

"We're going to butterflies," she tells him.

"So you are. Well, then, I'll get out of your way." He steps aside and shakes hands with Uzi. They clasp each other's elbows, a ritual guy's embrace. I put down my carry-on bag and give him a full-on hug.

"You have an exceptional place," I tell him. "And the best family in all of Cayo."

"Tell all your friends about us!" Victor says, squeezing my shoulders. "We'll make a nice time for them here!"

"I will!" I say, and it's true. In the coming year, we'll both make good on our promises. "Thanks again for taking us to San Antonio," I tell him as I pull the car door closed.

"It was nothing!" he says. "It was right down the road! Next time, we visit the Mennonites. Don't forget!"

The tapir, the national animal of Belize, is a relative of the horse and the rhinoceros, looks like a cross between an anteater and a pig, and goes by the nickname "mountain cow." I wouldn't have known any of this, having never before heard of a tapir, but the wood railing outside the Chaa Creek Natural History Centre displays a lineup of seven animal skulls, and Maya immediately points to the largest one and asks "What's *that*?" We're the only visitors at the center this morning, and the young female guide is eager to be of use.

The Natural History Centre is a mandatory first stop on the way to the Blue Morpho Butterfly Farm, which is fine with us, since the two-room cabin is packed with user-friendly information about local animals and plants. It's the kind of museum Uzi likes: small, rustic, unpretentious, and not out to make a buck. Photographs and illustrations of native reptiles and amphibians, mammals, and birds are paired with captions printed on laminated index cards and affixed to large sheets of posterboard and painted plywood. A windowsill holds a lineup of glass jars filled with formaldehyde. Each one contains a single, tightly coiled snake. "Ucch," Maya says, but I find them fascinating in their states of permanent suspension: the venomous coral snake with its bands of yellow, black, and red; the fangless tropical king snake; the aggressive and reviled dirt-colored fer-de-lance.

One corner of the front room is set up as the interior of a traditional Maya stick–and-thatch hut, a *xanil na*. The stone hearth is pushed up against a wall, and a working loom, empty gourds, and sacks of food and clothing hang from the ceiling. The only furniture in the room is a tan hammock slung on a diagonal and a simple table fashioned of sticks. Most of Maya life, as Rigoberto told us, was public and outdoors, which makes it possible to look into this barren facsimile of a room and imagine a colorful plaza on the other side of the wall, teeming with human activity.

At a desk in the back of the museum we buy our tickets to the butterfly farm. When we step outside, Jeronie is leaning against the porch railing, arms crossed, talking to the guide. He checks his watch when he sees us. "I'll meet you back here in half an hour, okay?" he says, and we trudge over to the next building, where the butterfly tour begins.

Some facts about blue morpho butterflies, known here as the "Belizean blue": they're among the largest butterflies in the world, with wingspans of up to eight inches; they taste food with their legs; and their shimmering wings are believed to have inspired the famous Maya-blue pigment found on pre-Columbian offerings, artwork, and murals at sacred sites.

The on-site naturalist at the butterfly farm looks like a camp counselor, with khaki pants, a Chaa Creek resort T-shirt, and brown pigtails. We sit at an outdoor green picnic table while she shows us a diagram of the blue morpho life cycle and opens a series of six white plastic buckets to show us caterpillars in various stages of development, all clinging to small piles of leaves. Inside the screened-in room just behind us, she explains, we'll see the cocoons, and if we're lucky, a butterfly will be emerging from one as we watch.

"Are you understanding all this, Maya?" I ask.

Maya nods. "Where are the butterflies?" she whispers.

"Over there. We'll see them in a minute."

"Listen to her," Uzi says. "It's interesting."

The full blue morpho life span, from the day the egg is laid on a leaf to the moment of death, is 137 days. Of that, only a month—less than a fourth of its existence—is spent as an adult. That's got to be the most protracted adolescence in the natural world. But all of these details are only prelude to the main event. The butterflies are what everyone comes here to see, and they're the last stop on the tour. I check my watch. Jeronie will be back in fifteen minutes.

I raise my hand, which reminds me of Brian, and again I feel a pang of nostalgia. He'll be bouncing down the road past San Antonio Village right about now. Shakti and her son are probably speeding along the Western Highway toward Belmopan, their focus already shifting to images of starfish and fine white sand.

"I'm sorry," I tell the naturalist, "but we only have fifteen more minutes. Is it possible to see the butterfly house now?"

"Oh, sure, sure," she says. She puts the sixth bucket back on the shelf and leads us over to the screened-in pen but stops before opening the door to the small anteroom that prevents the butterflies from getting out. Through the screen door I can see dark wings flapping everywhere.

"Maya, maybe you'd better get in the backpack," I say. I'm thinking about protecting the fragile butterflies, but I add, "You'll be able to see the butterflies better from up there," to convince her, and she eagerly climbs in.

The butterfly house is no more than a large framed box, with wire mesh for the walls and roof and a crunchy white-gravel floor. Hundreds of butterflies half the size of my hand cling to the screens on our sides. The wings, when closed, are a dull brown with large black eyespots ringed in yellow, making the insects look more like giant moths than butterflies. Every now and then, one releases from the roof and sails over to a screened wall or to cafeteria trays loaded with slices of watermelon and cantaloupe, revealing small flashes of blue as they fly, like airborne scraps of sky.

The naturalist bends down and plucks a dead one from the gravel. "Their outsides are brown for camouflage," she explains. She delicately peels the wings apart and props them open with her index finger. "Ohhh," Uzi, Maya, and I exhale. Inside, the wings are a stunning shade of metallic blue edged with a thick rim of rich brown. It's a shade of blue I've never seen in nature before, less purple than indigo, more violet than cerulean, lighter than cobalt, darker than aquamarine. I've never seen it in a flower or a child's eyes, or the sky. Maybe in an abstract oil painting, or a neon sign. Blue-morpho blue: it's a shade uniquely its own.

"This one was a female," the guide says.

"How can you tell?"

She outlines the wings' outer edge with an index finger. "The females have two rows of white spots on the brown edges. Males are mostly blue."

"Look over here," Uzi says. He's standing in front of a simple wooden hutch near the door, where five rows of cocoons hang from horizontal sticks. They're smooth and emerald, shaped like perfect little nautilus shells. Each one has a date marked on a piece of tape, indicating the day it's expected to hatch. Some of the cocoons in the bottom row have already peeled open, and a large, newly minted butterfly clings to the empty shell of one, still slightly wet and recovering from her efforts.

"Like Mommy's," Maya says, pointing, and she's right. The newborn butterfly, in profile, looks just like the one inked onto my left hip. I had just turned thirty when I walked into a tattoo parlor on Sunset Boulevard with my sister, and I was looking for a way, on the eve of a new decade, to mark my body with the universal sign of transformation, to commemorate the birth of something as yet unformed and new. It would be another year before I'd meet Uzi, and Maya was still the barest outline of an idea, but I sensed such connections waiting ahead, and even though I know it sounds odd coming from the pragmatic cynic I was, I wanted to somehow prepare my body to be ready to receive them.

A butterfly lands lightly on the back of Uzi's hair, parallel to Maya's face, and she tips her head and stares at it with a look of pure wonder. She holds both hands out and flexes them open and shut, as if to mimic the opening and closing of their wings. It's one of the most innocent, loveliest gestures I've ever seen. A second butterfly swoops down and alights on Uzi's shoulder. He turns his head around to catch a glimpse of it and grins.

"They like you," I say.

A third lands on the rim of the backpack, a fourth on Maya's shoulder. "Watch, Maya," I say, extending my index finger to a point just in front of the one on Uzi's hair, gently encouraging it to step onto the perch. Its delicate legs grip my finger. The butterfly is no heavier than a feather, so light I can barely feel resistance when I lift my hand. So much in so little. I hold it up to eye level and watch it slowly flap its wings. It's a wonder of concealment, the hidden blue paradise tucked inside.

This is how Jeronie finds us when he walks into the cage: surrounded by butterflies, drunk on butterflies, awestruck by the way they perch on our heads, our shoulders, our hands with such lack of guile, such trust. He chuckles to see us pivoting in slow circles, our arms stretched wide, trying to attract elusive fragments of iridescent blue.

When I see Jeronie, I flap my arm just a little to let a blue morpho set sail.

"Ready?" he asks.

"Just about."

"Rosita can see you in a little while, if you want," he says.

Rosita can see us? In a little while?

"I'm sorry, I didn't catch that," I say.

"Rosita can see you in a little while, if you want," he repeats.

There are so many bewildering elements in that sentence, I don't know where to start being confused. "Rosita" must be Dr. Rosita, from the book. But why would Jeronie be bringing her up at the butterfly farm? And how can she see us, when we already missed our appointment with her? And *why* would she see us, when we were told she didn't have any more appointments this week? I stare dumbly at Jeronie, trying to make the pieces fit.

"Okay," says Uzi, who's a couple of beats ahead of me.

"We can walk there," Jeronie says. "It's right down the hill."

Down the hill? This hill? Oh—that's *right*. The owners of Chaa Creek resort are Rosita's neighbors and friends—she mentioned it in her book—which means we must be adjacent to her farm right now. And the other night Jeronie did say he knew her. Which means . . . when he left us for the half hour, he must have been going down to find her, to ask if she could see us.

I'm so moved by this act of generosity, I turn into a stuttering fool. "Jeronie," I tell him. "I can't—don't—I don't know what to say. This was—is—so incredibly kind—and thoughtful. Of you."

"It's nothing," he says, heading toward the door as if to escape the force of my gratitude. "If you're ready, we can go."

The waiting room at Ix Chel Farm is an octagonal pavilion with a red tin roof right at the forest's edge. A molded white concrete bench wraps around two thirds of the interior, capable of seating a dozen people easily, but when Jeronie drops us off the only other patients waiting are two bearded Mennonite farmers in broad-brimmed straw hats. The suspenders of their black trousers stretch up and over cotton workshirts that are, I notice, a shade very close to blue-morpho blue. We sit across from them and exchange solemn nods. Neither of them looks sick but then again, probably neither do we.

The center is named for Ix Chel, "Lady Rainbow," the Maya moon goddess of midwifery and healing. From what I can see, the center is a collection of low white buildings with peaked thatched roofs surrounded by jungle on three sides. Unlike Canto's cabin, this seems to be more of an operation, an outdoor clinic of sorts. Every now and then, people in white shirts walk into or out of a rectangular, two-story building across the gravel driveway with a sense of officious duty. It gives me a small sense of safety to see there's a system here with observable structure and rules. How much can go awry in a place with an appointment schedule and a waiting room?

I glance at Maya, who's busy flipping through a children's book about rain-forest reptiles and murmuring some unintelligible words. We're about to see one of the best-known healers in Central America, but to Maya she'll be just another woman in the rain forest. Maya doesn't know why we're here, and she doesn't know to ask; to her, there's nothing to anticipate, and so there's also nothing to fear. Me, I have enough apprehension for both of us. Whatever excitement I feel about meeting Dr. Rosita is muddied by the worry that what happened in Canto's cabin will happen again.

I look at my husband to see if he shows any indication of feeling the same, but he's sitting on the bench as serenely as if he were waiting for a regularly scheduled crosstown bus. I place my flat palm against his thigh and give him a little nudge.

"This is very exciting!" I say, trying to provoke a response.

"Mm-hmm." He smiles and nods benignly. It's just another happy day in Uzi's rain forest. Whatever response I'm looking for, I'm not going to get here. I smile back and remove my hand.

Maya reaches for the water bottle, and I unscrew the cap and hand it to her just as a young woman steps into the pavilion and motions for the Mennonites to follow her. She checks her watch and turns to us. "Rosita will be ready for you in about forty-five minutes, maybe a little less," she says. "If you'd like, you can look around in the gift shop or take a walk on the medicinal trail and come back in half an hour."

"Okay," Uzi says.

We wander over to a small white hut with another octagonal

red roof, a smaller, enclosed version of the waiting area. Inside, a local woman standing at a cash register greets us with a cheerful *"Buenos días!"*

"Buenos días!" we reply.

Low wooden shelves hug the perimeter of the room, displaying embroidered white shirts and colorful Guatemalan belts and wallets. Maya picks up a little Guatemalan worry doll and instinctively rubs her thumb across its chest. Neat rows of small jars and bottles stripe a center table. I pick up a three-inch glass cylinder filled with a light green ointment. The label says JUNGLE SALVE. A pamphlet nearby says it's one of the natural health care products produced at the farm from local herbs and leaves. I roll it over to read the label's back. "For insect bites, itching, poison ivy, fungal infections, and skin irritations. Ingredients: Jackass Bitters, Gumbolimbo, Chicoloro, pure vegetable oil, beeswax." A slim brown bottle with an eyedropper cap wears the label BELLY BE GOOD. "For gastritis, constipation, and chronic gas pains. Man Vine, Ginweo, Guaco." It's like hearing pidgin English: half I understand, half I don't.

"We should buy some," Uzi says.

We should, but it feels lopsided to be having that desire now, as if here, of all places, we shouldn't succumb to the desire to consume. "Maybe later," I say.

Outside the gift shop, posted arrows direct us around behind the pavilion, where a dirt path hugs the edge of the rain forest for fifty steps, passing between a towering palm and a large grapefruit tree heavy with fruit, before it enters the woods. A sign says the medicinal rain-forest trail, created by Dr. Rosita after Don Elijio died, preserves many of the plants he used for healing. As we step into the rain forest, the aperture of the outside world shrinks until it's just us, the plants on both sides of the trail, and the soft dirt beneath our feet. There is no sound in here at all except for the light crunches of our sneakers treading on the earth. It's dimmer and more enclosed than any of the trails at Tikal. I slip off my sunglasses and slide them into my shirt's front pocket.

Every twenty feet or so, a small printed sign sticks out of the ground at the base of a medicinal plant or tree. I bend over to read the first sign on the right. This plant has spiky, variegated leaves that stick straight up from the earth like green and yellow flames. It's a snake plant, also known as *lengua de vaca* in Spanish or *Sansevieria trifasciata*, its Latin name. It's used here as a snakebite remedy. I used to have three of these plants on top of my kitchen cabinets in New York, where we called them "mother-in-law's tongue" and used them as decoration.

Farther up the trail we find the chicoloro plant, also known as *Strychnos panamensis*. "I wonder if this is where strychnine comes from," Uzi says. Rat poison. "Don't let Maya touch it."

I pull a leaf from an adjacent allspice plant, rub it between my fingers, and hold it up to Uzi's nose. "Remember?" I ask. This makes me think of Rigoberto, which makes me think of yesterday at Tikal, and oh, damn it, *now* where did Maya go?

She's already way ahead of us, rounding a bend in the path. It makes me a little crazy to see parents at amusement parks with children on nylon leashes, but after this trip I understand the impulse, I really do. I leap up four wooden steps and whiz past a Spanish elder and a white poisonwood tree. The further in I venture, the dimmer the path gets, even in daytime. I wouldn't want to be lost in here alone, certainly not at night. At the thought, a slight chill of apprehension radiates from the back of my ears all the way down to my calves. I walk faster. I am Martin Sheen cruising up the Nung River into Cambodia's heart of darkness, except that instead of a Navy patrol boat and a four-man crew I've got a pair of Nike sneakers and a rambunctious three-year-old. So maybe it's not such an apt metaphor after all.

I find Maya scuffing her toe into the dirt in front of a wild yam vine and carry her out past a ceiba tree, a wild pineapple, and a dysentery bark. How many medicinal plants can you fit in an eighth of a rain-forest mile? More than I've heard of before, that's how many.

The path loops back around to the farm and deposits us in front of a reproduction of Don Elijio's hut, which looks like a larger, darker version of the *xanil na* we saw at the Natural History Centre up the hill.

But there's no time to compare and contrast the interiors, because the woman who asked us to come back in half an hour is looking for us now. She motions us across the lawn in the direction of two white plastered cottages. "Over here," she says.

The consultation room is a wooden deck behind one of the white buildings. As we approach, a middle-aged, deeply tanned Caucasian woman rises from a lawn chair to greet us, and any lingering preconceptions I have about what a shaman should look like officially self-destruct.

Rosita wears a flowered cotton sundress that skims her knees and a wide, round straw hat. Her eyes turn down just slightly at the outer edges, just as in her photo, giving her an expression of weary compassion, but then she smiles, revealing two rows of perfect white teeth, and her whole face comes alive.

"Hello," she says, motioning to some empty chairs in front of her. "I'm Rosita Arvigo." Her voice is thinner and reedier than I would have expected, pleasant yet also commanding. "Please sit down."

I get the impression that when Rosita says sit, you sit. We sit. Maya climbs up on my lap and sticks her index and middle fingers into her mouth.

"You're from America?" Rosita asks.

"We're from California," I say, and Uzi adds, "Topanga Canyon. Near L.A."

"Thank you for fitting us in today," I say. "We had an appointment with you for the twenty-fourth, but we missed our flight down here, and our travel agent said you didn't have any more appointments this week. So we appreciate you making the time for us."

"Sometimes that happens," she says. I'm not sure if she means the missed flight, the packed appointment calendar, or making time for last-minute clients. I think she means the flight. Or maybe all three.

"So, what brings you here today?" she asks.

"We came for our daughter," I begin, motioning toward Maya, "who has an imaginary . . ."

Maya's mouth flies open into an angry O and her dark brows pinch into a perfect cartoon-character V, an expression of sudden outrage. Her face unequivocally says, "You're going to talk to *her* about *me*?"

I can guess where this is heading. "Maybe one of us should take her away for a little while," I say.

I look at Uzi. Uzi looks at me.

"I'll do it," he says. "You should tell the story."

After they've rounded the corner of the house, I turn back to face Rosita. "So," Rosita says. "She has an imaginary . . ."

". . . friend. An imaginary friend that she talks to and says she can see. He goes everywhere with her. It gets a little out of control at times. That's why we're here."

"Does the friend have a name?"

"Dodo."

"Dodo." She gives an amused little laugh. "That's a good one."

It's been a long time, such a long time, since I've sat and talked one-on-one with a woman of Rosita's age. She's probably just a few years younger than my mother would have been. No matter how old I get, in the presence of an older woman I automatically become submissive and adoring, obsessively eager to please, with an almost desperate need to be understood. This usually makes my mouth start working overtime, as in, *You didn't understand what I just meant? Please—let me explain it nine different ways. Because I need you to understand me completely.*

"There are a lot of Dodos, according to her. Good ones and bad ones, boy ones and girl ones. She says she can see them and hear them all," I continue.

"That's a little unusual."

"You're telling me. There's one in particular that's been giving her trouble. She says he's a bad one, and that he's a boy." I get the feeling I don't need to say the word "spirit" with Dr. Rosita. It's already implicit in my description.

"How long has this been going on?"

"It started in September," I say. "I was working in my office one day, and she ran in and hit me, and blamed it on him. That was the first time I heard her mention him. She's never had an imaginary friend before. I had one when I was a kid, but mine was pretty benign. Maya's doesn't seem so tame. Hers goes everywhere with her. Whenever she acts out, she blames him. There are other behavioral things going on, too, like she doesn't want anyone other than my husband or me to touch her . . ."

"Maybe that's not a bad thing."

"Maybe not. But it makes going to a doctor or dentist almost impossible. And sometimes she has night terrors, where she screams in the middle of the night but doesn't fully wake up. I've caught her a few times speaking to Dodo in a language I can't understand, which really, really scares me."

"Can you remember any kind of emotional upset around the time this all began?"

"In her or me?"

"Either. But we're mostly talking about her."

I tip my head to the left and try to think back that far. September was the month Maya started preschool at the Montessori, and Uzi was working absurdly long hours, but I can't think of a specific incident that could have caused Maya any trauma.

"Not that I can think of," I say.

Rosita takes her hat off and lays it on the ground next to her chair. I notice that she's wearing flat brown sandals with straps that crisscross the bridges of her feet and that her shins are unshaven and her toenails unpolished. I also notice she has beautiful, shapely calves for a woman her age, and for some reason, this makes me start to choke up. She strikes me as someone perfectly at ease with her environment, secure in her own authority, with no need to flatter or impress anyone else. The sentence that forms in my head is, "This is how I want to be when I grow up."

"Has she always had a good imagination?" Dr. Rosita asks.

Who? Oh. Right. We're talking about Maya. "Always," I say. "Extremely. Very articulate for her age, that's what everyone says."

"And what have you tried to do for her before now?"

I raise my eyebrows to indicate *a lot*. "I started with what I thought

I was supposed to do. I spoke with the preschool teacher, I spoke with the pediatrician, I consulted with a friend who's a social worker. Everyone said imaginary friends are normal for three-year-olds to have. But it didn't feel normal to me. She would be acting like her usual self, and then suddenly, like the flip of a switch, her personality changed to stubborn and defiant and impossible. She has a nanny from Nicaragua who assessed the situation, said she had a spirit attached to her, and did a ritual to get rid of it."

"What did she do?"

"She told me to run an egg up and down Maya's arms and legs, and then she took some basil from the refrigerator and told me to squeeze it in Maya's bathwater and pour it over the top of her head."

Rosita nods slowly. "That's a good start," she says.

So Carmen had known what she was doing. "She took the egg outside and did something with it. Said a prayer, I think," I continue. "It worked for a few days. But then Dodo came back even stronger than before. That was the first time I started thinking maybe we were dealing with something out of the ordinary. My husband was already there in his mind, he believes in all that, but it's taken me longer." I get the feeling that I'm going on for too long, which makes me talk even faster, trying to fit in as much as I can before Rosita indicates I should stop. "And then just before we were scheduled to fly here, Maya came down with croup, which isn't that unusual for her, she gets it a lot, but this time she had it pretty bad and after a week she wasn't getting better. By the time we got to Guatemala City she was dreadfully sick, and she wouldn't take any of her cough medicine. She was screaming that Dodo didn't want her to take it and that Dodo didn't want her to get well. That's when everything went from being just weird to being scary."

I'm definitely talking too much, I can tell. "We already had a vacation planned to Belize, because my husband is a diver," I continue, "so we thought we'd look for someone to see down here. I ordered your book up in the States and I started reading it, and we booked an appointment with you from California, but when the flight was overbooked and we had to fly here a day later we missed the appointment and the travel agent said you didn't have any more openings." I'm really babbling now. "So the day we got here we went to San Antonio Village instead and saw a bush doctor there. His name was Canto, Ovencio Canto. Do you know him?"

She nods. "I know of him," she says. "He's good."

"But Maya went crazy the moment he touched her wrist, and I couldn't calm her down."

"Pulse prayers," she says. "Then what happened?"

"She started screaming and kicking and making horrible noises. She was having trouble breathing to begin with, and then she was choking and gasping for breath. I couldn't sit there and let it go on like that, so I stood up and ran outside with her. He gave us a bag of leaves so we could make her a tea and also to put in her bath that night, but she didn't want anything to do with it when we tried. He also gave me an ointment to put on her chest, which seems to be helping her cough. That's the story. And then Jeronie brought us here."

Rosita purses her lips a little, thoughtfully. "And since you saw the bush doctor?"

"She's been better, physically. But Dodo's still around."

"What do you think is going on?" she asks.

Me? Throughout everything that's happened over the past four months, this is the first time anyone has asked me what I thought. I've been so preoccupied with soliciting other people's opinions, and acting on their suggestions, I've never stopped to ask myself the same question. What *do* I think is going on?

Maybe it's because Rosita is an American and a mother like me and we're speaking in our native language. Or maybe it's because she has the same haircut my mother did, shorter on the sides than on the top, which cracks open a young, vulnerable place inside of me. Whatever it is, I trust her. Which is probably why I tell her the truth.

"Something's going on with my daughter," I say. "I don't have any doubt about that. Her behavior changed dramatically a few months ago. Everyone could tell. I don't know if it's a spirit, I don't think I even know what that would mean. But I don't want to get sucked into convincing myself it's a mental issue, either, because that's an even more frightening prospect. And then there's this whole other part of the equation, which is that my husband works really long hours, but since this all began he's been much more interested in being with us, more engaged in the family, which makes me wonder if I've been unconsciously pumping up the drama so he'll stick around. So," I feel myself pulling for something from her—a reaction, or a connection—and the rawness of this need embarrasses me. I make myself stop talking, mid-sentence.

Rosita has remained expressionless throughout my litany. She doesn't seem fazed by anything I've said. Nor does she seem moved. I feel a small plunge of disappointment, like a dial being turned down a notch. I thought my admission would at least have elicited—what? Congratulations? A maternal pat on the back? A compassionate frown? I guess that's not how these appointments work.

"Well," she says. "Maybe your child has a spirit attached to her, or maybe you just have a child with an overactive imagination. I'm not sure. But if it's a spirit, we'll take care of it. All right, then," she says, standing from her chair. "Let's go pick some plants."

Two raised garden beds near the parking lot hold a voluptuous array of colorful flowers and plants. Rosita strides across the grass toward the first one. I trot along behind her. I'm in reasonably good shape, but I have to really move to keep up with her. In front of the first bed, Rosita reaches down for a white plastic grocery bag lying on the ground.

"We'll start with marigolds," she says. "They're good for children." She reaches down and twists a large bunch of perfect yellow marigolds off their stems and stuffs them into the bag. The motion of her hand is deft and sure, an act of mastery. If someone told me to pick marigolds, I'd daintily pluck them by the stems one by one. Rosita has hands that know how to handle flowers.

"Then some roses," she says. From a large, bountiful rosebush nearby she extracts a handful of pink flowers. Some of the petals separate and scatter as she slips them into the bag.

"We have roses at home," I volunteer, just to have something to say, although our soil is sandy and dry, nothing like the tropics, and our roses bloom for only a few days a season before their petals start to drop.

"Next, some basil," Rosita says, striding around to the other bed.

"Like our nanny used," I say.

"Yes, but this is coming straight from the garden. It works better that way. And finally, some rue."

"What's rue?"

"It's an herb. Also called *ruta.* I use it a lot." She takes a large handful from a tall, delicate, pale green plant and adds it to the bag. "That's enough," she says and hands the bag to me. I look inside. Yellow and pink flowers are all jumbled up with dark and light green leaves. I tie the plastic handles in a knot to keep the plants inside.

"How much time before you have to leave?" she asks.

"Not much," I say. "We're driving to Placencia, and then Jeronie has to turn around and drive himself back."

She purses her lips as if she's thinking. "All right, then you'll have to do the bath yourself. Can you give your daughter a bath in Placencia tonight?"

"I don't know if there's a bathtub in our hotel room. If there isn't, I'll figure something out."

"Good. When you're preparing the water, I want you to squeeze all the leaves and flowers into it. Really get in there and mash them up. During the bath, splash the water around her a little, like this." She makes tiny splashing gestures in my direction with her hands. "And pour some over the top of her head, like you did before."

"I don't know if she'll go for it," I say. "She wasn't so hot on the idea the other night."

"Tell her she's getting a flower bath," she suggests, "and get her involved in the preparations. You can make it into a game. Children usually love that."

"I'll try it," I say.

"Also, when you're preparing the water, remember to say prayers into it. It doesn't have to be anything complicated, just some prayers while you're squeezing the flowers to bless the water."

"Out loud?" I ask. The idea horrifies me slightly. What if someone walks in and sees me praying? I'll feel foolish beyond belief.

"You can whisper them, if you want," she says.

"Can I say them in my head?"

"If you have to. It's just important that you say them."

"What if I don't know any prayers?"

"Then you can make them up. It's not that hard. You'll manage."

"Okay," I say, a little doubtfully.

"Go get your husband and daughter, and we'll finish up," she says. "I'll meet you back over there."

I head across the grass and up a gravel path, where Uzi and Maya are playing in front of an enormous nopal tree. I don't know what to make of Dr. Rosita. The nature of our meeting required me to open the book on our family and to lay out all my fears, but then her approach to treatment was so businesslike and directive I had to quickly suck all that emotion back in to absorb the instructions. I understand why it has to be this way, how practitioners need to enforce strict boundaries to protect themselves, but I hate this rawness I feel, this self-doubt, this sinking feeling that practitioners like Rosita need to protect themselves from people like me, who otherwise might try to get more than any one person can give.

What is it I want? I wonder as I motion for Uzi and Maya to come back to the deck. *Me. Just me. What do I want?* I watch my husband and daughter crossing the grass to join me, she running just a few steps ahead, he rushing to keep up. *What do I want?* The answer comes so fast and so easily it startles me with its simplicity. I want my family, this family I've created, to feel healthy and whole. That's all.

"What did you talk about?" Uzi asks, as we walk back to the deck.

"I told her about Dodo. Then she gave me flowers and plants for Maya's bath tonight."

"What's she like?"

"She's a tough cookie," I say. "But I like her."

On the deck, we sit on the two chairs Rosita and I just vacated. "You can hold the child on your lap," she instructs me. "Will she let me put my hand on her head?"

Maya shrinks into my chest just from hearing the question. "I don't think so," I say. "Can we get around that part somehow?"

"That's fine. I can just keep my hand above you. Okay, move closer together."

"All of us?" I ask. "Uzi, too?"

"I need to do it for the whole family," she explains, raising her right hand until it hovers about four inches above our heads. Then she starts whispering rapidly in Spanish and slowly circling her hand above our heads. I catch the word *dios*—God—and I think I hear *espíritu*, spirit.

There is something utterly calming about waiting patiently in a warm jungle clearing with my husband and child while a woman drenches us in prayer. Even Maya sits quietly while Rosita prays. In the trees behind us, a bird makes a loud tapping noise. I shift my body a little to the left to reduce the pressure of Maya's weight on my knees. When the rubber sole of my shoe drags across the wood deck, it makes a squeaky, scuffing noise. It's neither irritating nor interruptive. It just is.

When she finishes, Rosita holds her hand above our heads for a few seconds more, then takes it down.

"Before you leave," she says, "I want you to get some copal incense from the gift shop. We sell it there in little bags, and you might also want to pick up some charcoal rounds. You light the charcoal and then sprinkle the copal on top so it creates some smoke. Let it get really smoky, and walk around your whole living space with it, into every room, every bathroom. Make sure you do under all the beds and inside the closets, too, any place that's dark or cramped. You need to do the whole house nine times."

"Nine days in a row?" I ask.

"Sure, you can do it nine days in a row, or you can do it three days in a row three times. Whatever combination you want. It doesn't matter. Just make sure it's a total of nine times."

"Nine times," I repeat.

"Nine times," Rosita says, cementing it. "Okay, then. You're good to go."

We're good to go? That's *it*?

"We're done?" I ask. After the drama in Canto's cabin, it doesn't seem that Rosita has done anything at all.

"That's all it takes," she says.

I stand up, shifting Maya to my left hip. The serenity I felt during the prayer has evaporated as quickly as it came on. I can't believe we're done.

"How much do we owe you for the appointment?" Uzi asks.

Rosita gestures in the direction of the gift shop. "There are envelopes in there for donations," she says. "You leave whatever you can."

"Thank you, Rosita," Uzi says.

She swats the air and smiles a little. "It's no problem," she says. "It's what I do. Thank you for coming. And good luck with that friend." She makes a little shooing motion toward the gift shop.

"Thank you," I manage to squeak out. I don't want to appear ungrateful, but I'm still trying to understand how so much anticipation led to so little: a fifteen-minute conversation, a bag of leaves, and a prayer?

In the gift shop, Maya again runs to the woven basket of little worry dolls and sifts through them with her hands. I find the copal resin, sold in small, striped Guatemalan drawstring pouches. It's hard to imagine myself carrying a smoking bowl of incense through all the rooms of our house and feeling serious about it. Uzi picks up a little manila envelope near the cash register and stuffs a folded fifty-dollar bill inside.

"I can't believe we're paying for that," I say.

"I thought it was interesting. And helpful."

"Helpful? Which part?" I hold up the bag of flowers. "This is probably worth five bucks, which means you just paid forty-five for a prayer."

"I think it's worth it," he says. He looks at what's left in his wallet. "I should have given Canto more," he says. "Do you think if I leave money for him here, they can get it to him?"

"I don't know. Maybe."

I steer Maya away from the little Rainforest Remedies bottles and back toward the Guatemalan textiles. I pick up a small zippered purse on a long shoulder string, and tie a knot at the halfway point. Then I slip it over Maya's head and sling it across her chest. "For all your monies," I tell her.

Over her shoulder, I see Uzi trying to ask the shop worker about sending money to Canto. She doesn't seem to know who we're talking about.

"*Canto,*" Uzi says. "*En San Antonio. El doctor?*" as she regretfully shakes her head.

"Rosita said she knew of him," I say. "I can go ask her if there's anyone here going to San Antonio."

"Good idea," Uzi says.

I step outside into the sunlight, and head back over to the deck. I don't think this is the best way to get money to San Antonio—I think we should ask Jeronie instead—but there's something I want to ask Rosita. I'm not being truthful when I say nothing happened on the deck. Something happened to me. When Rosita said she needed to pray over the whole family, it felt as if a taut balloon were deflating inside my chest. I want to ask her why this was and why she thinks we all needed to be healed. But when I get back to the deck, it's empty. Even the chairs we sat on just a few minutes ago are gone. I look around the lawn but I don't see her anywhere, and the door to the cottage is shut. The appointment is over. I can't feel certain it even happened the way I remember it. Already, all the evidence is gone.

chapter twelve
Placencia, Belize
December 27, 2000

There are two distinct groups of mothers, I've come to believe: the Ones Who Trust and the Ones Who Do. The Ones Who Trust maintain an unwavering faith in their children's inherent perfection. They keep intervention to a minimum, operating with the belief that most problems naturally resolve on their own. If Uzi were a mother, he'd be one who trusts. Carmen would be a mother who trusts. Shakti, for sure, is a mother who trusts. Mothers who do take a more active role, believing a child's happiness depends on the steps a parent takes to ensure it. They intellectualize, they research, they weigh options, they plan. I am a mother who does—the tinkerer, the fixer, the perpetual aide—and ever since Dodo appeared, I think I've been Doing too much. The degree to which he dictates Maya's behavior unnerves me, yes, but even more, it threatens me to see her under his control. If my primary task as a mother is to protect my child, Dodo's supremacy renders me impotent and insubstantial, and so the stronger he comes on, the harder I fight back. (My God, I realize, I've been entangled in a power struggle with an illusion.) Yet the alternative to this struggle, which is riding out Dodo's presence and hoping he'll eventually fade away, feels like too much of a risk. That's what's been driving my insistence on having control. I'm afraid if I don't fight back, I'll lose. If faith is a willing surrender to the unknown, which I believe it is, then the opposite of faith is not cynicism, or disbelief. The opposite of faith is fear.

All this I think, on the four-hour drive between Dr. Rosita's farm and the Caribbean coast.

The couple who run the Mariposa Beach Suites in Placencia could not possibly be more gracious. Marcia is an Englishwoman with stylishly short blond hair and a tropical muumuu, and Peter is every bit the bespectacled, retired San Francisco businessman in his short-sleeved polo shirt and pressed khaki shorts. A few years ago, they bought a beach lot on the Placencia peninsula and built their retirement home here, a two-story hacienda with a large owners' apartment on top and two smaller guest apartments underneath. After we say our good-byes to Jeronie and carry our bags into the guest apartment on the left, they offer to drive us a mile south in their golf cart to the heart of the village, but Uzi would rather walk there on the beach. Four hours in the Trooper, the last third of it bone-jarringly bumpy, has made him eager to get his limbs working again.

"You're sure?" Marcia asks. "It's a long way there and back."

He's sure, though he says we'll take them up on the offer to borrow bicycles another day. I don't really feel like walking right now—I don't feel like doing much of anything after this morning's encounter—but I also don't want to keep Uzi and Maya cooped up inside, and ever since we left Dr. Rosita's farm, she won't let me out of her sight. She wants to be touching a part of my body at all times, even if it's just a shoulder pressed lightly against my arm. She wants security today, but there's no obvious reason why. She doesn't seem frightened or threatened or sick, she had no visible reaction to Dr. Rosita, and the ride to Placencia was long but uneventful. So I'm stumped by this one.

Before she goes upstairs, Marcia warns us about sand flies, so I pull some insect repellent from my backpack and smear it on our ankles and calves. While I'm rubbing it on Maya, Uzi goes into the bathroom, then sticks his head back out the door.

"They have a bathtub here," he reports. "And a shower."

"I want a bath tonight!" Maya shouts. "Please, Mommy, a bath!"

"Good thing you bring it up," I tell her. "Because I have a really nice bath you can take tonight. A flower bath." I glance at the kitchen sink across the room, where I've placed the plastic bag of flowers Dr. Rosita handed me . . . was it only four hours ago? Already, it feels as if days have passed. Time reshapes itself into a completely different geometry down here.

Maya scrunches up her nose. "Whaaht?" she says, dragging out the syllable with a perfect New York accent. She sounds just like my beloved ninety-year-old Cousin Billie, who says it like "Whaaht? Are you crazy?! Whaaht?" and hearing it makes me laugh out loud, because Maya must have picked up the inflection from me.

"It's a bath with flowers in the water," I tell her. "Roses, like the ones we have at home. It's pretty. You'll see."

"No flowers. I don't want a flower bath."

"Why don't you see it before you decide? We've got a whole bag of pretty flowers, and you can help me put them in. The Hursulas can go with you."

"*Hursulas!*" she shouts in a panic, looking wildly around the room. Oh, no—did we leave them in the Trooper?

"Uzi!" I call toward the bathroom. "Do you know where the Hursulas are?"

"They're on the big bed with the bags!" he shouts back. "I found them when I double-checked the car!"

Maya runs to the larger of the two beds and unearths the dolls from the pile. She clutches them to her chest with an expression of pure relief, then glues herself back onto my leg. We sidle over to the kitchen together, where I wipe my hands on a dish towel and investigate the cabinets. They're the definition of fully stocked, right down to the vegetable steamer and the box of cornflakes I asked for via email when Marcia volunteered to buy food for us in advance. I open the refrigerator door to find a quart of milk, two pint-sized containers of orange juice, a jar of peanut butter, a stick of butter, and six eggs. On the counter there's a box of cornflakes and a bowl of oranges and bananas, next to a loaf of homemade zucchini bread baked by Marcia—which happens to have been my mother's name, even the same spelling—with a note card propped in front of the plate: "Welcome and enjoy! Marcia and Peter."

I pick Maya up and carry her across the room, although at thirty-five pounds she's almost too heavy for me now. Across the apartment, two sets of French doors open to a tiled patio. Two steps down, and there's the beach. A warm ocean breeze wafts across the room to the open window above the kitchen sink. The patio has a small table, two chairs, a hammock, and a view of a palm tree growing straight from the sand. Its oblong coconuts bunch up like smooth green testicles at the base of its fronds. A few have dropped onto the sand, where they lie half submerged from gravity's pull.

Uzi steps out of the bathroom, his hair wet and gleaming from a quick shower, and greets us with a friendly *woof*.

"Meow," Maya responds. He tosses his head back and laughs, and in that moment I catch a rare glimpse of the boy inside the man. For what must be the 178th time since we married, I wish I'd known him back then, before companies and deadlines and strollers. Although, as we often remind each other, if we'd met as the seventeen-year-olds we once were, there's almost no chance we'd be together now.

He clutches the outside of his front pocket to make sure he has his wallet. Affirmative. "Have you seen my sandals?" he asks, just as he finds them exactly where he always leaves them, inside the front door. He smiles sheepishly at me.

"Whenever you're ready," he says.

Between the two of us, Uzi and I have traveled on the most visited street in the world (the Champs-Élysées), the longest (Toronto's Yonge

Street), and the most crooked (Lombard Street in San Francisco). After today we can add the narrowest to our list, although I'm not sure you can legitimately call Placencia's Main Street a street. It's more like a four-foot-wide concrete sidewalk on top of the beach. As the story goes, it was built thirty years ago so fishermen could transport wheelbarrows of the day's catch into town without having to wrestle with the sand.

Today the sidewalk runs three quarters of a mile through the heart of Placencia Village, past yards on both sides overflowing with bougainvillea and garnished with full laundry lines. I can reach out and touch picket fences or pluck hibiscus flowers from trees growing so close in they brush the sides of my face. If I really stretch, my fingertips can skim a windowsill, even the sides of clapboard homes. When all three of us walk abreast, Uzi has to keep one foot in the sand. I imagine what we must look like from behind, the two matching tall, dark-haired parents on either side, each holding the hand of the child in between, like a 212 area code out for a stroll by the beach.

The village of Placencia sits at the southern tip of an eighteen-mile-long peninsula that juts away from the mainland like a downcast finger. Most of the walk to the village is along fine, pale sand past modest beachfront resorts with screened-in cabins plotted in W formations to maximize the usage of each lot. Mature palm trees jut and swoop out of the sand. Closer to town, chunky, square homes painted purple, yellow, royal blue, and mint green balance on pylons that jack them four feet above the sand. They all have white wraparound porches, giving each row a delectable, lollipop appeal. At virtually any spot on the walk I can make two right angles with my thumbs and forefingers and frame a picture-perfect shot. I've never before been to Hawaii or Polynesia, or any tropical destination that could reasonably be called paradise, even as hyperbole, but this comes close to how I imagine it would be. The air here is warming rather than warm, the scent of salt water neither overbearing nor too slight. Fewer than five hundred people live in Placencia, but as we walk by at least a dozen of them stop to wave at us from their porches and front yards.

"I want to stay here forever," I tell Uzi, who's heard that one before.

We pass an octagonal Anglican church that looks like a white yurt on stilts. A local girl comes skipping barefoot down the path and we step off the sidewalk onto the sand to let her pass. She has the flawless ebony skin of the Creoles, who've run Placencia's fishing operation for the past hundred years, and startlingly blue eyes, which mean there's likely to be a Scot somewhere in her family's story. In the eighteenth and nineteenth centuries, most of this land was owned by English and Scottish families, whose surnames still appear in the local phone book. Stretch the town's story further back to the 1600s, and the town was settled by English Puritans from Nova Scotia, or even further, and fourteen Maya settlements once dotted the lagoon, making it an important pre-Columbian site for salt making and coastal trade. This strip of beach is rumored to be one of the oldest continually inhabited areas of Belize.

We cross over to the peninsula's only paved road, where a pink-and-green family-run restaurant advertises a late lunch. It's a one-room clapboard building in the direct path of afternoon sun, where a barefoot waitress brings us the day's special of fresh red snapper with sides of coleslaw, coconut rice, and beans. Brian, who spent three days in Placencia before heading up to Cayo, told us we'd need to develop a taste for rice and beans since we'd eat so much of them down here. After lunch, when we stop in one of the village's markets, I learn why. The bins reserved for fruits and vegetables hold only a few onions, a small pile of potatoes, and a couple of browning bananas, and the refrigerator along the wall has been picked clean, while the dry-goods aisles are well stocked with canned foods and ten-pound sacks of rice and beans.

"I have no butter, and I don't know what I'm getting tomorrow," the salesclerk behind the counter is saying into her telephone. Her bread shelves are barren as well. When I ask about cucumbers, she says, "Maybe tomorrow. Come early, vegetables and dairy go fast."

"I love it," Uzi tells me. "People use only what they need, and this way there's no waste."

"This way there's no vegetables," I say. Maya walks over and hands me a bag of macaroni and a squat can of *chiles jalapeños*.

"I'm helping," she announces.

"Thank you!" I hand the can of chilis back to her. "Can you put this one back where you found it?"

"Do you think you'll have bread tomorrow?" I ask the clerk.

"What kind?"

"Any kind. Doesn't matter."

"Pedro!" she calls toward the back of the store. "*Tenemos pan aquí para la mujer?*"

A boy emerges from a back room with a loaf of white bread and puts it in my hands. I start to thank him, then realize it might be coming from the owner's private stash.

"It's okay," I say. "I can come back tomorrow. *Puedo venir mañana.*" I push the loaf back into the boy's hands.

"It's okay," the woman says. "*Daselo a ella*, Pedro." Pedro pushes the bread back at me. It's soft and pliable, like something in the process of forming. Already it bears the imprint of both our hands.

"*Gracias,*" I say. I make a mental note to come back tomorrow to make sure more bread has arrived.

Maya comes skipping across the store and hands me an onion. "Thank you very much," I say. She wraps both arms around my right leg. I buy the loaf of bread, the onion, and the bag of macaroni.

Outside, we embark on a search for an Internet café. I promised my father, brother, and sister that I'd contact them after we arrived, but Crystal Paradise didn't have connectivity and we've been out of touch with everyone at home for five days now, since we left L.A. Across the street there's a soccer field with what looks like a pickup game in progress. About a dozen boys and men lope back and forth across a lawn that's as much dirt as grass. It's impossible to tell who's on what side or if there are teams. One of the boys jogs over in our direction, kicks an empty soda can through the white post-and-rail fence, and jogs back onto the field.

A man with long, swinging dreadlocks and a red soccer jersey is crossing the road toward the field. "Excuse me," Uzi says, intercepting him. "Do you know where we can find an Internet café here, or a public computer with Internet connection?"

The man flashes us a blindingly white smile. "Ay, mahn, what you need da Internet for?" He taps a forefinger against his forehead. "You gotta whole world in 'ere."

"We need to reach our families in the States," I explain.

"Ah, den you need da Space Monkey, mahn. Right dere." He points down the road to a big open-air palapa on the left. Its shaggy thatched roof extends over the front steps like ragged bangs.

"Thanks," Uzi says. "Have a good game."

"Ah, it's just fun, mahn," the man says, giving us a two-finger wave. "But danks anyway."

The Purple Space Monkey Internet Café opened just three months ago, but it's already a popular pit stop for expatriates and tourists with its four dial-up computers and satellite transmission of American TV. From the outside nothing about the place resembles a restaurant, but under the heavy thatched roof lie a sports bar and café with two televisions, a wooden bar backed by shelves of alcohol bottles, and a deafeningly loud espresso machine. Off to one side there's a book exchange where travelers can choose a well-thumbed paperback from the tall wooden shelves and leave one of theirs behind.

The computers are lined up against the back wall on the left, two of them vacant. Uzi takes the seat on the far right. Maya and I weave our way through the tables and peruse the bookshelves. I need to find something to occupy her, so I can get some computer time. The road between Cayo and here was too bumpy for me to write in my journal, and I haven't yet put down my impression of the morning's events. The details are still swimming around shapelessly, lacking defined borders. One at a time, they randomly shoot up to the surface—the rows of smooth green butterfly cocoons, the Mennonite farmers in the waiting room, the marigolds in Dr. Rosita's flower bed—to remind me how differently the second half of this day is shaping up from the first. It's as if we emerged from a green womb before noon, to buy bread and onions in Eden before the sun sets.

I scan the Space Monkey's shelves: *The Great Gatsby*, *Harry Potter and the Sorcerer's Stone*, Ayn Rand's *The Fountainhead*, and Herman Hesse's *Siddhartha*. Heady beach reading in this town. I find an old Spider-Man comic book for Maya, not the most suitable choice but the only illustrated option they've got.

I sit in front of the one available computer and try to log on. The connectivity here is so slow it might as well be nonexistent. Maya sits at my feet and pages through the comic while I wait for the Yahoo! home page to load.

"I've been trying for half an hour," says the woman on my right, frowning as she gives her enter button three steady pecks. "Eventually it works, but you can't predict when. It's BTL—Belize Telecom—we call it 'better try later.'"

She's a small blond slip of a thing in flip-flops and short shorts. Her name is Monica, she tells me, extending her hand for a shake, and she just drove down from Wisconsin in her pickup with a friend. Tomorrow she'll meet up with her boyfriend, who's captained their new sailboat down from the States. He lives here most of the year; she goes back and forth.

"It's complicated," she says. I nod.

"How long have you been coming here?" I ask. I mean Belize, not the Internet café.

"I followed a guy down here when I was eighteen, so that was 1980. He said the place was already ruined by tourism back then." She glances around the café and pokes at the enter key two more times. "Actually, that was a great time to be here."

If she was eighteen in 1980, that makes her . . . two years older than me. *Really?* She looks at least five years younger. That must be what no children and enough sleep can do for you. I'm just guessing about the no children part, since I can't imagine how she could go back and forth between Wisconsin and Belize the way she does if she had one. Even without a child, I wouldn't have the moxie to make that drive.

"Mommy." Maya pulls on my leg. I scoop her up and plunk her on my lap. Her mouth is stretching down and out like she's about to cry and . . . here it comes. "Yasheee," she wails. "I miss Yasheee."

"You miss *Yashi*?" I say. What did I miss here?

"Who's Yashi?" Monica asks.

"Our cat in California. I have no idea why she misses her now."

Monica raises her eyebrows. "Oh-kaaay," she says.

"You don't have kids?" I hold Maya's head against my chest and rock her.

Monica shakes her head no. "Dogs. Two of them. They're my babies."

"Did you bring them down with you?" I try to picture how that would work, two dogs, two women, and their luggage in a pickup truck in winter.

"You don't even want to know."

Maya pushes me away, darts across the restaurant, and drops herself dramatically onto the middle of the serving floor. "Yasheee, Yasheee," she moans.

Several of the diners turn to look at the source of the noise. At times like this I'm supposed to feel empathy for my child, I know that's what mothers are supposed to feel, but mostly what I feel right now is embarrassed.

Uzi leans back behind Monica. "What's going on?" he asks.

"She misses Yashi."

"Yashi? Now?"

"Don't ask me. I'm just the mother." I stand up and push in my chair. "I'll go to her. I'm not making any progress here, anyway." As I walk past his computer, I notice that Uzi has managed to log on to his email account. "Quick, before you lose the connection—can you email my family?"

"What do you want me to say?"

"Tell them . . ."

What *do* I want to tell them? The details of the past five days come to me in one big anachronistic rush: the endless treetops at Tikal; a mirrored bathtub in Guatemala City; Sri Lankan curry in San Ignacio; the tiny, luminescent frog in the shower at Crystal Paradise; iridescent blue butterfuly wings; Orion the night of the Christmas party; Dr. Rosita's instructions for burning copal; zucchini bread on a kitchen counter; the worn floor of Canto's cabin; a square orange house on a white-sand beach. I wouldn't know where to start.

"Tell them we made it here fine," I say. "And that we're coming back Monday as planned."

"Yasheee," Maya moans. "Dodo. Dodo-oh-oh."

My grandmother used to say, *"Oy gevalt."* My mother would say "Sugar!" to keep herself from uttering worse. I'm less tactful than the women who preceded me. I never lapse into euphemism when a good, strong expletive succinctly hits the mark.

"Oh, shit," I say.

Monica raises her eyebrows. She wasn't expecting that from me.

"You don't even want to know," I tell her.

By the time I cross the restaurant, Maya has crawled underneath an empty dining table. I push the tablecloth aside and crawl underneath beside her.

"What's going on?" I ask.

"Dodo!" she cries.

"What happened to Dodo?"

She looks up at me in a panic and scuttles backward like a crab, bumping into the leg of an adjacent table, where two tourists are waiting for their meal. The water in their glasses sloshes up and over the rims and onto the tablecloth. They don't look pleased.

"I'm sorry," I say, getting up on my knees and wiping the water off the table with my hand. "I'm so sorry. I'll get it cleaned up for you."

The woman makes a little annoyed *kuh* sound in the back of her throat and scoots her chair an inch to the right, as if we might contaminate her. How did she wind up here, in the laid-back capital of Central

America? Some travel agent must have made a terrible mistake. I reach out to pull Maya away, but she tips her shoulder in front of her chin and leans as far away from me as she can without falling over.

"Maya," I say. "*What* is going on? Tell Mommy what's wrong."

"Nyah!" she shouts.

"*Excuse* me," the woman says.

"We'll be gone in just a minute," I tell her over my shoulder, then turn back to Maya. "I need you to come over there with me now, right now, or I'm going to have to pick you up and carry you."

"How old is she?" the woman at the table asks, not kindly.

"Eleven!" I snap. "What do you think? She's *three*."

The woman recoils in distaste, but I don't care. What kind of stupid question was that? If she thinks a child needs to be dragged away by force in public, let her try it with her own kid. And good luck with that.

Maya scrambles away on her hands and knees, dragging both Hursulas along with her. She curls into a ball under a television in the corner where a female newscaster somewhere in America is talking straight at the camera with the sound turned down.

"All right," I say to Maya. "You know what? We need to go outside. Let's go see the fishing boats. You want to come with Mommy to see the fishing boats?"

She lifts her head and glances toward the exit. I sense a slight opening and stick my foot in. "They're probably coming back from a day on the ocean right now," I say. "When the boats come in . . . they're filled with fish. You can see them all piled up on the deck. Fish flopping all over the place. You want to go see?" I have no idea if this happens here, but it sounds as if it could, so it's not completely a fiction.

"Okay," she says.

"Good," I say, extending my hand. "Let's go tell Dad where we're going."

Just two blocks away, at the southern tip of the peninsula, both the road and the sidewalk end at the Placencia dock. The dock is a path of weathered wood extending straight into the sea, surrounded by a gaggle of white motorboats. A half-dozen dive shops aggregate at its base. The Natural Mystic Guide Service is our favorite, Maya and I decide, with its rainbow lettering and a tropical sea mural painted on its front wall. There's also a raucous bar with reggae music spilling from its open door, a variety store selling fabric hammocks and Guatemalan shoulder bags, and an open-air Shell station that's little more than two pumps under a corrugated tin roof and a big, hand-lettered NO SMOK-ING sign.

The motorboats coming in to rest on the beach unload snorkelers and divers who disembark noisily into the shallow water with their flippers and gear in their hands. The divers look like bipedal seals in their black wet suits and catch enough of Maya's interest to distract her from noticing that I haven't produced any fishing boats. We noodle around barefoot at the base of the dock for a while, looking for starfish. Behind us, the sun hangs low in the sky. I didn't pay much attention to the sun's path in Cayo, where our days were so carefully planned, and it occurs to me that this is the first time since leaving Los Angeles that we've gone off a schedule. No one is picking us up or expecting us for dinner, and our only plans for tomorrow are to sleep late and eventually walk outside. The next four days extend ahead of us, as pristine and untainted as an open field of snow.

When Uzi finds us, we're swinging our feet off the edge of the dock, watching tentacles of seaweed undulate in the clear water below. I give him a *Where have you been?* look with my eyebrows. We have a long walk back, and we didn't bring a flashlight.

"How much daylight do you think is left?" I ask him.

He looks back at the shops and trees behind him. "About thirty minutes," he guesses. There don't seem to be any cabs here, and if any of the motorboats resting half in the water and half on the sand can function as water taxis, it's not clear.

"By the time we ask around and find out no one can take us, we'll be in the dark," I say. "I think we should start walking."

How is it that every journey to get to a destination feels longer than the way home, except at sunset in Placencia, where exactly the opposite is true? Uzi picks up Maya and starts walking up the beach so fast he looks like a windup machine, and still, every five minutes when I stop to catch my breath, I feel compelled to announce, "I can't *believe* we walked this far before. Are you sure we're going the right way?"

The sand is mostly deserted at this hour, except for a few intermittent couples wrapped in each other's arms, gazing at the gently breaking surf. The ocean is calm tonight, perfect for midnight dives. A thick stripe of seaweed marks the high-tide line, forming mounds that look like piles of brown fettucini doused with liberal amounts of salt. We zip past the candy-colored houses; past the palm trees scooping out and up over the ocean like capital letter Js; past Francis Ford Coppola's beach resort under construction; until, in the last few waning moments of the day, we see the small, thatched cabanas of Kitty's Place, the resort adjacent to our guest apartment. Uzi gratefully relinquishes Maya to the sand, where she breaks free from us and gallops ahead.

She gets only about thirty feet before coming to a dead stop. A heart-piercing wail of anguish cuts through the day's last veil of light.

A child's cries are a distinctive vernacular of their own, a language only a family can speak. Maya's scream of pain is unmistakable, making me drop everything midsentence and instinctively hurry in her direction. Her howl of outrage is released when a child grabs her playground toy or when she's given a time-out. When she's tired her cry sounds like a worn-down siren, and when she's faking for attention it's a whine that comes in broken pieces from the back of her throat. This cry isn't any of those. This one is high-pitched and panicked, her wail of shock and grief when she's just realized something is lost. As soon as I hear it, I know what it means.

"Which one?" I call out to Maya, as I run up to her on the sand.

She stands at the water's edge with her shoulders slumped toward the sand. When she sees me, she looks up with an expression of pure sorrow. "Hursula One!" she cries, clutching the solitary Hursula Zero in her hands. "She's gone!"

Tonight's moon is a waxing crescent, a thin sliver of a smile barely shining any light onto the sand. We'll never be able to find a lost doll on the beach tonight.

"Do you remember where you saw her last?" Uzi asks. I try to think back to any time this afternoon when I registered the presence of two dolls. She had them at the Space Monkey, when she was crawling on the floor. Did she have them both at the dock? I can't remember.

"Did you have her at the boats?" I ask.

"I don't know," she sobs. "We need to find her!"

"I can get the flashlight," Uzi offers.

She could be on the road between the Internet café and the dock or on the dock or in the water by the dock or anywhere on the beach between there and here. Or someone could have picked her up in the past half hour, which means she could be anywhere in town by now.

"I don't know," I say. "Maybe we can look right around here for now, and then we'll walk back down the beach in the morning."

"Hursula will want me!" Maya cries. "We need to find her! She will be scared!"

"I hope she didn't get pulled into the water," I say, thinking out loud, which turns out to be the worst possible thing I could have said within earshot of Maya.

"No!" she screeches, hopping up and down in the sand. "No!"

"Maya, calm down," Uzi says. "We'll find her."

"No! Hursula can't swim!" Faster than I can grab her, Maya takes off for the ocean, and my rib cage follows her as if it's being yanked by a thick rope. She's not water safe yet, but that idea doesn't even have time to register as a thought before my body is catapulting through the dark toward the moving shape of hers. I tackle her on the wet sand, landing on the hip that's still sore from yesterday's fall. Sand is softer than limestone, but the impact still sends a dull pain shooting through my pelvis.

I grasp Maya tightly and roll us up to sitting. The water is barely lapping at my feet. There's a good twenty-foot margin before Maya would even have been ankle-deep, plenty of room for Uzi or me to have intercepted her, and I can't help feeling silly for making such a dramatic rescue.

"Good catch," Uzi says anyway, sounding impressed.

"Hursula," Maya sobs against my chest. "I want Hursula."

Uzi helps us up to standing and we stagger diagonally across the beach to the apartment. The backs and sides of my legs are covered with wet sand. Uzi holds Maya while I peel off my khaki pants at the door.

"I feel like such an idiot," I tell him.

"You couldn't help it."

"That's why I feel like an idiot."

"No, I mean you couldn't help it because you love her. I had the same instinct, just not as fast as yours." He smoothes my hair behind my ear and kisses me on the left temple. "You're the mother," he says. "It's how you're wired."

The day of our wedding, I told the rabbi that I was marrying Uzi because he was the kindest man I'd ever met. His eyes tonight are tired and tender, yet in them I can still find the generosity of spirit that drew me to him four and a half years ago. Maya sticks her second and third fingers into her mouth and leans back against his shoulder, crying softly. He bounces her up and down just as he did those first ten weeks when she had colic. He bounced her so much back then, he almost ruined his knees.

"The Maya Dance," I say.

He laughs a little at the reminder, and Maya looks up, startled, as if the unexpected sound of laughter awakens a primordial memory. "Heh?" she says through the tears.

"Daddy's doing the Maya Dance," I tell her. "That's what we called it when you were a baby," and around her fingers, she forms the barest outline of a smile.

"Why don't we get her changed, and I'll take her next door for dinner," Uzi says. "You can rest here for a while and join us later if you want."

"Hursula," Maya injects.

"We'll look for her on the way," Uzi promises.

I push open the door to the apartment, and step inside. "Hey!" I say. "Did you notice that before?" I point to the wall in front of us, where three tin butterflies are arranged in a triangle above the queen-size bed. Two of them are orange, the other royal blue. I must have missed them the first time, and now their presence seems significant, more than just a coincidence. "There are *butterflies* on the wall. Do you see?"

"Well, the place is called Mariposa," Uzi says, zipping open Maya's suitcase to find her clean clothes. That's butterfly in Spanish.

"You know some Spanish?" I say. He speaks Hebrew, French, Danish, some Arabic and Sanskrit, I knew about all those, but Spanish, too? That's been a pretty well kept secret for four and a half years, not to mention for the past four days.

He taps his index finger against his forehead and gives me a lopsided smile. "I gotta whole world in 'ere, mahn," he says.

From the beach, the three curved archways on the upper veranda of Kitty's Place Beach Resort glow warm and gold above the low-lying palms. To reach the restaurant, I'm directed up a flight of outdoor stairs. Inside there are football pennants and Bob Marley posters on the walls but no father and daughter waiting at a table, the hostess says, so I head down to the lobby and gift shop, hoping to find Maya and Uzi there.

I hear them before I see them. The peal of Maya's laughter rings out from around a corner. I haven't heard that sound for weeks, but I'd recognize it anywhere. I slow down, curious to know what's making her laugh like that yet reluctant to interrupt whatever might be provoking it.

A potted palm is stationed at the next corner, and I sidle up alongside it. Through its feathery green fronds I can see Maya and Uzi sitting on a porch swing near the gift shop. Uzi rocks the swing from his feet on the floor.

"Okay, kitty?" he asks. "Are you ready?"

"Ready."

"All right, then. Everyone put on your moon goggles." They both mimic the motion of adjusting goggles over their eyes.

"Meow!" Maya says.

"Now put on your moon belt," he says. They pretend to lock on seat belts.

"Meow!"

A hard lump lodges at the base of my throat. All the times I've badgered my husband for his absences, all the times I've belittled him for not knowing the intricacies of parenting Maya—and there he is, pulling her out of the Hursula funk by himself. That takes creativity and no small amount of patience, I know.

"Everybody put on your moon boots," Uzi announces. They both lift their legs and waggle their feet in the air.

"All right," Uzi says. "Are. You. Ready?" He pushes back against the floor until his legs fully extend. "Ten, nine, eight, seven, six, five . . . "

He lifts his feet and the swing swoops forward, creaking loudly as it goes. Maya squeals loudly with delight. When she was barely two, Uzi would sometimes swing her upside down by the ankles like a pendulum, singing "Tick, tock, tick, tock, I'm a little cuckoo clock." Before he even stopped she'd be shouting, "Again! Again!" Uzi used to call it "the energy of More."

The porch swing sways back and forward, back and forward, starting to slow down. "Again!" Maya shouts, "Again!" and I see a look of recognition sweep across Uzi's face, stretching his mouth into a slow smile.

If a father and daughter reconnect on a swing and a mother isn't there to see it, does it really happen? Quantum physics tells us that the act of observing a particle pushes it out of the realm of probability and into something actual. Only when a consciousness is directed toward it with an intention does it become something real. Put more simply, the act of being observed changes the properties of that which is being observed. Can the same be true with human behavior? It's impossible for me to know if this moment between Uzi and Maya would be unfolding exactly like this if I weren't here to see it. Possibly it might not. The three of us are so intertwined that the absence of one alters the behavior of the others. The presence of all three of us matters even more. It makes a triangle out of what would otherwise be just a line.

I step out from behind the palm and walk over as if I've only now arrived.

"Mommy!" Maya calls out, waving when she sees me. "I'm a moon kitty! I'm going to the moon!"

Uzi gives me the thumbs-up sign to indicate *Things have turned around.*

"Excellent job, Jim," I say in my best *Mission: Impossible* voice.

"We just went on a moon voyage," he says. "Apparently, we're going on another. Want to come?"

"Sure," I say. Maya slides closer to Uzi to make room for me, picks up my hand, and licks it when I sit down. "Good kitty," I say, patting the top of her head.

"We didn't find Hursula," she tells me.

"It's okay," I say. "I'll help you look tomorrow."

"Okay," Uzi announces. "Here we go. Everybody put on your moon goggles." We pull the imaginary goggles over our heads.

"And everyone put on your moon belt." We mime locking our seat belts in place.

"And don't forget your moon boots." We lift our legs and waggle our feet in the air.

"And now your moon . . . help me out here."

"Your moon hats," I say.

"Moon *hats*?" Maya asks.

"Sure, why not? It's cold up there," Uzi says, giving me a little wink. We plant our imaginary hats on our heads. "All right," he says, pushing the swing as far back as it can go. "Everybody ready for take-off? Count with me, Maya. Ten. Nine. Eight."

"She doesn't know how to count backward," I say.

"Yes, she does. I just taught her. Seven. Six."

"Five. Four. Three. Meow," Maya says.

"One. Blast off!" they shout. Uzi pushes hard against the porch floor and releases his feet. "Hold on, everyone!" he says. I grip the armrest and scream along with Maya as the swing takes off toward the beach, then dips back toward the porch, two times, three times, four, a heavy pendulum tick-tocking across the tiled floor.

When was the last time the three of us played together just for the fun of it, without a predetermined objective in mind? I can't think of a single time in the past year when we spent an hour in the pursuit of nothing more than a good time. How can that be? I run through a fast slide show of images of the past few years, trying to find one that fits— does taking Maya to Sea World together count?—and then the strangest thing happens. My line of thinking just stops, right there. I completely let go of the need to come up with evidence to support my theory.

Whatever I need—what *we* need—is right here on this swing. Sitting. Playing. Now. And I realize, in this moment, that this is how a family grows. Not by the addition of more children or through the race to endlessly accumulate more or from my constant attempts to guard against loss, but in ordinary moments like this one. Deceptively simple moments that manage to be worth everything while appearing to be worth nothing at all.

Uzi cups his hand over his mouth as the swing slowly rocks back to neutral. "Hou-ston," he says, in his best robot voice. "We-have-a-landing."

"Again!" Maya shrieks. "Again!"

Some people believe every plant species contains its own intelligence, designed for its own healing purpose. People who eat the hallucino-genic root of the iboga tree speak of being visited by a man made of branches and leaves who listens to their troubles, and Carlos Castaneda described the spirit of mescaline as a black dog that inspires play. By tapping into this higher level of intelligence, it is said, ancient shamans discovered which plants to use for what. This could explain how healers who lived continents apart learned the same uses for similar plants.

If the copal tree has a spirit, it must be a dancer of the rain forest, a mercurial, diaphanous creature tumbling gracefully through the air. A female form wrapped in white skirts of gauze, beckoning us to follow. The ancient Mesoamericans who used copal resin in their religious ceremonies and for inducing trance states called it *pom* and believed it to be the food of the gods. They offered its smoke to their deities as sustenance, believing it could magically transform into divine and edible food. Today, Maya groups in Guatemala, Mexico, and Belize ritually pass copal smoke across a person's body to cleanse the spirit and drive away bad influences and bad luck, and although it's not a hallucinogenic, shamans inhale its smoke to help them enter trances for healing and divination.

The copal we bought at Dr. Rosita's farm looks like tiny rough pellets of light amber tossed with dried needles of rosemary. When we sprinkle a pinch of the mixture on top of a burning charcoal round, the pebbles turn shiny and gummy and the rosemary blackens. They combine to release a piney, woodsy fragrance that spirals upward in thin tendrils of smoke. When Maya was barely a year old, Uzi lit an incense stick and she reached out and tried to grab the smoke with her hand. She does the same thing with the copal smoke now, laughing as she relearns the futility of the act.

"Are we supposed to do it five nights here and four nights at home or nine times in each place?" I ask Uzi.

He's holding one of Marcia's saucers that we wrapped in aluminum foil before placing the charcoal on top. A small cloud of incense precedes him as he walks around the room. The apartment walls are ringed in a thick border of hand-painted Maya glyphs, encircling us in colorful, ancient script.

"I don't know," he says. Thin pulses of smoke rise from the saucer and partially obscure his face. It's not a very big room, and my eyes are already starting to sting from the smoke. He gets down on his knees and waves the saucer underneath Maya's twin bed.

"Don't forget the closets," I tell him, remembering what Dr. Rosita said. I scan the other side of the room. "You think we should do the kitchen cabinets?"

"It couldn't hurt." He opens the door under the sink, waves the saucer around, closes the door, and opens the cabinet that holds the pots and pans. Maya crawls behind him meowing. Every now and then I reach down and pet her head.

I volunteered Uzi for the censing job, thinking I would feel foolish waving a saucer of incense around. Now as I watch him moving through the room with a sense of calm purpose, I wish I'd offered to do it myself. The tight outsider's self-consciousness I felt just a few days ago has started to unravel. Until now, I've been unable to apply real conviction to my actions here, as if to do so would make me just another American eager to role-play being indigenous for a few days. If I couldn't take the spiritual actions of a culture seriously, I felt, it seemed false and misguided—disrespectful, even—to partake in them at all. But the meeting with Dr. Rosita this morning has changed that. The more I've had time to think about it, the calm consideration she gave my story without trying to force any labels on it, her matter-of-fact attitude about the problem and how to solve it effectively, has started to peel back my layers of resistance. I can't say I'm eager to give Maya the flower bath tonight, but I'm not feeling reluctant or skeptical about it, either. That alone is a noticeable change.

When Uzi finishes smoking the apartment, I bring the bag of flowers and a tall glass from the kitchen into the bathroom. Maya crawls behind me and puts her paws up on the bathtub's rim. I don't have a separate bucket for squeezing the plants into water, so I'll have to do it right into the bathwater in the tub.

I open the plastic bag and display its contents to Maya. "Isn't it pretty?" I ask. The leaves and petals inside have gone limp after six hours, but the colors are still lucid and bright, creating a botanical salad of yellow, white, red, and green.

"Mm," Maya says. "Can I touch them?" She sticks her hand in the bag and rummages around.

"You can help me squeeze them in the water," I tell her. "Let's get your clothes off first." I run the bathwater as we pull her lime green Teletubbies T-shirt over her head. Then I help her out of her plaid shorts. Uzi is standing in the bathroom doorway, and I motion with my head for him to join us.

He shakes his head slightly. He's got a funny look on his face. What's wrong? I'm only taking off her clothes. Am I doing it too fast? Am I wasting too much water filling the tub?

"What?" I ask.

"I don't think I belong here right now," he says.

"Belong where?"

"In here. I can't explain it. But I've got the feeling that whatever's going on is between the two of you. I'm just going to be in the way."

"Are you insane? I'm just giving her a bath. Come on in."

He shakes his head again and steps back from the door with a little wave good-bye. "I'll come back later," he says.

I sigh, a big, deep sigh, and turn the water off. One day, I hope, I will understand this man, but there's probably one flower bath and twenty-something years between now and that time.

"Daddy's going?" Maya asks.

I lift my shoulders and frown as if to say, *Who knows?* "Looks like it's just you and me tonight, kitty," I say. I lift her up and into the warm water. "In you go."

"Hursula," she says. I pick up Hursula Zero from the floor and place her in the water with Maya, where she floats faceup.

"Where's the flowers?" Maya asks.

"Right here." I pull a handful from the bag and let them tumble into the water. Each segment of plant and flower separates from the others as it drops, creating a kaleidoscope of falling color. I do this two more times. Then I turn the bag upside down over the tub and shake it twice to make sure everything goes in.

The plant pieces float on top of the water. Maya takes a couple of steps in place, then squats right into the middle of the floating garden. I skim some of the petals and leaves into a small pile in the water in front of her.

Okay. What now?

"I guess we do it like this," I say. I squeeze the plant material until it forms a wet clump in my hands and then release it back into the water. "You can do it, too." Maya gives it a try and giggles. "Flowers in the water," she sings as she mashes petals and leaves in her fists. "Flowers in the water." Dr. Rosita was right: she's turning it into a game.

Dr. Rosita also told me to pray while I squeezed the flowers, and I feel my chest constrict a little in resistance when I remember this part. Prayers are for churches and synagogues, for mosques and Seders, hospital corridors and group Bible lessons. Twenty solemn people gathered around the table. I'm kneeling on a bathroom floor up to my elbows in bathwater. It's hard to imagine anything that will make me feel more ridiculous than bursting into prayer right now.

Can I say them in my head? I asked Dr. Rosita. *If you have to,* she told me. *It's just important that you say them.*

If I don't pray inside my head right now, nobody else will ever know. But wouldn't it be cheating?

It's just important that you say them, Dr. Rosita said.

If I'm not going to do this right, what's the point of doing it at all?

I stop squeezing for a moment and try to think of a prayer that might be appropriate. I know the Hebrew prayers for bread, wine, and Hanukkah candles, but I can't imagine those would apply. I don't know any prayers about plants. What about a prayer for children? Or something neutral? How can I have lived for thirty-six years and not know a single generic prayer?

Then I remember: ten years ago, when my father's drinking had reached its highest pitch, a friend took me to an Adult Children of Alcoholics meeting. "Just try it once," she said, so I did, and I met a couple of nice people, and then I went again, and after a while I was going every Thursday night. At the end of each meeting the group members would hold hands in a closing circle and recite the Lord's Prayer. This was in Knoxville, Tennessee, where everyone knew the Lord's Prayer by heart. I had to fake it the first dozen or so times until I learned all the words, but I think I can remember most of them now.

I squeeze a handful of flowers and silently think, *Our Father, who art in Heaven, hallowed be thy name.* Maya starts sorting the floating plants into four separate categories: rose petals, marigold petals, rue sprigs, basil leaves. She's a Montessori child to the bone. *Thy kingdom come, thy will be done, on Earth as it is in Heaven . . .*

On Earth as it is in Heaven . . .

On Earth as it is in Heaven . . .

What comes next? I start over again, hoping the sheer force of the first two lines will propel me into the third, which it does. *On Earth as it is in Heaven. Give us this day our daily bread, and forgive us our trespasses.*

There's a saying that a tree's branches can grow only as wide as its roots, and when I walked into that first ACOA meeting twelve years ago, I'd been feeling without roots for a long time. The friends I made there became my family between families: Roger, who cooked me dinners in his Victorian house; Jason, who took me rock climbing in North Carolina to address my fear of heights; Phoenix, who owned the local crystal store and gave me a hunk of quartz to help me sleep; Gayle, who tried to teach me how to sing. They kept me calm and nurtured me, until I moved to the Midwest the following year. *Forgive us our trespasses, as we forgive those who have trespassed against us.* Those meetings were the first time I ever stepped outside of my self-reliant little box, admitted I needed help, and accepted it from anyone. *And lead us not into temptation but deliver us from evil, for thine is the kingdom, the power, and the glory, forever and ever, amen.*

At the end of every ACOA meeting the Lord's Prayer would flow right into the Serenity Prayer, as if we were resurrecting a forgotten stanza, and I find myself automatically reciting that one now, too. *God, grant me the serenity to accept the things I cannot change, the courage to change the things I can, and the wisdom to know the difference.* It's a good one, so I say it again as I squeeze the plants. And then, like a magician's handkerchief pulled from a hat, one piece of fabric knotted tightly to the next, the second Serenity Prayer segues right into the Shema, and I find myself silently reciting, *Shema yisrael, adonai elohainu, adonai echad.* Hear, O Israel: the Lord is Our God, the Lord is One.

That, I did not expect.

The Shema is the holiest prayer in Judaism, a declaration of faith in a monotheistic God. In synagogue it's sung like a mournful, ascendant wail, each phrase winding its way further up the register like a road toward redemption. It's the first prayer a Jewish child learns and the last prayer a dying person is supposed to say, both the route into consciousness and the path out. Jewish Holocaust victims recited the Shema together as they were marched naked into the woods, an act that tells us, *they knew, they knew.* I look at Maya's smooth, wet little body in the tub, surrounded by floating flowers and leaves, and if I weren't already kneeling, the simple beauty of her existence would bring me down to the floor. I wonder if my mother, the sole believer in our family, recited the Shema when she lay in the hospital bed during her final days, if she had time to whisper its words in Hebrew or in English before slipping into a coma, or if the horror of what was happening prevented her from finding the words. At that final moment of reckoning, do we instinctively grasp for familiar words to ride on as we're carried away from everything we've ever known? Or in our final breath, do we discover the opposite to be true: that life as we knew it was the dreamscape and now we're heading home?

Since the morning my mother died, I have never been able to hear the Shema without spontaneously starting to cry. The tears slip down my cheeks now and drip into the water as I keep squeezing the leaves and flowers. Maya dips her head down and turns her face up underneath mine.

"You're crying, Mommy," she says. "Why are you sad?"

I squeeze the water from another handful of flowers and press the mushy clump against her rounded stomach. It sticks to her skin and she giggles.

"Mommy's not sad," I tell her. "Mommy's just thinking. Sometimes people cry when they're sad, and sometimes people cry when they're happy, and sometimes people cry when they think. I know it sounds funny, but sometimes that's how it happens."

"Are you thinking about a sad thing?"

I lean over and kiss her forehead. "No, sweet thing," I say. "I'm thinking about something that was good." I pull my arms from the water and wipe the petals and leaves off my forearms with my hands. "Let's pour the water on you now, okay?"

So fast, it happens. Her body goes plank rigid in refusal.

"I don't want to," she growls.

I back off so fast it feels as if I'm being sucked into a vacuum. Whatever nostalgia I was just feeling gets pulled back in, too.

"Okay," I say. It's hard to regain an emotional balance after feeling yanked like that. "Then . . . let's try just splashing around a little." I make tiny waves with the water against Maya's stomach and back. I make tiny waves near Hursula, too, who bobs on the water's surface like a rubber cork. Maya lifts her hands in the air and brings them down against the water with a resounding smack. Drops shoot out on both sides, splashing the front of my T-shirt.

"Hey!" I say, splashing her back.

She laughs tentatively and smacks the water again. I splash her stomach. "See?" I say. "It's fun." We do this for a while, churning up the bathwater so the pieces of flowers and leaves swirl around and stick to the sides of the tub at the waterline. The motion of the water seems to calm her down. She picks marigold and rose petals from the water and presses them against her arms and chest.

"Look at me! I'm a flower! Daddy!" she hollers. "Come here! I'm a flower!"

"What about your head?" I ask her, thinking of Carmen and the basil bath at home. "We didn't get any in your hair yet."

"Okay," she says agreeably and stands up. "Do all of me," she instructs.

I dip the glass into the water, letting it fill to the rim. "Okay, kitty," I say, lifting it above her head. "Here you go."

I pour. The water streams down her face and shoulders, separating into thin rivers that run down her stomach and legs. "Pfft!" she says noisily, spitting water out of her mouth and blinking hard. White rose petals and tiny sprigs of green rue stay plastered against her hair.

"Again?" I ask, and she nods. I dip the glass and pour it over the crown of her head again, this time holding my hand against her forehead to divert the water from her eyes and mouth. I do it again. The bathtub is a self-contained loop. We can do this a hundred times and not lose any water. I dip the glass and pour, in even, steady, mechanical motions. Dip, pour, dip, pour.

"Mom?" Maya says.

"Yes?" I lift the full glass, ready to pour.

"Bad Dodo has to leave now, but the good ones are going to stay. Is that okay?"

I freeze in position, with my arm in midair. Did I just hear her right? I'm certain I heard her right. But . . . how could I have just heard that right?

"Bad Dodo?" I repeat.

"Bad Dodo has to leave," she says. "But the good ones will stay. They are my friends."

A strange sense of weightlessness fills me, as if my thoughts are disconnecting from my skin. I don't feel my hand shaking but I can see it, because the water in the glass starts moving from side to side.

The bath works? It fucking *works*?

"Okay, Mom?" Maya asks again.

Pour the water over her head, I tell myself. *Pour the water.* I lift the glass and pour.

"Okay," I say.

"And then we will be happy! Meow!" She does a little dance in place, clearly pleased with herself, and sits back down in the water.

I hear a slight scruffing noise behind me, the sound of Uzi's shoulder against the doorframe.

"Did she just say what I think she said?" he asks tentatively, keeping his voice low.

"Uh-*huh*," I say. The second syllable comes out squeakily high. I dip the glass and pour again.

"She just said . . ."

"Uh-*huh*." I keep dipping and pouring the water on Maya's body like a battery-operated machine. I don't know what will happen if I keep pouring, and I don't know what will happen if I stop. I just keep going.

"Holy shit," Uzi says.

"Uh-*huh*."

A deep well of laughter starts bubbling up inside me. It spurts out in coughs and gurgles that feel like tiny convulsions. Maya looks at me curiously and starts maneuvering Hursula through the floating petals like an icebreaker. I put the glass on the floor and lean against the rim of the tub, laughing and crying in equal measure, in a hysterical, ecstatic release of wonder and elation and relief.

Maya smiles at me benignly. "Good Mommy," she says.

I feel Uzi's hands on my shoulders. "I can't believe that just happened," he says. "Can you explain how that just happened?" I shake my head no. And here's a new twist in our story: Uzi angling for a way to make sense of an incident that, for once, I don't feel the need to explain.

By their seventh night in the Holy Temple of Jerusalem, Judas Maccabeus and his followers would have known they were witnessing an extraordinary event. The single vat of purified oil they found in the recaptured temple should have been enough to keep the eternal flame lit for only twenty-four hours, yet on that first day of the month of Tevet, it had been burning for seven days straight. The flame would stay ignited for another day, exactly the amount of time the Maccabees needed to prepare more oil. Did their steadfast faith in a divine protector make them nod their heads in affirmation as the flame kept burning, thinking *of course* as they restored their temple and worked the olive press? Or did any of them take a break to walk outside, like me, and wonder what the hell was going on?

You think you understand the simple, observable laws of cause and effect, until one of them goes and breaks rank right before your eyes. One pot of oil equals one day of light, until suddenly the flame burns for eight. A bath is just a way to get clean until it reveals a property you never knew it had before. Or five plus five equals only two full hands, until someone invents zero and place notation and a whole new way of counting spreads throughout the land. And then, at just about the same time the oil burns in Jerusalem for longer than it should, a band of Indians in Mesoamerica creates a complex calendar that predicts the end of time.

The ocean in front of Mariposa is tranquil tonight, its waves rustling softly against the fine sand. Uzi sent me out to the beach to pull myself together, because my hybrid of laughter and tears was starting to scare Maya and, I imagine, looked slightly maniacal to him. My eyes are still watering from the copal smoke, and I'm grateful for the clean, warm night air on the beach.

The crescent moon is nowhere to be found. The only light on the beach comes from Mariposa's ambient glow and the head of my flashlight. Above me, Orion still stretches across the sky as if he's lying facedown on a plane of glass. I shine my light up in his direction, which creates the illusion that the beam can reach the stars. When I shine it out toward the ocean, it illuminates only about twenty feet ahead, right where the waves sizzle out against the fine sand. I click off the light to save the battery. Way out on the dark horizon, it's nearly impossible to discern where sea separates from sky.

The Maya Indians who fished and camped on this beach might have stood right here a thousand years ago, also gazing out to sea. According to legend, their hero-god Kukulkan sailed off on a raft of snakes, promising to return from the east. In human form he was said to be light-skinned and bearded, a myth the Spanish conqueror Hernán Cortés exploited to his benefit when he first arrived in Mexico and was mistaken for the returning deity by the people living there. By the time they realized Cortés was no god, it was too late. And so perhaps some of the indigenous peoples here are still waiting for Kukulkan's return, just as the Jews wait for their Messiah; the Christians for the return of Christ; the Hindus for Kalki the avatar; the Muslims for the Mahdi, their divinely guided one; and the Hopi for Pahana, their Lost White Brother from the stars. Imagine the global party if they all show up at once.

We're all waiting for something, aren't we, as the cogs of this new millennium have started to turn? The year 2000 has crackled with the imminence of now as one great cycle on the Gregorian calendar ends and a new one begins. The Maya also measured time in cycles, though not the same way we do. Our hundred- and thousand-year cycles move time forward in a linear manner. They saw time as a series of elongated cycles that loop back around to fixed starting points and then begin again, a past that keeps returning. The 5,125-year Great Cycle of their Long Count calendar ends on December 21, 2012, prompting some apocalyptic thinkers to say the Maya were warning us about the end of the world as we know it. Other thinkers dismiss the drama, saying a new Great Cycle will begin without fanfare on December 22, like an odometer resetting to zero. And some researchers believe the end date, which lands on a winter solstice, marks a rare astronomical event that occurs only once every 26,000 years. On this morning, they say, the Milky Way will rim our eastern horizon in such a way that its Great Rift will appear to be touching the Earth, and the solstice sun will rise straight through its dark center.

The ancient Maya could see the Great Rift, the dark area in the middle of the Milky Way, with the naked eye. They described it as the mouth of a serpent, the birth canal of the Great Mother, and the Dark Road, Xibalba Be, that carries souls to the Underworld after death. This is the place the Maya king-priests believed they visited in their trance states. In Maya cosmology Xibalba Be is a portal between the worlds, and it's said that on the day the calendar ends the wisdom of the ancestors will travel back along this road to return to us on Earth. In Maya mythology this day marks the beginning of the Fifth World, the world of ether, and ushers us into the Fifth Dimension, where our linear experience of time will come to an end.

I don't really understand the fine points of the astronomy here, and I don't expect time to grind to a crunching halt. (I bought into the whole Y2K madness at this time last year, and that turned out to be an enormous nonevent.) But I like the idea of ancestral wisdom finding its way back home. If I've been waiting for anything this year, it's the same thing I've been waiting for since Maya was born: for my female ancestors to notice me waving up at them frantically from below, shouting, "Hey, guys! Down here! It's me! What do I do next?" They left before I had time to find out about their labors, ask about my early childhood, or even learn how to roast a chicken. The idea that some of their knowledge might filter back down comforts me in a small way.

Farther down the beach, someone lights a cigarette and the flame from a lighter flares and vanishes in the dark night. Tonight is the seventh night of Hanukkah. The holiday is almost over. Every Hanukkah throughout my childhood we spent at least one night at my grandparents' house, where I spun dreidels on the kitchen floor with my sister and my cousins, using pennies for ante and sucking on chocolate coins, while our grandmother, mothers, aunts, and great-aunts shuttled hot chicken soup and dripping plates of brisket from the stove to the dining room table. I grew up a long way from the secular home Uzi and I have created in California, far from our extended families and their traditions. I once thought I had to move away to establish myself as an individual, but I'm not so sure that was a good idea anymore. Despite my dreams of picking an exotic locale and staying there forever, I could never pack up my family and move to another country permanently, as my husband has done. California already feels too far from home.

I turn the flashlight on and point it back in the direction of Mariposa. Maya will be getting ready for bed soon. As I walk toward the apartment, the cone of light shining ahead of me fastens on a white rock in the sand. From a distance it looks like a small skull, but up close it's more like an irregular hunk of Swiss cheese, full of holes. I pick it up and run my fingers across its rough surface. When I shine the flashlight on it, I see the holes are about the circumference of my pinky. I count them. Eight. It would make a perfect menorah for tonight. I've still got the candles in my bag.

Through the open French doors of our apartment, I can see Maya jumping on the bed in her nightgown while Uzi pours a glass of water in the kitchen. Twelve more paces, and I will reenter the trinity that is my adult life: woman, mother, wife. Before I step onto the patio, I turn around to take one last look at the sky.

When I was pregnant with Maya and couldn't sleep at night, I used to lie on my bed and look through our bedroom window at the stars above Topanga. If the place after death and the place before life were one and the same, I thought, then my mother and my unborn daughter were in that place together. But then Maya was pulled from my body and placed on my chest, and my mother remained somewhere . . . well, somewhere that stretches the limits of my mortal comprehension.

What would it take to get there, so far beyond this physical world? More than climbing to the top of a pyramid, I feel certain. It would mean traveling beyond the sky, past the clouds. Through all the layers of atmosphere. Into a place beyond space, beyond discovery, even beyond recognition. A place beyond time.

chapter thirteen
Placencia, Belize
December 28, 2000

I n the highlands of Guatemala you can still find Maya daykeepers, the Ah K'in, who have been keeping time for their people for more than two thousand uninterrupted years. They use the sacred 260-day Tzolk'in count, a calendar of thirteen numbers and twenty days. Unlike our Gregorian calendar, which divides a solar year into twelve chunks of roughly thirty numbered days—January 1, January 2, January 3, and so on—the numbers and days of the Tzolk'in advance at the same time. The first day of a Tzolk'in year is 1 Imix, followed by 2 Ik, and then 3 Akbal, all the way up to 13 Ahau, which is always the final day of a Tzolk'in year.

Every day on the Tzolk'in calendar is believed to have its own unique characteristics, which means certain events are best aligned with certain days. Today, for example, is 9 Kan, a favorable day for planting. Yesterday, 8 Akbal, is known to be a good day for contemplating the stars. Traditionally, the village Ah K'in consulted the Tzolk'in for divination purposes and to schedule rituals and events, similar to the way Vedic astrologers in India consult their clients' natal charts to determine compatibility and propitious dates for a wedding. It is said, among the Maya, that a person's disposition is determined by the Tzolk'in day on which he is born, and women in the highlands take their babies to an Ah K'in shortly after birth to learn their children's predestined traits, weaknesses, and strengths.

If I'd taken Maya to a daykeeper when she was just a few days old (and you'll have to stretch your imagination here, since I've never heard of a daykeeper in Topanga—though Topanga is exactly the kind of place that *could* have one), I would have been told she'd been born on Chuen, the day of the monkey. Children born on this day are known to be attention-getting, clever, and artistically expressive. They communicate well and learn at a fast pace, and they're often natural performers whose desire for attention can make them overact to win the spotlight. A daykeeper might have told me to expect Maya to have a short attention span, with a mind that moves nimbly from topic to topic rather than zeroing in on one idea and sticking to it. While raising her, he might have said, I need to help her be creative and to explore the secrets of nature to balance out worldly distractions.

If my mother had taken me to a daykeeper soon after I was born in 1964 (and you'll really have to stretch the imagination now, since I'm certain there were no daykeepers in Westchester County, New York, back then), she would have learned that my birth at 1:25 A.M. took place as the energy of one day was transforming into the next, which can give a child traits of both. Since the days in question were Ahau (pronounced ah-HAW) and Imix (ee-MISH), the daykeeper might have told my mother that a child born on an Ahau day, whose symbol is the sun, would be destined to become an artist, musician, dancer, or singer with high expectations for self and others, while the influence of Imix, the day of the alligator, would mean she'd grow up to have a strong nurturing energy and work hard to achieve emotional security for herself and her family. But she'd also have a tendency to become too overprotective or overly dominating, with the potential to become emotionally volatile at these times. That's because by relating to the world through their feelings rather than their intellect, Imix children tend to be reactive to change.

The verdict is still out on Maya's future personality, but those traits come exceedingly close to describing me. They might explain why, when Marcia invites us up to her house in the morning for coffee and Maya picks up a butterfly ashtray from the coffee table and then Marcia immediately pulls it from her hands and then Maya screws up her face and starts crying from the surprise, my first instinct is to hustle Maya back downstairs. Her cry isn't exaggerated or whiny, it's just the innocent cry of a child who didn't know she'd done something wrong, and because it's so natural and not orchestrated for effect, I feel a rush of anger toward an adult who'd treat her that way. I breathe deep as Uzi has taught me to do and wait a respectful five minutes—it's Marcia's ashtray, after all, and Marcia's house, and she has every right to protect her possessions from a preschooler—before suggesting that perhaps I'll take Maya down to the beach, since a quiet morning coffee isn't a terribly attainable goal when a three-year-old is in the mix.

"Let's go look for Hursula," I suggest as Maya and I head down the tiled stairs to the sand. I'm sure the doll is gone by now, but I don't have a better plan for the next half hour. And I did promise her we'd look for Hursula today.

"Okay," she says agreeably.

We head under the palm trees in the direction of the ocean, holding hands. Peter is down by the water, raking a night's accumulation of seaweed off the beach in front of the house, a Sisyphean task if I've ever seen one. He waves at us and calls out, "Good morning for a walk!" as we pass by. I've noticed that Maya hasn't mentioned Dodo once since waking up two hours ago. I feel that something very, very unusual, maybe even bordering on mystical, happened in the bathtub last night, but I don't know if it's supposed to stick or what to expect next. I'm not sure if I'm supposed to mention Dodo today or wait for Maya to bring him up. Maybe I should call Dr. Rosita to ask? Then I realize I don't have a phone number for her. I couldn't even find the road back to her farm myself. Maybe I'm not supposed to do anything at all? I debate this as we walk along the edge of the surf. As we wander in the direction of the town, I halfheartedly look for a rubber arm or leg sticking out of the sand, a macabre image even for an imagined one.

Finally, I can't hold back my curiosity any longer. "Maya," I say. "You haven't said anything about Dodo lately. I'm wondering if he's okay."

She stops to pick up and inspect a rock washed up on the sand. Then she hurls it in the direction of the water.

"Maya?" I ask. "I just asked about Dodo. Is he okay?"

"I don't know," she says, then adds, "Maybe he is with Hursula."

"Dodo's with Hursula?" I say.

She shrugs. "Maybe." She doesn't seem terribly interested, either way.

A small flock of seabirds peck at the wet sand just ahead of us, and she runs into their midst, flapping her arms and cawing. I let her run in circles for a while before I notice the sun is lifting and her cheeks are turning pink. This morning is shaping up to be warmer than yesterday's. I don't have a water bottle with me on the beach, and I don't think we have any more in the room, so I suggest we double back toward Kitty's Place to buy two water bottles at the gift shop there.

The items on display at Kitty's are the same items we've seen everywhere else in Belize, except here they're bumped up one notch on the price scale. Ceramic mugs illustrated with tropical fish; dark Belizean hardwood shaped into small, hinged jewelry boxes and shallow bowls; T-shirts that proclaim, YOU BETTER BELIZE IT!; and endless plastic bottles of Marie Sharp's Habanero Hot Sauce. I find a row of water bottles lined up against a wall and bring two up to the counter. While I wait on line to pay, I admire a carved Guatemalan mask hanging on the low wall beneath the cash register. It's a horse's head painted red with yellow stripes on the cheekbones like war paint.

"Mom." Maya tugs on the leg of my striped cotton pants.

"Just a minute," I say. I flip the mask over to see the price—U.S. $45, ouch—and hang it back on the display nail.

"Mom." Maya tugs harder.

"What?"

She pulls on my arm until I bend down to her level. "That girl," she whispers in my ear. She points across the store at a girl not much older than her who's wearing a blue T-shirt and denim shorts and holding Hursula One.

At least I *think* it's Hursula One. It's a Water Baby doll that looks just like Hursula One, except where Hursula was last seen wearing a pink-and-yellow nylon bathing suit, this doll is swaddled in a scrap of fuzzy pale blue cloth. I can't tell what it's wearing underneath.

I take Maya's hand and walk over to the child, who appears to be in the shop alone. She looks as if she could be American or Canadian, maybe European.

"Excuse me, honey," I say. "Is your mom in the store?"

She shakes her head no after just the right interval. She understands English.

"We saw your doll," I say. "Did you bring her from home?"

Her eyes go a little wild. Someone's told her not to talk to strangers. I take a step back so as not to frighten her. "It's okay, honey," I tell her. "I'll wait till your mom comes in."

"Can I help you?" A man in a navy baseball cap sidles up next to her. They have the same thin nose and the same hazel eyes, except her father's are more calculating, I notice right away.

"My daughter had a doll just like your daughter's that she lost on the beach yesterday. We were wondering if maybe your daughter picked it up."

The girl pulls the doll close to her chest and presses up against her father's leg.

"Sorry," he says, twisting his mouth into a *too bad for you* frown. "This one's hers."

Fifty dollars says he's a studio executive or an entertainment lawyer from L.A. No—a hundred.

"Are you *sure*?" I say. "Because my daughter's got its twin right here, and as you can see, it's the same doll."

The father glances at Hursula Zero in Maya's hand. "Not exactly the same," he says.

"Dad," the girl says, tugging on her father's shorts just like Maya tugged on my pants.

"Shh," he says, waving her off. "I'm sorry," he tells me with a tight little smile this time. "But this is my daughter's doll."

"Mom?" Maya says, sounding confused.

In my other life, back in Los Angeles, I'd stand my ground, cross my arms tight, and tell him, "I don't *think* so." Or I'd ask Uzi to deal with him in a manner much more diplomatic than mine. But right now, I don't feel the need or the impulse to do either. The doll is Hursula One. That's very clear. It's Maya's, and she deserves to have it back. Yet at the same time, looking at the father and his daughter feels like peering into a reflection pool and seeing a slightly earlier version of ourselves. The possessiveness, the insistence, the ego. And it is then that I see how each step of the past five days has occurred in an almost choreographed lockstep, each one leading perfectly into the next, to usher us into this room. If we hadn't missed the plane to Guatemala, we would have seen Rosita on our first day here, and if that had happened, she probably would have given Maya the bath herself, and I would have attributed the outcome to her as a healer, instead of to forces larger than myself. (Even though I'm the one who administered the bath, I can't take credit for anything that happened. I know I am no healer.) And if we'd seen Rosita on our first day here, we would have missed traveling to San Antonio and meeting Canto, and we might not have gone to Tikal on Tuesday or met Rigoberto, and Uzi and I wouldn't have had the same chances to rediscover what we love most about each other. And maybe I wouldn't have seen Uzi and Maya together on the swing last night. They might not even have been on the swing last night. Maybe the reason the bath worked is because we met Rosita and gave Maya the bath only after all these other events had occurred and I'd had time to absorb them one by one. And because everything happened exactly, precisely, uniquely as it did, Maya and I are standing here right now in front of this other child who holds Hursula One in her arms.

I understand now what Uzi meant when he chose to leave the bathroom last night, right before the bath. When you're lucky enough to witness events unfolding with their own intelligence, you need to get yourself out of the way.

"Maya?" I say, placing my hand on her shoulder. "I think this is the girl's doll now. It's not Hursula One anymore." I add *now* and *anymore* for the father's benefit, to show him I understand what's going on. "Let's go back to Daddy now, honey," I say, and I gently steer her toward the door.

Just before we exit the shop, I can't help it: I turn around for one last look. The father is still glaring at me, his jaw set in a hard line. His daughter hugs Hursula One to her chest. The fuzzy blue cloth has slipped down the doll's back, revealing the straps of a pink nylon bathing suit.

What a strange new world this is going to be, where events can be inexplicable yet real nonetheless, where I know that subtler levels of reality exist even when I can't quantify or see them.

Over my shoulder, I flash the father what's meant to be an encouraging smile.

"Good luck," I say, and we walk out the door.

Marcia and Peter have two bicycles for guests to use, and by tucking Maya into the basket on the back of Uzi's we manage to get all three of us to the village in half the time it took us to walk there last night. It's not the safest solution we've ever come up with, given that the road is only a lane and a half wide by American standards, but we encounter only two or three cars on the way, and Maya whoops and shrieks with excitement the whole ride into town.

Uzi wants to use the Internet café again, so we head straight for the Space Monkey. As we pass the market from yesterday, I call ahead to Uzi, "I'll meet up with you in a minute!" and pull up my bicycle in front of the store. I lean it against a wooden fence post near the door and duck inside. The same woman from yesterday is behind the front counter, and Pedro is refilling the refrigerated dairy section.

"Cucumbers!" the woman says when she sees me. But that's not what I'm here for. The bread table has at least fifteen loaves piled on it today. I had a feeling it would: that's why I didn't bring the unused portion of our loaf with us. I just wanted to make sure.

An hour later, on the way back to Mariposa, the road is more heavily traveled and Maya doesn't want to stay in the basket. "Do you think we can ride the bikes on the beach?" I ask Uzi.

"It'd be hard." A supply truck passes us on the left, coming close enough for my hair to push back in its wind. "Let's try it," he says.

I've never tried to ride a bicycle on sand before, and now I know why. It's not anywhere close to easy. But it's a beautiful day, and I don't mind disembarking after a few minutes to walk the bicycle along the water's edge. I roll up my khaki pants to just below my knees and hang my Tevas from the handlebars. In front of me, Uzi pushes his bicycle with Maya balanced on the seat so she can pretend to be riding it herself. She still hasn't mentioned Dodo, except for the time I brought him up this morning.

I pick up the pace and push my bicycle up next to Uzi's. "Watch this," I mouth to him.

"Maya, how's Dodo today?" I ask her.

She shrugs. "I don't know about him," she says.

I raise my eyebrows at Uzi, who raises his eyebrows back at me. Then he squints over my shoulder at something in the distance.

"Hey," he says. "I think that's Coppola."

We've reached the part of the beach where Francis Ford Coppola is building his second luxury resort in Belize, the twenty-four-cabana Turtle Inn. This'll be in addition to his other property, Blancaneaux Lodge out past San Antonio Village. At the open-air bar across the beach, a husky figure with dark hair sits bent over a glass. When he turns his head just slightly, I catch a glimpse of a dark beard. It *does* look like Coppola.

"You should go talk to him," Uzi says.

"To say what?" In Los Angeles, this would be a writer's ultimate serendipity, the chance to have a private audience with a screenwriting legend who runs a literary magazine and an annual writer's workshop. But here in Placencia, he's just a guy sitting alone at a bar enjoying a late-morning drink.

"I don't know. Tell him you're a writer. It's a relaxed place. I'm sure he'll be happy to meet you," Uzi says.

I could tell Coppola that in college, when I had to write the obligatory literature paper comparing Joseph Conrad's *Heart of Darkness* and *Apocalypse Now*, I watched the movie three times in a row and walked around shell-shocked for days with my thoughts stuck in the moral quagmire of Kurtz's compound. Or I could tell him that the film's central premise, that journeying deep into a different spiritual landscape—in the movie's case, a moral no-man's-land—muddies the distinctions between self and other, matter and spirit, sacred and profane, until such dualities no longer exist. That's when you realize good and evil are only constructs created by man. Nature intended for everything to be the same. But he's probably heard this four thousand times before. It's better—and more respectful—to leave the man alone. It may not even be Coppola sitting there at the bar. So little here turns out to be what it first seems.

After we resecure the bikes at Mariposa, we walk a short distance north along the beach to have lunch at the Rum Point Inn. This was the "in" place to stay in Placencia in the 1970s, and the resort has retained some of its retro charm. The two-story main house is a weathered white clapboard affair with green window frames, a red roof, and a large and comfortable main room filled with upholstered chairs, books, and board games.

Lunch is served at a polished wood table in a long, narrow dining hall with a wall of windows. It's a pretty room, paneled like the hull of a well-worn sailboat, with wooden shutters propped open to reveal a view of the ocean. The server carries over a high chair for Maya. She's too big to fit in it, so we flip the tray back and push the seat close to the table to lift her to bar-stool height. Just last week she would have complained about the unconventional arrangement, but she doesn't seem bothered by it today. I keep stealing glances at her to make sure she's not on the edge of an eruption, but so far she seems happier and more content than we've seen her be in months. Uzi gives me little reassuring smiles every time I look at him.

He pulls a blank sheet of paper and a pen out of his day pack and engages Maya in a game of connect the dots. I watch the way she sticks the tip of her tongue between her lips in concentration as she draws her lines, the way her slightly sunburned cheeks contrast with her mop of dark curls. She looks so much like my mother at the same age. At home, we have a photo of my mother sitting at a piano keyboard at the age of two, an iconic photo in our family since she went on to study music and become a music teacher. When Maya was about eighteen months old, we took a black-and-white picture of her in which, quite accidentally, she was sitting in the same position with the same expression as my mother's, and we hung the two photos side by side. Everyone who comes to our house thinks they're both photos of Maya, even though one was taken in 1940 and the other in 1999.

The food takes awhile to come, and as I watch Uzi and Maya methodically passing the pen between them, I feel calmer than I can remember feeling for a long time, although it's a calm that incorporates a form of movement, like a river flowing steadily and serenely downstream. Sitting here in the dining room of the Rum Point Inn, watching my daughter and my husband absorbed in a simple, homespun game while the December sun bears down on a sandy beach behind us and the Caribbean glistens over Uzi's shoulder in a bright hue of aquamarine, I can feel something stirring beneath my surface, a new awareness, maybe, or a distant recognition, of something new and something good.

Could it be the intuition, soon to be proved true, that after today Maya will never speak of Dodo again? Or is it the very first glimmer of her sister, whom we will find the courage to conceive three months from now in a pension in Prague, a trip we do not yet know we will make, and who will arrive a week early to be born almost exactly one year from today, squeaking in just before 2001 comes to an end? She will start trying to dance before she can walk, just as Terry and Linda, the Psychic Twins, told me she would.

But I sense it's something else I'm feeling now. Maybe it's humility. Maybe it's even the first stirrings of faith. Or maybe it's something as simple as grace.

The server arrives with our orders and puts the plates down in front of us. Uzi quietly lifts his hands over his plate and closes his eyes. I open my mouth to say something. Then I shut it. Whatever he's doing is between him and whoever he is reaching toward. He opens his eyes, and when he sees me watching him, he smiles and lifts his fork in a small salute.

"Bon appétit," he says.

I look at the food on my plate, broiled tilapia with a side of rice and beans. This meal. This room. This family, this day, this trip. This life. It fills me.

The thirteenth-century German mystic Meister Eckehart said that if the only prayer one ever uttered was "Thank you," that would be enough. For Uzi, such gratitude comes naturally. For me, not so much. Still, the desire I feel right now is mine. I'm not quite up for holding my hands above my plate, but I allow myself to close my eyes. And for that single moment on December 28 in Placencia, Belize, time stands still.

Far above us in the Upperworld, in the celestial heavens, the unseen forces of the universe work their secret magic.

Somewhere in the ether of the Underworld, where the ancestors reside, a grandmother and a great-grandmother gaze upon this scene and smile.

Here in the Middleworld, in the realm of ordinary existence, a mother presses her palms together underneath a wooden table, bows her head, and thanks them all.

acknowledgments

To my editor, Marnie Cochran, for her enthusiasm for this story from the very start, and for helping me turn it into a much better book than it otherwise would have been.

To my agent, Elizabeth Kaplan, for sixteen years of advocacy, friendship, and advice.

To my spectacular Tuesday writing group—Elizabeth Berman, Melissa Cistaro, Amy Friedman, Deborah Lott, Samantha Robson, and Christine Schwab—whose feedback and encouragement sustained me from start to finish.

To Julia Drake and Jamie Scot, for unerring hard work on the marketing and promotion fronts and for living outside the box with me for eight shining months.

To Susan Corcoran for bringing this book to its audience.

To members of our extended family, from New York to Florida to California to Australia to Israel, and other points in between, especially Michele Edelman, Amy Jupiter, Glenn Edelman, and Allyson Edelman.

To the friends and colleagues who read early versions of this book or helped in so many other ways. I am blessed to have you in my life, and proud to list you by name: Jeff Wynne, Mary Swander, Carl Klaus, Bruce Bauman, Sue Schmitt, Kate Vrijmoet, Shelly Cofield, Electra Manwiller, Teri Carcano, Sky Kunerth, Noel Alumit, Leslie Schwartz, Meghan Daum, Leslie Lehr, Monica Holloway, Sherry and Melody Raouf, Julie McInally, Betty Budack, Hazel Williams-Carter, Paula Derrow, Joyce Maynard, Karen Bender, Rachel Resnick, Rolonda Watts, Nancy Wartik, Michelle Taub, Dana Hilmer, and Jane Marla Robbins.

To all the friends and colleagues who so generously took part in the hardcover salon tour: Kamy Wicoff and the SheWrites.com crew, Wicki Boyle, Allison Gilbert, Gretchen Newcomb, Jennifer Margulies, Bill Young, Jim Crowley, Ellie Searl, Val Evans, Jennifer New, Robin Hemley, Jan Weissmuller, Betsy Rippentrop, Spike Gillespie, Robin Chotzinoff, Trudy Zimmerly, Corrine Porterfield Brown, Kimberly Chisholm, Heidi Trilling, Carrie Link, Jodie Block, Sophie Paik, Abe Peck, Lisa Solovay, Dawn Suss, Sandy Schainuck, and Tami Muller (esteemed inventor of the Possibilitini).

To Diesel Bookstore in Malibu, Village Books in Pacific Palisades, and Prairie Lights bookstore in Iowa City, for being champions of local authors. We appreciate you hugely.

To Water Lily Café and Mimosa Café in Topanga; Mogen's Café in Pacific Palisades; The Office in Brentwood; and the Santa Monica Library for letting me sit for hours so I could have the illusion of human companionship while I wrote.

To the Will Geer Theatricum Botanicum in Topanga, for quiet office space.

To Jessica Hernandez, Wendy Berman, Jenny Mulligan, and the middle-school staff at Calmont and New Roads schools, for teaching my children what I could not.

To Amy Margolis, our Grand Poobah of the Iowa Summer Writing Festival, and to my students there every July.

To Belen Ricoy for help with Spanish and children.

To all the scholars of Maya history and culture whose writings offered me a route into another world, especially the works of Michael Coe, Anthony Aveni, David Friedel, and the late Linda Schiele.

To Van at Indigonight.com for the star maps.

To all the students in the 2008 Maya Spiritual Healing workshop—Trudy, Leah, Nicole, Gloria, Charlotte, Hayley, Breanna, Eva, Megan, Ticia, Margaret, Jen, Valerie, Steve, Sondra, Andrew, Patricia, Elizabeth, Carol, Michele, Graciela, Kas, Jennifer, Lizzy, and especially Heidi and Seth for making the trek back to San Antonio with me—and to Vanda and Diane, for helping to make it happen. Knowing you're all out there doing the good work you do inspires me, every day.

To Docio and Francelia Juarez for taking good care of us in Belize, and to Hugo for safe transport.

To Ovencio Canto, for sharing your knowledge with those who come to you from so far.

To the Tut family for sharing your resort, your knowledge, and your beautiful spirits with so many who are lucky to find their way to you. (Go for a visit!)

To Rosita Arvigo for your generosity, your experience, and the extraordinary community you have created. May we all be as wise as you one day, and may you be ten times wiser.

To Eden, for your patience and sweetness.

To Maya, for letting me tell our story and for always, always making me laugh.

To Uzi, for everything else and more.

the
possibility *of*
everything

HOPE EDELMAN

A READER'S GUIDE

a conversation with
Hope Edelman

Random House Reader's Circle: Taking your child to a Maya shaman seems like a dramatic attempt to solve your problem. What compelled you to go this route?

Hope Edelman: I don't know if I can adequately convey what an unlikely character I was to make this trip. I was not in any way the kind of person who would've come up with the plan on my own. But my husband is very alternative-minded, and my daughter's babysitter at the time, who had grown up in Nicaragua, strongly believed that we were dealing with a matter of otherworldly origins. Also, I was at a very low point in my life, struggling in my career, having difficulties in my marriage, homesick as a New Yorker in California, and the idea of taking a magical, adventurous journey held a great deal of appeal. I definitely felt the need for some magic in everyday life. In retrospect the choice does seem like a dramatic attempt, but at the time—it just felt as if events were unfolding in a sequence that naturally led us down to Belize, almost as if that were the inevitable conclusion to the story.

RHRC: When did you realize you had a story to write?

HE: Not until after we came back. I went to Belize as a mother and a tourist, not as a memoirist or journalist. After we'd been back for a few months we started sharing the story of our time there with some of our friends, who encouraged me to write it as a book. It was then that I realized I had a complete story, with an easily identifiable beginning, middle, and end; a character arc; and terrific supporting "characters." But I wasn't thinking in those terms at all when I was down there.

RHRC: You were a self-described skeptic before you made this trip. How did the time you spent in Belize change your outlook?

HE: Before the trip, I was very scientifically minded, completely wedded to empirical thinking, and I believed in very little other than what could be visibly proven. Whenever I had an experience that didn't fit in this box, I'd come up with a new way to rationalize it so my worldview didn't have to change. When I came back from Belize, I was a person more willing to believe in an unseen world. That doesn't mean I jumped right into living a spiritual life, or that I wholeheartedly began to embrace mysticism or religion, but that I became far more comfortable living with ambiguity. Now I can accept that some phenomena can't be proven or explained to scientific satisfaction, but are nonetheless real.

RHRC: How have you managed to write with such vivid detail and immediacy about a trip you took almost ten years ago?

HE: I'm glad the result is vivid, because pulling it off was tricky! I'd kept a journal and taken about a hundred photos on the initial trip, so I was able to rely on those somewhat when writing, although they tended to be mostly of quirky, nondramatic moments. Some of the events had left an indelible impression on me, and I was both pleased and surprised to discover that when I went back eight years later with chapters in hand, I'd gotten most of the broad strokes and many of the fine strokes right. My first trip back was in the spring of 2008, when I attended a workshop on Maya Spiritual Healing to learn more about what we'd experienced and also to revisit the sites in the book and track down the people we met on that first trip. We went there as a family later in the year, and I went again in 2009 to finish up the research. And because memoir, by nature, is infused by memory, my husband and I talked a great deal about what we remembered from the trip in 2000. I also interviewed friends and family members to ask them what they remembered about the months leading up to our departure.

RHRC: How much does Maya remember from this trip?

HE: This is the number-one question readers ask! She remembers bits and pieces of it, mostly from the second half. The first few days after we left L.A. she had a high fever and was sleeping much of the time. I think she experienced most of the activity that occurred then in a dream state. She does have some very clear memories about the time along the beach in Placencia, which followed the rain-forest portion of the trip. Interestingly, she's always remembered being on the porch swing and pretending with her father to put on their moon boots and go to the moon. In the book, I say that these simple moments are the ones that help a family grow, and although I recognized this at the time, I came to understand its profundity later, when I realized it was one of the few moments from the trip that Maya never forgot.

The first dozen or so times I heard this question I was fascinated by it, because my intuition told me there was another question behind the question. As I've talked with more readers, I think what they really want to know is how much of the magic of childhood persists into the preteen years and beyond—and whether it's possible to keep it alive. I believe it is.

RHRC: How is Maya now?

HE: She's a perfectly normal twelve-year-old, a seventh grader, into musical theater and hula hooping. She has a strong appreciation for nature and an unusual affinity for native plants, which I like to think comes from having been helped by them in the past. She's also interested in a spiritual dimension, but I can't tell if that's a result of her time in Belize or of growing up in Topanga Canyon.

RHRC: Even though your book takes place in Central America, it has a certain universal appeal that other mothers can relate to. What do you think that is?

HE: In the writing classes I teach, I encourage students to identify the stories behind their stories. Typically that means delving into the realms of archetype and myth. It was only after I'd completed *The Possibility of Everything* that I realized my story had quite a bit in common with the myth of Demeter and Persephone. Demeter was the Greek goddess of the harvest whose daughter, Persephone, was kidnapped by Hades, the god of the underworld. Demeter was so distraught about being separated from her daughter that she traveled to the underworld to retrieve her and cut a deal with Hades to have her daughter returned to her for part of each year. In Greek mythology, that's the story behind why we have seasons: when Persephone goes back to the underworld the weather turns cold and dry, and when she returns spring begins.

In some ways, it felt that I'd made a similar trek (in my case, deep into the rain forests) to retrieve the piece of my daughter that had departed when her imaginary friend arrived. I don't think of myself as any kind of heroine—I actually think some of my actions were cowardly rather than heroic—but I recognize that the story has some of the qualities of a classic hero story, in which a protagonist ventures out into the unknown and returns home safely but fundamentally changed. So I'm hoping that sharing my story will inspire other mothers to talk about similar experiences they've had that have changed them, whether their travels have been to another culture or a new neighborhood or a different state of mind.

RHRC: Most of your writing up to this point has been about early mother loss. What is it like, as a writer, to shift your focus to a story about searching rather than losing?

HE: To me they're two sides of the same coin. Those who've lost someone close to them become people who are forever searching to recapture what was lost. I didn't expect—didn't even want—my mother to make an appearance in this book, but it was impossible to write about going on a spiritual journey without examining what I was searching for, which brought me back to the story of her early death and its aftermath. You can't find something unless you first have a sense that it's missing, right? And that brought me back to memories of my grandmother, who had been a very important and loving influence in my childhood. I realized that what was missing most from my own experience of motherhood was the opportunity to draw from their knowledge, and so in a very unexpected sense, the trip through Maya lands, where ancestor worship has historically been so important, became an opportunity to reconnect with the women who'd preceded me.

RHRC: The book contains many detailed descriptions of Belize, Maya historic sites, and Maya culture. Why did you choose to include them in the book?

HE: As I began writing the manuscript, I had a strong impulse to ground the story in something larger than myself. Through reading books about the geography and history of Belize and the Maya, I discovered that the experience my family had there was very much a function of the place, its history, its native people, and their relationship to the land. You can't really understand the simplicity or the power of Maya healing unless you understand the fundamentals of Maya cosmology and mythology, much of which is literally written in the stars. So I made the decision to put that material in the book to give readers a sense of the bigger picture, even though I knew I risked having some of them skip over those passages to get back to the main story line. That's why I wrote those sections in a modular fashion. They're easy to leap over, if a reader is so inclined.

RHRC: What kind of relationship, if any, do you have now with the people or places in the book?

HE: I've reconnected with the Belizeans I wrote about, and have since formed personal and professional connections with others in San Ignacio and San Antonio. As I mentioned above, when I went there on vacation in 2000 I was wholly focused on helping my daughter and on seeing what I could of the country along the way. I was moved by the kindness, the generosity, and the humor of the people we met back then, which I tried to convey in the writing. I was also struck by how rich the culture was in so many ways, and how spiritually impoverished I felt in comparison. When I returned eight years later, I traveled with a different set of eyes: both because I was wearing a researcher's hat, and also because my worldview had changed so much as a result of that first trip. This time, it was impossible not to notice and be kicked into action by the bone-crushing poverty of the region, and it immediately became clear to me that I couldn't take money from a publisher without giving back to the people and places that gave me the story. So I've been using a portion of my book earnings to support programs in the Cayo District that advance literacy and education for children, as well as foundations dedicated to medicinal rain-forest education and preservation. I also organized a book drive for the San Ignacio library, and a portion of my book earnings went to paying high school tuition for two Cayo students during the 2009–2010 school year. Hopefully next year I'll be able to increase that number to three or four.

RHRC: Was faith required for you to lay bare some of what could be perceived as less-than-great parenting moments—for instance, your occasional lack of patience with Maya, or the struggle to force-feed her cough medicine?

HE: I think of writing as an act of faith. Every time I sit down at the computer I have to believe both in my own invisible abilities and in the power of words to create something out of nothing. Telling this story was absolutely a leap of faith, and sharing it even more so. I knew it was a personal risk to publish a book like this, and that I might well come under fire for my spiritual beliefs. I didn't expect that a storm would erupt online over my parenting practices, although in retrospect I can understand why it did. When I committed to writing the book, I made a promise to myself that I wouldn't try to sugarcoat the story to make myself look good. I wanted to write a true, authentic story that honestly revealed who I was—or who I think I was—ten years ago, even if I feel that I'm not exactly the same person now. That part was very difficult for me, since there were moments during the writing when I found myself judging my own behavior in the past, and I had to struggle against the impulse to change or soften some of those moments to save face on the page. Even more than faith, it felt like I had to find courage and humility to write those parts of the book. Because if I was judging myself as I wrote, I knew that readers might feel the impulse to judge me, too.

Writing about the night in the hotel in Guatemala City when I forced medicine down my daughter's throat was by far the hardest part of the book to write, and I really debated whether or not to put it in. It illustrated an important moment when I came very close to hitting bottom from frustration and fear, but I knew it ran the risk of depicting me as violent and maybe even unhinged. Some memoirists worry about throwing other people under the bus when they write, but I think I threw myself under the bus with this scene. I decided to put it in because I knew that nearly every mother has a moment in her past when she had to resort to physical force to get a child to take eardrops, or eyedrops, or oral medication against the child's will but for the child's well-being. Most of us are afraid to talk about those moments because we worry what others will think, so in addition to this being an important part of the story I hoped that it would help other mothers feel all right about the choices they've made, too. And perhaps not surprisingly, those pages in the book have wound up being the ones that mothers want to talk about the most.

RHRC: What are you working on next?

HE: In the interest of giving my family a break, I've just started writing my first novel. After five nonfiction books, it's wonderful fun to have permission to make things up.

reading group questions
and topics for discussion

1. In the beginning of the book, Hope and her husband have very different belief systems, which give them very different ideas about how to address their daughter's imaginary friend. Did you identify more with Uzi's character or with Hope's? Why?

2. How would you describe Hope's definition of trust at the beginning of the story? How would you describe it at the end?

3. Did you find Maya's behavior surrounding her imaginary friend normal or troubling? Was there a point in the story where your opinion of this changed or solidified? Did you still have the same opinion at the end?

4. If you're a parent, have you ever had a time when your intuition told you that the "experts" were wrong about your child? Did you follow your intuition or take their advice? What was the outcome?

5. Did any parts of this book make you laugh? Which ones? Did any make you cry?

6. The theme of being an outsider in a foreign and unfamiliar culture is important to this story. How did this dissociation affect the narrator's experience, and possibly the outcome of events? How do you imagine that this story might have unfolded if it had taken place somewhere else?

7. Some readers have said that the passages about Maya history were their favorite parts of the book. Others have said they found themselves skipping over those sections to get back to the story of the family. What did you think about these parts of the book?

8. Why do you think Dr. Rosita was the one who had the greatest effect on Hope, and on the whole family?

9. At one point, Hope says, "If faith is a belief in the unseen, as I believe it is, then the opposite of faith is not disbelief. The opposite of faith is fear." Do you agree with this statement? Why or why not?

10. Have you, like the protagonist of this book, ever been faced with a situation that you had difficulty explaining with contemporary language or scientific reason? How did you react?

HOPE EDELMAN is the author of five nonfiction books, including the bestsellers *Motherless Daughters* and *Motherless Mothers*. Her articles, essays, and reviews have appeared in numerous publications, including *The New York Times*, the *Chicago Tribune*, the *San Francisco Chronicle*, *Huffington Post, Glamour, Real Simple, Parents, Writer's Digest,* and *Self,* and her essays have been widely anthologized. A graduate of the University of Iowa Nonfiction Writing Program, she teaches every summer at the Iowa Summer Writing Festival. She lives in Topanga, California, with her husband, their two daughters, a cat named Timmy, and their pet tarantula, Billy Bob.

www.hopeedelman.com
www.thepossibilityofeverything.com

about the type

The text of this book was set in Janson, a typeface designed in about 1690 by Nicholas Kis, a Hungarian living in Amsterdam, and for many years mistakenly attributed to the Dutch printer Anton Janson. In 1919 the matrices became the property of the Stempel Foundry in Frankfurt. It is an old-style book face of excellent clarity and sharpness. Janson serifs are concave and splayed; the contrast between thick and thin strokes is marked.